Praise for Ben's War with the U. S. Marines

What critics said about the first edition,
Dad's War with the United States Marines

Given current demands on the American military arising from the 'war on terrorism,' *Dad's War With The United States Marines* is very highly recommended to all general readers and a welcome addition to the growing library of military memoirs and biographies."
    –James A. Cox, Midwest Book Review (Oregon, WI USA)

In the home office of architect Peter Green sit six ring-bound volumes with the wartime letters of his father, Marine Pfc. Benjamin Green. And in a letter written from Guam on Aug. 14, 1945, the elder Green tells his family that he scooped the world on getting out the big news of Japan's surrender."
    –Harry Levins, St. Louis Post Dispatch
    on the 60th anniversary of V-J Day, Aug. 14, 2005

This highly recommended read places the operation of a wartime AFRS Pacific Ocean Network outlet in the context of the family story of Ben Green, plucked from his senior radio advertising industry job in Chicago and going through Marine boot camp before becoming 'the highest ranking private on Guam' and running WXLI."
    –David Ricquish, Chairman, Radio Heritage Foundation,
    Wellington, New Zealand

Ben's War
with the
U. S. Marines

by Peter H. Green

GREENSKILLS PRESS

AN IMPRINT OF GREENSKILLS ASSOCIATES LLC

Ben's War with the U. S. Marines by Peter H. Green
GREENSKILLS PRESS
Publisher, an imprint of
GREENSKILLS ASSOCIATES, LLC

Ben's War with the U. S. Marines
First published as Dad's War with the United States Marines.
Seaboard Press, an imprint of James A. Rock & Co., 2005

Copyright © 2005, 2014 by Peter H. Green

Cover Design by Jennifer R. Stolzer
Book design by Greenskills Press

All applicable copyrights and other rights reserved worldwide. No part of this publication may be reproduced, in any form or by any means, for any purpose, except as provided by the U.S. Copyright Law, without the express, written permission of the copyright holder.

This is a work of nonfiction.
Historical figures are treated fictionally. based on historical research, letters and their writings.

Address comments and inquiries to:
GREENSKILLS PRESS
P. O. Box 11292
St. Louis, MO 63105

E-mail: writerpeter@peterhgreen.com
Internet URL: www.peterhgreen.com

Library of Congress Control Number: 2014936579
Kindle e-book: ISBN 13: 978-941402-00-9
Amazon Paperback: ISBN 13: 978-1-941402-01-6
Trade Paperback: ISBN 13: 978-1-941402-02-3
Printed in the United States of America
Second Edition: March 2014

Dedicated to

*Connie, who listened patiently
to my stories all these years,
Lisa, Richard Kennedy and Max
Lori, Jeff, and Brandon;
to Linda, who lived it with me, and her son Eric,
And to family and offspring to come.
I hope this will give you a chance to love Dad
as much as he would have loved you.*

TABLE OF CONTENTS

1. The Californian 1
2. San Francisco Chronicles 25
3. Home Economics.. 45
4. The Politician... 61
5. Transported to Guam 81
6. Cambridge Beach 103
7. Armed Forces Radio Station WXLI 123
8. Here's Guam 135
9. The Highest Ranking Private on Guam 145
10. The Scoop 155
11. Waiting for B. J. Day.. 165
12. Liberty Ships: The Privateer... 179
13. Homecoming: Scrambled Eggs 187
14. Making Up for Lost Time 201
15. What Makes Benny Run?... 217
    Endnotes. 249
    About the Author.. 255

CHAPTER 1

THE CALIFORNIAN

When you're little you can't see where you're going.

We worked our way through the crowded, cavernous waiting room. I saw just a swirl of pants, coats, a baby stroller—a sea of people in continuous motion. My only unblocked view was upward. A vaulted roof loomed far above the milling, dashing crowd. Its huge, arched windows stared darkly, increasing my fear of the oncoming night.

A large Elgin clock with Roman numerals, centered under an arch, warned us that it would soon be time. High on the wall straight ahead, I saw some shiny cutout metal letters, all capitals, spelling out, "NICKEL PLATE ROAD." Although I knew each of these words, I looked up at Mom to see if she could explain the sign. But she was busy holding my baby sister in her arms and trying to keep up with Daddy, who led the way quickly through the hall, bobbing, weaving and dodging people as he headed toward one of several large doorways in the end wall.

We turned right into a much lower hall with a steel roof extending far off into the distance. Along the wall between the doorways we had just passed through were fruit and cigar stands, lunch counters with uniformed waitresses and newsstands with dozens of papers and many brightly colored magazines. On our left was a row of doors that must have led to the outside; I could see rail cars through the small windows.

"See, Peter, the trains are through here," Mom, said, as we hurried along. Now the murmur of the crowd in the great hall had given way to different sounds. I could hear the "CHOO... Choo,...choo, choo, choo" of a steam engine starting to haul out of the train shed; uniformed men at the gates calling "All aboard!" to passengers, and a man's deep bass voice coming through the loudspeaker: "Train... leaving ...on Track Nine... for Detroit...Cleveland...Buffalo ... and New York."

The crowd had changed too. Now I could see men with suitcases coming out of the gates from arriving trains, lines forming at the doors to the train shed and small families like my own, couples and larger groups, making their way toward their gates. The name of each train was shown in white letters on a lighted sign that stuck out from the wall. Where people stood in line waiting to board, a man in a dark blue uniform—Mom said he was the conductor—was looking at their tickets and letting them through the open iron gate, past the double swinging doors and out to the train platform and the cities beyond.

There were men and women hugging and kissing goodbye, men guiding four-wheeled carts piled high with trunks, suitcases and duffel bags, red-capped Negro porters pushing dollies and more groups like ours, looking for the right gates, anxiously now, as the time of departure neared. Suddenly we found the sign we were seeking, The Californian, and we joined a swiftly moving line.

"OK, Pete," said Daddy, "you're the man of the house now. Take care of your mother and Linda."

"Yes, Daddy, but come back soon!"

I'll never forget how Daddy picked up Linda and squeezed us all in his widespread arms in one last big hug. He turned, grabbed his suitcase and walked through the swinging doors, smiling and waving as he disappeared. We waved until he was out of sight, turned slowly, went down the stairs to the entry level, crossed the street to the parking lot and Bluey, our 1940 Ford beetle, and headed for the empty house on Blackstone Avenue.

The freeze-frame photo of that scene is still vivid in my mind. Up to that point in my life, I had enjoyed Dad's love, support and enthusiastic guidance in our shared activities. On weekends he took me to the Museum of Science and Industry, one of the few remaining structures from the 1893 World's Fair. Because the site of the huge domed building cuts off 57th Street at Stony Island Avenue, I used to think it was called the Museum of Science and In-the-Street. Dad always bragged that we had spent a "month of Sundays" there. We would climb the classical staircase beneath tall Ionic columns; enter through monumental bronze doors, pass between stainless steel walls with round brass buttons punctuating the joints where the panels meet and wander through the exhibits in vast classical halls with stone pilasters, vaulted ceilings and marble floors. I would watch scale-model freight and passenger trains traverse the intricate landscape of a layout that filled an entire wing, with its hills, tunnels, rail yards, industrial districts, houses, stores—complete cities with trees, cars, lighted windows and real streetlights.

You could also look down on it from a balcony that overlooked the huge hall, although Dad had to lift me up and hold me so I could look over the railing. Even down on the main level, Dad complained that something designed for children was too high off the ground for them to see. He would always have to borrow a large solid wood bench and slide it over from the wall to a vantage point next to the base of the display so I could stand on it and see the trains. As I got a little older, we would go upstairs and climb on a huge steel structure from the balcony. Periodically a shrill steam whistle sounded, reverberating from the hard, smooth surfaces of the high-vaulted space. On the level below, an engine with flywheels and belts would start up, wind cables from pulleys on top of the structure onto a huge rotating drum and lift an elevator from beneath up to our level. We climbed some steel steps and into the steel lift cage; wire gates shut us in, and we descended down, down, down: past steel walls which, I later learned, moved upward, seeming to plunge us thousands of feet into the bowels of the earth.

When the gates opened again, we emerged in a dim tunnel carved out of solid coal. We were conducted by gruff, old coal miners through a series of rooms, where they demonstrated how various huge machines drilled into the coal seam, broke off and crushed coal and loaded it into rail cars. We then got into a three-car train, where we once again were enclosed by wire mesh. A coal miner with a lantern on his head, goggles, blue striped overalls and big work gloves climbed aboard an electric engine and started driving us through the tunnel. It was noisy and scary; at one point, the dim lights on the train blinked out: there was nothing but the rattle of the train and what sounded like the car scraping against the tunnel's side walls of coal.

At the end of the ride we were led into a lighted room and sat on benches, where a miner explained about safety lamps. He demonstrated how they burn with an eerie brightness in the presence of deadly coal gas to warn miners of the danger and explained how they test them. He showed us a lamp with a hole in the protective screening that was supposed to prevent the flame from igniting the gas in the mine. He put a good lamp in a test cabinet, closed the door and turned on the valve that sent coal gas into the chamber; other than burning more brightly, nothing happened, and the lamp passed the test. Then he put in the defective one and pumped in the gas. With a huge bang the top blew off the test cabinet, sending a puff of smoke and flame toward the ceiling. Even though I knew it was coming, I always jumped at this point. This marked the end of the coal mine tour. Even though we thought we were thousands of feet under the earth, amazingly enough, we walked out of the room into the world of the museum, another exhibit area, which turned out to be in the basement, just one flight below the main level.

An even earlier memory of Dad—and I must have been no older than three—was in the family's first apartment on Woodlawn Avenue. On Saturday mornings, he would set me in a wooden high chair we had, which was hinged so that the seat portion could sit on the floor, while the high-leg portion would fold in two sections out of the way behind. He sat me on the chair, closed me in with the drop-down tray and set up my watercolor paints and coloring book, my dish of water and brushes. Thus hemmed in, I nonetheless had plenty to occupy me. I watched as Dad said goodbye and told me, "Now you paint me a nice picture and don't wake your mommy!" And I would sit there and paint by the hour, while Dad worked at the office and Mom got her extra beauty sleep.

In the morning before work Dad would get dressed out of his tiny closet with a mirror on the door, in the light from the bare bulb hanging by its cord from the closet ceiling. Positioned before the door mirror in just his gartered socks and boxer shorts, he put on his starched white shirt and cufflinks and then his tie. I would stand and talk to him, watching every

Chapter 1-The Californian

move he made. In my "sleepy suit" with feet, I still had gold ringlets in my hair and stood only as high as his shorts—as he tied a big Windsor knot. Then he'd reach to the top shelf, put on his wide-brimmed, brown felt hat blocked with dimples and say, "Okay, Pete, I'm dressed. I'm going to work now." And I would laugh and say, "But, Daddy, you don't have any pants on!" My earliest memory of time spent with Dad was playing with blocks with him on the living room floor. Victoria, the young black woman who cooked and cleaned for us one day a week, came in with a plate of sweet-smelling chocolate and vanilla sugar cookies she had made with cookie-cutters shaped like diamonds, hearts, spades and clubs. I still remember the wonderful taste of those warm, fresh cookies. I don't know if I thought of any of these things as we said goodbye to Dad that morning, but I held onto them long after he was gone, because we weren't going to have any more times like that for a while.

While his senses adjusted to the evening chill of a Chicago spring and the din of the train shed, Ben scanned the platform. Proceeding quickly alongside the cars, further ahead he spotted a uniformed Marine sergeant shouting orders to a crowd of men. He pushed through the crowd and confronted the man in charge. The non-com, annoyed at the interruption, looked up quizzically from his clipboard and inquired, "And who are you?"

"Ben Green reporting for duty, Sergeant."

"It's about time, Green," he barked. He checked the paper on his clipboard.

"Green, you're in charge of this group all the way to San Diego. Keep 'em on the train, settled down, out of fights, and make damn sure that they all get there. Understand?"

"Yes, sergeant!"

Jolted into his new role, and never one to be shy in a crowd, Ben assessed his group—about 40 men, tall, short, slim and paunchy, some neat, some sloppy, some tough-looking, many of them confused and scared. He reflected proudly on the Marines' decision to put him in command. He knew what to do. The sergeant addressed the men, told them Ben was in charge and faced him again. "Well, what are you waiting for? Get this crew moving, on the double!"

Without a second's hesitation, he said, "Okay, men, my name is Ben

Green and I'll see to it that we all get to San Diego and show 'em what Chicago's troops are made of. Let's board this train!"

His letter home the next morning was ebullient: "This is Benny speaking from Compartment A on the Californian just outside Kansas. Being head man I had choice of accommodations and they're wonderful. Charlie Newhall of the First National Bank, my assistant, is with me and we're living royally. But no doubt the honeymoon will soon be over and a Marine sergeant will tell us just who the hell we are. We'll probably arrive late Monday or Tuesday. This is quite a gang— about half of our group of 41 men are kids—the others are between 30 and 36—a couple look a little sad-eyed but the rest are spry enough to shoot craps, etc. So far they are so excited about being on a Pullman train that they haven't had a chance to get bored. When they do—it's going to be a little harder to keep them nailed down." He then took the men on a Cook's tour, telling them where they were and where they were going, so they could brag to the folks at home.

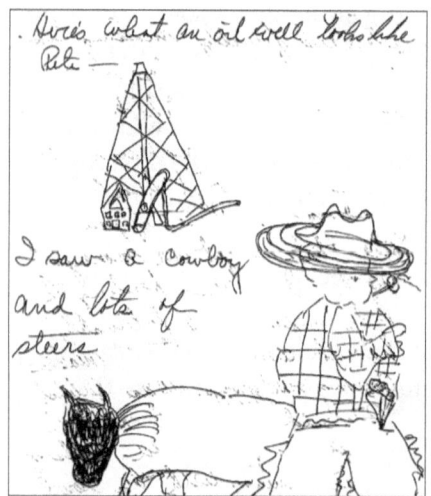
Ben's view from the train

The food on the train was generous and good, but he had to get tough with the porters and waiters to prevent them from "chiseling the boys" by passing a plate for tips. He thanked Alice for sending him off with a bag of goodies, "How did you ever do it? Each detail was perfect: cookies, matches covered up to keep them dry, some swell books, and cigarettes wrapped in a funny page from a radio script—but especially those wonderful cookies. Of course I mustn't forget the pictures of the circus and the Easter eggs. You and Pete certainly gave me a lot of laughs." He felt wonderful and collected the mail to be put off at Kansas City. He read his Time magazine for a while and then dozed off. On this eventful day the troops were just getting organized for Ben's war with the United States Marines, but clearly the battle was joined.

Arriving at Camp Pendleton, no longer "in charge," he fell in with his

Chapter 1-The Californian

fellow travelers to draw his clothing issue. He quickly distinguished himself in a matter of minutes by his attack on a sea bag. He described the logistics marvel of an enlisted man's sea bag: "an instrument of the devil, originally intended for seagoing personnel to stow away personal gear in a compact and transportable single unit. It is only slightly more unwieldy than the cumbersome footlocker officers tote around the four corners of the earth. Properly loaded, a sea bag is nearly round, hard as concrete and can be bounced, rolled, bumped, dropped and stacked, without doing any more to the contents than to make them virtually unusable.

"The very first step in making a Marine out of a civilian," he explained, "is to issue him personal gear including clothing for the tropics, for Alaska, for the United States, for bivouac and for guard duty. All to be neatly stowed away in the sea bag, which is exactly 33-and-a half inches tall and 14 inches in diameter. Actually, I was very pleased to have all this shiny new Marine Corps gear pushed upon me." The group of 46 men who arrived in San Diego, most of them under 23, accurately spotted his 36 years and designated him "Pops."

"Hey, Pops, how you gonna look on Michigan Avenue in these rags?" they taunted. He was too absorbed in the task of packing the enormous stack of seemingly useless clothing to respond. Suddenly, everyone was gone. Looking up, he noticed that they were marching—or the others were. He struggled to lift this dense mass off the ground onto his back, shoulders, head, or wherever it would land. His sea bag, for some reason, seemed to bend in the middle. This forced all the clothing at the top half back onto the ground. By the time he had the bag off the ground and secured in somewhat portable fashion, his outfit was two blocks ahead of him and he was staggering in pursuit. His years of training in meetings and plush offices had somehow failed to prepare him for this. As he lurched along he recalled his favorite quote from George Jean Nathan, who said that all the exercise a man needed was getting in and out of taxicabs and waving to people on the other side of the street. "But," he muttered to himself, "not if he wants to carry a sea bag."

He had made his way only a short distance up the company street when his plight was observed by a loud-talking Texan, who began a running commentary on his progress. He soon was joined by numerous other wags and observers lining the street. By actual count, he dropped the bag

17 times. "Roll it with your nose," urged one helpful Harry. "Sneak up on it—it won't bite back," suggested another. "Kick it to death—it's alive," warned a third.

After the latest drop he was bent over retrieving the monster, when he felt a surprisingly gentle tap on his back. "Hey, Mac—don't pay any attention to those jokers. They weren't any better when they got here. Here, let's do it right." Ben looked up. A man mountain was at his side.

He rearranged him, repacked his bag, taught him the trick of balancing the load on one shoulder and said, "Where you headed for?"

"With them," he informed him, pointing.

"With who?" he countered. He looked down the company street. Ben looked down the company street. There were no recruits in sight. "Well, let's hunt for 'em," his new friend volunteered. Minutes later, with a kind word, he headed Ben down his own company street, where the D. I. was ready for him. "A drill instructor," he explained for the uninitiated, "is a strange animal, produced by cross-breeding a hyena with a mad dog and then, just before he's made a D.I., he's starved for a week and given a company of recruits to see how many he needs to satiate his appetite."

"Where do you think you've been? This is not a party. From now on, you get where you're going on time! Any more of this stalling and you'll be running around the parade ground at three a.m. Now, get that gear stashed and be back out here in three minutes." Ben's war with the Marine Corps was on and he didn't start it.1 The mountain man who showed Ben how to heft a sea bag hailed from Chicago, where he worked in the steel mills. His name was Jimmy Morrow.

It was Ben's second week at boot camp. After noon chow, they formed up at the barracks for mail call. Pfc. Hart called out the names. "Green, ah don't know 'bout you," the tall, muscular southerner drawled, "You're a mighty popula' fellow. Heah's anotha' bunch." Ben strode forward and claimed two letters and a big package, which he was eager to open later that night when he had time. One was his daily letter from Alice; the second had an official printed return address on it from the Marine Corps. He tore it open, and winced as he quickly scanned the contents. "Damn!" he exclaimed.

Jimmy Morrow craned his neck and looked over his shoulder, "What is it Ben?"

Chapter 1–The Californian

"Doggone it. It's my commission. I'm too old," he moaned. "That slot in Marine intelligence is only open to men under 35, and I just turned 36 in March."

"Gee, that's tough," said Jim, the most kind-hearted man Ben had ever met. "I know how much you wanted that!"

"Yup, and it looks like it's too late now. Let's face it: we're already in the Marine Corps!"

"It's a sure thing we aren't going to get promoted around here," Jimmy offered in commiseration. "There's no opportunity to do so, and the first crack at ratings will come on new assignments. Those of us who go into the infantry will get short shrift. This base is known in the Marine Corps for considering a private first class the equal of an Army lieutenant."

"Jimmy," Ben confessed, "I'm disappointed, but not one-tenth as much as I would've been if I hadn't had a week of this first, especially with guys like you around."

Ben's sense of patriotism was strong—but almost everyone felt that way after the Nazi invasion of Europe and the last straw, Pearl Harbor. He was scornful of those who did not share his feelings, especially of well-known celebrities who shirked their military duty. "I see John Hodiak continues to ride to glory on his draft dodge," he wrote, "and Ralph Edwards, having reaped the benefits of all the publicity in which he nobly said he was ready to go if his country needed him, has now sought and obtained a 'war supporting industry' deferment! Phooey! Oh well—I've got clean hands and we can always feel good about ourselves."

Now that he had accepted his fate, relying on his wits and quick instincts to make the best of a difficult situation, he settled in and began his Marine life in earnest. Boot camp in itself presented plenty of challenges, which he met in his own way. "This chow is wonderful," he remarked to Alice in his daily letter, but he was alarmed at how fast it had to be eaten: no talking the mess hall, with everything regulated, including three inches between the trays on the dining table. For Peter's benefit he made a sketch of a divided tray. You could go back for as many

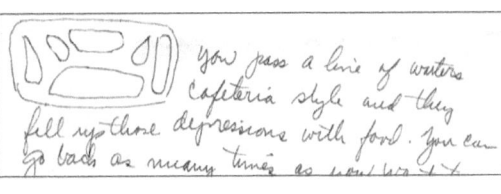

Divided chow tray

second helpings as you wanted. "For breakfast there are always, coffee, cereals, sometimes beans, toast some kind of fruit and potatoes (no orange juice, of course, this being California)," he noted. "Dinner's at noon: meat, potato salad, vegetables, ice cream bread and milk or cocoa. Everything is well-prepared, and supper is as large as dinner except the main course is likely to be stew or chili or spaghetti and sardines."

"I did well on my aptitude tests," he reported, "and if the first couple of weeks don't kill me I'll be a Marine. So far we have been getting our outfits, doing some drilling and getting used to routine. Tuesday, we start in earnest on a regular daily schedule. Don't be disturbed if you don't get letters. We literally have no time to ourselves from morning to night." On the previous night their outdoor theater, consisting of no more than a few rows of benches and a big screen under the open sky, had been turned over to the troops for an informal prize fight competition. Platoon 484 pitted its most promising candidates—including gentle Jimmy Morrow, whose 220 pounds and massive frame at least looked impressive—against the best contenders from rival platoons. Predictably, Jimmy got knocked out. He was nursing a jaw so sore that tonight he didn't even bother to go to chow call. Later, Ben opened the package from Alice, which included lots of useful items: hangers, candy, towels, money belt, apron, soap, a watch and a box of wonderful nuts from his sister Ruth. Although he had discouraged Alice from sending food, because everything had to be stored in the sea bag, he was glad to have the cocoa she sent. Ben fixed Jimmy a canteen of Nestlé's and brought him an apple from the mess hall.

He sat in a lower bunk of a 21-man hut—they had just moved from a tent. "I did well on my aptitude tests," he reported, "and if the first couple of weeks don't kill me I'll be a Marine. Later, Ben opened the package from Alice, which included lots of useful items: hangers, candy, towels, money belt, apron, soap, a watch and a box of wonderful nuts from his sister Ruth. Although he had discouraged Alice from sending food, because everything had to be stored in the sea bag, he was glad to have the cocoa she sent. Ben fixed Jimmy a canteen of Nestlé's and brought him an apple from the mess hall.

He later wrote: "Your cookies were opened at 6:15 and were gone by 6:25. They tasted wonderful and the boys sure loved them. I don't know what they do to them at the post office—probably drop them from 10-story

Chapter 1-The Californian

buildings—they were all broken, but it didn't mar the taste one bit."[3] Between her newsy letters from home and her shipments of cookies and treats, she soon became the sweetheart of Platoon 484.

Ben found it easy to escape notice. "As I see it, I won't be conspicuous in any way with the management while I'm at this base. One reason is that my size puts me at the end of the column, where the small youngsters are—and curiously, they aren't very good. Our drill instructor calls them "feather merchants." However, in many ways I'm just what you said I'd be to a lot of the kids, and I answer questions for them all day long. We have a professional chiseler—a kid from Baton Rouge, a merchant marine sailor and a De Met restaurant manager. It's a good crew and I think we're regarded as having the makings of a top-flight platoon."

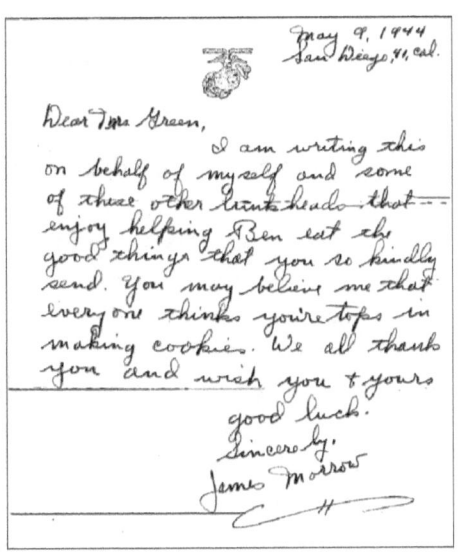

Jimmy's thank-you note

Meanwhile, Alice wrote that she had an offer from the New York Post to publish her column, which Ben advised her would probably not materialize until the fall. But he suggested that she use it with a Mr. Wester from Irna Phillips's office to get an appointment with this important person, who wrote most of the programs on daytime radio. It also brought tidings of Peter's fifth birthday party, which featured movies (courtesy of Peter's Uncle Mel, Ben's sister's husband, a photography enthusiast) and a puppet show.

The troops were then issued their rifles, bayonets, backpacks, mess kits and canteens, introduced to outdoor movie theaters and told to be ready to move out to their next activity in a week. They experienced bayonet training—in which a tobacco-chewing Marine confided that his best bayonet technique was to spit tobacco juice into his opponent's eyes— and the obstacle course. They complained of aches, bruises and blisters.

Ben began to have early skirmishes in his war. "I got my back up on our single trip to the P. X. We aren't allowed to have anything in bottles because the bottles break in our sea bags—a very reasonable and practical rule. The D. I. keeps ink for us. Since two of us have Parker 51's, he instructed me to buy ink. A corporal at the P. X. got very snotty about it and I wouldn't back down, finally telling him I had my orders too. He knew that our D. I. outranked him. So finally, he told me I couldn't have it unless the D. I. was with me. So I went over and got him and got the ink. Such tremendous problems fill our hours. Isn't that something?"

Early on, Platoon 484 had what Ben described as "a peculiar run of luck." It seemed that Hart, the Private First Class that everyone liked, was placed in command of the platoon, with an assistant who was very easygoing. "You have no idea how much difference there is among the men. We have seen sergeants cuff, kick and slap at men on the parade ground. Punishments such as picking up 500 cigarette butts, standing with nose and toes against the wall, carrying 20 buckets of sand in the hut, dumping them on the floor and then cleaning them up in 20 minutes—we have had none of this. Our inspection has been easy and, because we drill well, we haven't worked nearly as hard as some of the platoons do, but there's a rub:

When you empty a dish you are supposed to hold it up in the air until a waiter comes along and takes it to be refilled." Thursday, May 4, 1944 (Fourth day of boot camp).

Doing the Dishes

"When you're through you file out, drop silverware a piece at a time into receptacles, scrape your tray into a garbage can, wash it first in hot soapy water, then into tubs of clean hot water. MP's watch you, and the holder of a dirty tray does it over."

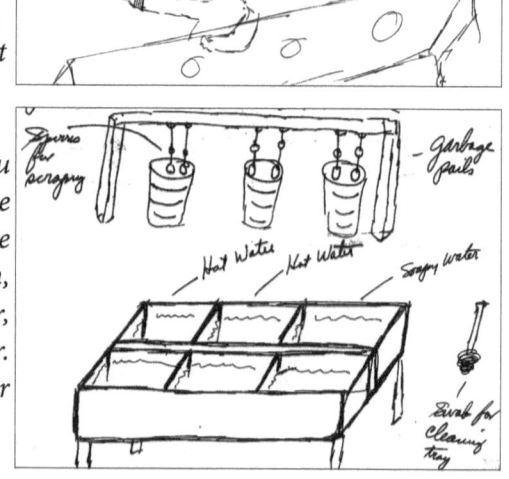

Mess hall etiquette

Chapter 1-The Californian

I'm afraid our platoon is getting a little sloppy."

He went on to express concern that, because Hart was somewhat inarticulate and poor in lectures, he hadn't communicated the stress placed on the platoon's behavior during the first three weeks. Ben was concerned that "something that we would do or fail to do would cause Hart to be placed on report, making him lose all privileges for two weeks. This would certainly turn this very nice guy into a mean bastard, since he would be sure to blame his misfortune on our ingratitude rather then on his own inadequacy." Later he commented, "Mentally, we have the most spirited platoon in this area. More noise, more music, more hilarity comes from our hut, particularly, than anywhere else on the base, as nearly as we can tell. We also seem to get more good food from home. So you can see our morale is high."

By Tuesday they had indeed started on their daily schedule. Ben indicated how busy it was by picking a Sunday and describing it hour by hour

5:35	Roll call	2:30	Lecture
6:10	Chow	3:00	Drill
7:15	Tetanus shot	3:30	Athletics
8:00	Haircut	4:00	Laundry, shower
9:00	Field jackets	4:40	Hang clothes
10:00	I.D. pictures	5:15	Chow
10:30	Drill	6:00	Clean rifle
12:20	Chow	8:00	Show
1:30	Platoon picture	9:00	Taps

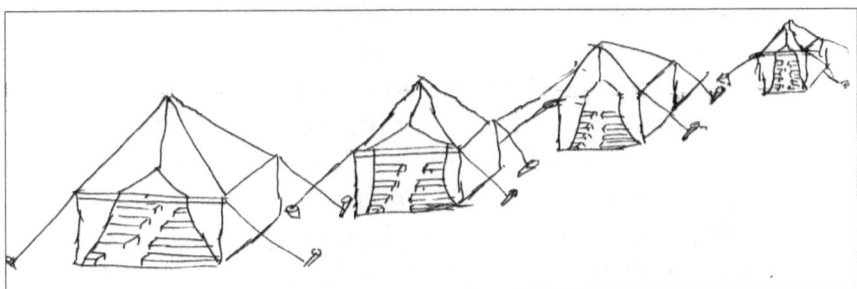

This is a tent row, and we live eight to a tent. When we go on bivouac, we live in shelter halves—two men put two together to make a pup tent. The tents aren't bad—we kind of like having only eight men to a tent for a change

He pointed out that, for each item on that list, they marched in formation anywhere from half a mile to two miles. "So if we do have a day when drill is light, we do enough marching to make up for it."

News from home included word that Alice's sister, Helen, who had undergone a period of extended distress and major surgery, was recovering. Alice had even considered putting the children in her mother's care and traveling east to help take care of her, but the danger had passed. It also included a clipping from the Sunday comic strip, "The Toodles." Its creators, Alice and Ben's friends Stan and Betsy Baer, who loved to feature friends of theirs in their cartoon strip, especially families affected by the war, had featured a boy named Peter Green. [4] "Peter, you're wonderful," Ben crowed. "All the men in the platoon think you are quite a celebrity, and I'm tickled that Stanley treated you so handsomely. The adventures around the house sound so natural and so full of fun, they make me very happy." He concluded with the description of another battle: "I had my usual incident today to the delight of my whole platoon." There was no milk and sugar at the mess table. He harassed the mess corporal who had been making the most noise yelling loudest at the men. Ben then told him "in no uncertain terms" that "we had to get back to our area and wanted our breakfast" and got away with it. "Instead of calling a waiter, the corporal went and got the stuff himself."

Along with more California dew—"damp, cold and chilly, and everyone is miserable"—came further training. Extended ordered drill, "running through the sand in skirmishes and throwing yourself on your face hugging the ground, then another run and 'boom' on your face again, double time back to the area and stand in the sun for an hour and a half learning to take apart a Browning automatic rifle." Other activities to be mastered included grenade training, jiu-jitsu lessons and guard duty. "I drew a stinker, which seems to cover half of the outskirts of Los Angeles, San Diego, the Consolidated Aircraft Corp. and two thirds of the base at night, but in the daytime consists of a 20 ft. strip of concrete up from the mess hall: three hours on and six hours off during a 24-hour period." O

On a work detail, cleaning the administration building Ben admitted he "polished brass and set all the clocks wrong, just for fun. Silly for a 36-year-old man to act that way, isn't it? Also, we made a

Chapter 1-The Californian

Peter Green as he appeared in "The Toodles"

French bed for Mike Aurelio last night, and Jim and I found out how to get free popcorn out of the vending machine." He adds, "I also tried my luck going to the PX, which is strictly prohibited except in conducted tours, of which there has only been one. But I wanted a pennant for Pete's birthday and needed stationery, so I risked it and got away with it."

Good news broke on May 17. Effective Saturday, all platoons would be given a furlough of 10 days upon breaking up, which for Ben would be June 24, assuming they were not assigned in the meantime to mess duty.

Then they had gas mask drill, had their boots surveyed—that is, inspected to see if they needed new ones—and packed for a move to the rifle range. They were also happy to learn that they would be among the first recruits to train with the Browning automatic rifle (B. A. R.). "Incidentally, Ben noted, "boots didn't fire these on the range until now. This is something new, and we are quite tickled."

Then, toward the end of their stay, they learned something else: "We've discovered the secret of the terrible scrambled eggs, which we have suspected of being dehydrated. But since I helped to load 200 cases on a truck a couple of weeks ago, I was fairly sure they weren't. The eggs are steamed instead of fried. We had the same eggs at guard mess, scrambled in the usual way, and they tasted fine. Steamed, they taste like somebody's socks."

Ben wore his new Marine wardrobe proudly. For work, they had two combinations: dungaree pants with dungaree jacket—Marine green, black insignia—made of herringbone cotton, denim type. Or, they wore the pants with a sweatshirt. During the day they always wore their tan pith helmets.

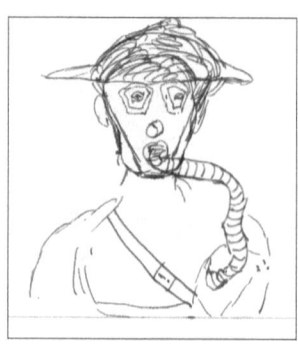
Gas mask drill

"When we dress for pictures or parade, we are wearing dress greens—a khaki shirt and khaki field scarf—and our green garrison cap. "That's the way we were dressed in the platoon picture," he explained to Alice. "Then if it's cool we wear our very smart field jackets, which are khaki, waterproof, zippered and lined, and smartly cut... Our overcoats are green, and we have not yet been issued our uniform blouses (coats) or dress shoes. We get those when we come back from the range and get outfitted for the trip home. A

Chapter 1-The Californian

well-fitted Marine uniform really looks like something, and they try hard to fit you—even take you to the tailor shop for alterations." Ben and his fellow recruits were now old hands at Marine dress, procedures and getting along in the Corps. They were ready for the final test; in addition to learning to fire the B. A. R. they would be learning to shoot with their M-1 rifles. With the preliminaries over. they headed to a camp at the rifle range.

Troop bus

"The ultimate achievement of Marine Corps boot camp," he wrote, "is shooting for record on the rifle range. The Corps is a fighting outfit and shooting is a way of life." A desultory camp named Mathews, permanently maintained in a temporary status, including its dysentery, sloppy mess arrangements and inadequate tent facilities, was the place where Marines finally came out of the cocoon of recruit life. To a degree they rejoined the human race. At Mathews their now tougher carcasses, calloused hands and indifference to berating and abuse met the challenge at the hands of a towering Scot named Angus MacPherson.

MacPherson had one burning ambition, which he was not reticent in describing to Ben's platoon. In their first lecture he declaimed with a thick brogue: "Sometime, somewhere I'll r-r-receive, instead of the usual assortment of dolts and clumsy, awkward goons, a company of natural riflemen. Men to whom a rifle will be simply an extension of their arms and body. Men who will clap the piece into their shoulders, squeeze, not pull, the trigger and who will respect with supreme reverence the only thing that can bring them back alive, their M-1 rifle."

He prayed for a company of men who would set an all-time rifle range record for the Marine Corps on record day. MacPherson never tired of telling them: "What a mar-r-r-velous instrument has been carelessly placed in yer hands: ye, who will never appreciate it; ye, who will never lu-r-rn to use it properly; ye, who are tew styupid to digest the rich fare of riflery that I spr-r-read before ye daily!"

For three long, hard weeks, prone, kneeling, sitting, standing—"Squeeze the trigger, get that elbow up"—they worked. "That's all there are to it," repeated MacPherson each golden day. Ten long days without ever firing the thing. Ten long days in which they proved over and over and over again—yes, they could take it apart and put it together again without a false move. Ten long days in which they prayed nightly that MacPherson would die in bed and fail to appear on the range the next morning.

MacPherson had a good heart. But as far as he was concerned, men were only put on earth for one purpose: to squeeze the trigger of an M-1 and to fire straight and true. Day after day, as Ben lay prone on the California sands, MacPherson's No. 12's came into view. "Get that elbow up," he bellowed. "Get your shoulder around the butt of that rifle. How do you expect to shoot for record?" About the fourth day, MacPherson began spending a disproportionate amount of his time at Ben's station.

He would sneak up behind and land all of his 227 pounds in the middle of his back and simultaneously jerk his elbow up. Nothing cracked, so Ben gave him credit that at least he understood about what a human back would take. On the ninth day, MacPherson swore. "Those damned short arms of yours." Ben was appalled: he felt exactly about his arms as Lincoln had felt about his legs: they were just the right length to reach anything they needed to. On the tenth day, MacPherson's mind was made up. Ben was summoned from the range and dispatched to an office. There was no explanation—there never was an explanation in the Corps, either because the man performing the duty was incapable of giving one, or in other cases, deemed you far below the echelon requiring one. Measurements were taken by a lethargic but seemingly knowing pair. They made notations. They looked at each other. They looked at the paper. They even looked at Ben. After a long silence, one spoke.

"I'll be God-damned," he said.

Ben's breaking back

Chapter 1-The Californian

"Yeah," said the other.

"The little feather merchant needs one."

"Write an order," said the senior.

"Okay," said the order maker. He wrote. He handed Ben a slip of paper. "Go to Building F." He went to Building F. He waved his paper. He wound up in a rifle supply room. "Hmmm," said the sergeant. "I'll be God-damned." He turned his back on Ben and disappeared into rows of racks filled with every imaginable type of small weapon supply.

By now, Ben was sure he had committed a cardinal Marine Corps sin and was about to be given some kind of excommunication. Finally, the sergeant reappeared. "Gimme your rifle." He gave. In seconds the man removed the butt and fastened another to it. "Try that," he said. He tried. It sank into position with ease.

"Hey what did you do?" Ben ventured.

"Gave you a half inch shorter butt. Almost never happens." With that he glared at Ben as if he were a deformed freak.

With his short rifle butt, he appeared on the range for his first live ammunition drills and found he could shoot like an angel. MacPherson began to treat him as if he were a hot quarterback on a Big Ten, Rose Bowl contender team. Ben was sure to shoot as he thought a Marine should.

As Allied forces stormed the beaches at Normandy on June 6th, Ben was ecstatic. "What a day!" he told any fellow soldier who would listen. They arrived on the firing line at 6:30 a.m. to hear H. V. Kaltenborn on the radio blaring over the public address system with the news of the invasion. This high-strung broadcaster had reported each day's battles in his frantic tenor throughout the war and was rumored to sleep on a bedroll in the studio in case a news bulletin broke. For the first time in many years, Ben was overjoyed to hear Kaltenborn's voice.

From then on in every spare moment he hung outside the huts of D. I.s that had radios and listened to all the news that he could catch. But the war news topped everything. He started to talk about it to a few of the boots near him, but the reaction was so slight that he hurried down the line 40 targets away to find Jim and Charlie Newhall to share his enthusiasm. Kaltenborn said that from there it looked really good. The bulletins carried a high note of optimism, and the German admissions seemed to confirm the official press releases. "Deep down, I hope, as everyone does,"

Ben wrote, "that I was wrong and that, instead of having to fight for every mile of the way to Berlin, the prayed-for collapse will come."[6]

Record day dawned. Dawn was only a guess. It was pitch black at 4 AM and pouring rain. "Do we have to shoot in this?" the kids wailed. Fading were their visions of Marine Corps glory, medals, the permanent attachment to their records of prowess in the handling of firearms. Certainly the Lord had conspired against them. Ben comforted them as best he knew how. The rain could stop. It would be hours until they would be on the range in position to shoot. Shooting in the rain wasn't impossible—lots of outfits must have had rainy days for records days. They wailed on: "How can you see the sights in this downpour?" Frankly, he didn't know. But inside his rain slicker, he had tucked two towels and a shirt torn into rags before they left the barracks. The gag men promptly asked if he was going to shoot for record or take a shower. He remained silent as they slogged off to the range in formation. It was 7 a.m. when they took the line.

The setup was simple. There were 30 targets, 30 stations. At the center of the firing line was an elevated stand, where the officers' staff operated. All signals came from this stand. In charge was an all-seeing colonel with powerful field glasses, who seemed to know what was going on at all 30 stations at all times. His brassy voice boomed over the P.A. system alternately with abuse, ridicule and encouragement. "Maggie's drawers" was the big disgrace—a red flag, waved back and forth in front of the target, meaning the shooter had made a complete five-shot miss and a score of zero for the position. Twenty shots were fired in all, five in each position. Varicolored flags signaled the control stand and the rifleman on the relative success of the endeavor. The day's shooting was miserable. The rain never stopped. The men literally couldn't sight their targets and blind firing simply had to mean low scores.

"Finally, I was on the line. I'd made up my mind," Ben reported. "I was going to shoot well if it took all day, and I had a plan. I took my position. With one of my towels, I carefully dried my rifle from sight to sight. Then I fired one shot. Again I dried the piece and fired. Behind me, impatient miserable men had given up all hope of shooting well for record. They were interested only in getting through with it, out of the rain and back to the barracks. They started to heckle me. I was holding up the line. But I couldn't even hear them. My first five shots were five bull's eyes." And then came the welcome sound—loud and clear on the P.A. system—of the colonel's voice. "On Target 19, nice going shorty, take your time, keep it up."

"The rest was a breeze. I fired and tried fifteen times more and I was in like Flynn. As Angus MacPherson had told us, 'That's all there are to it.' Before I left the range with my company I was handed an order. 'Report to Building F at once.' Merrily I sought and obtained transportation and waved the slip in the faces of the two lethargic overseers."

"Gimme your rifle." said the senior. Ben gave. The man removed the short butt that had helped him to perform and returned the original butt to the rifle.

"But I just shot high scores with that," Ben protested.

"Yeah, but you won't need that for killing Japs. We only got four of them short butts."[5]

In mid-June their qualifying rounds at the range were complete. Ben earned a Sharpshooter medal and only missed the Expert class by a few shots. "And now our work is done, I think—we finished our hand grenade course, gas mask drill and also finished combat tactics, or creeping and crawling in the sand with rifles for 100 feet or so. Then Odell, our tyrannical training officer, turned tail and became the nicest guy in the world. We had a bull session half the afternoon during which he answered 101 questions about furlough. All we can think about, all we can talk about is furlough—how to get there, what to do, dope on clothing and gear. We're like a bunch of kids with a new toy. Somehow the seriousness of the war never bothers us. Even when we buy newspapers regularly, as I have been doing since the invasion started, we slide right by. It seems to be going well, doesn't it? Soon, we can talk and talk and spend some glorious days together."

On Tuesday, June 20th, he sent home a short note with his travel arrangements: thanks to some help from a family friend in Chicago, he would be on a streamliner leaving at 4:30 p.m. on the following Saturday, with a possible arrival time in Chicago on Monday (June 26th). He cashed in the ticket issued by the government and took the faster train, about three days' travel, with a similar return on El Capitan; these arrangements at least allowed him to spend almost half of his ten-day furlough at home. He could pick up the ticket in Los Angeles. He had requested and received a shoe ration stamp from Alice, so he wouldn't have to wear his uniform oxfords while he was home on leave. He would buy some fine new dress shoes when he got to L.A. He had enough money in hand to pay for both the ticket and the shoes. While uncertainty and fear still hovered not far away, in the mindset that Ben and most sane people developed in the military—of living one day at a time—things couldn't be better: he was going home!

Chapter 1-The Californian

Ben's platoon, with names labeled

CHAPTER 2

SAN FRANCISCO CHRONICLES

Ben stood on the front walk looking sharp in his service uniform: olive drab wool blouse over his khaki shirt and matching tie, dress pants and saucer service cap with visor. He stood alternately at attention and at ease, smiling and clowning while Alice struggled with the Argus 35-millimeter camera. She took a few shots, asked her neighbor to photograph them together and then it was her turn. Playfully Ben removed his fancy hat, set it on her wavy, dark blond curls and shot frame after frame as Alice posed smiling contentedly in her flowered dress. He had about five days at home before the three day return trip. As her sister

Alice and Ben reunited

Alice in Ben's cap

Helen wrote, "It gives me a wonderful feeling, too, to think of you all reunited, but I know you and Peter must be beside yourselves. Only little Linda will take her Daddy's appearance with calm. I am sure you are killing the fatted calf and wearing yourself out baking goodies and cleaning the house much too thoroughly (as if Benny cared, when he has you)." She had warned Alice, "Don't hide the radio, too!" Helen was referring to the time Alice, in her zeal to neaten up the house, had hidden the kitchen receiver in a drawer and had to get help tracing the wire from the wall outlet box to locate it.

The ancient white oak still nestled gracefully into the curved section of cast iron picket fence along the sidewalk. The old Victorian house, with its wide, inviting eaves and tall, dark windows overlooking the street, welcomed him. To fix a steak dinner, enjoy it with the family and drink a beer whenever he wanted would be paradise. He was relieved that Helen was talking in her letter about taking a house somewhere on the Massachusetts shore for next August. He would not be nearly so worried about his family if Alice were with her sister and Peter and Linda had the company of their cousins, aunt and uncle.

The days flew by, and his hopes for a happy reunion reunion were fulfilled. But too soon it was time to tear himself away again and endure another sad parting.

He still had no idea where he was headed next: he would find out when he returned to Camp Pendleton. Helen hoped he would be assigned to training on the East Coast, but he dismissed that as wishful thinking. There was a war to be fought, and he had volunteered for it. "I haven't given a moment's thought to what lies ahead," he wrote, "which probably means that I have become like all the other GI Joes, interested only in what date the mess will be over." At least he was on a good fast train.

Aboard the *El Capitan,* he camped in the club car, where he spent the first day and a good part of the second with two WACs and a couple of soldiers from Chicago, drinking and playing poker, "a very handy arrangement,

Chapter 2-San Francisco Chronicles

since my poker winnings paid for my drinks, and as a result I'm a little ahead of where I expected to be." The second night he returned to the club car and "picked up with about half a dozen kids, girls on vacation, and we started singing. Finally, the entire club car joined in, and we kept at it until about 11 o'clock. I had enough beer so I popped off to sleep right away and thus feel fine this morning." While Alice was surely happy to hear from him and learn he was all right, she could hardly have been thrilled at his activities. His ability to be the life of the party in any situation was to her not always, especially not now, his most endearing quality.

Blissfully unaware of such concerns, however, Ben bubbled about *his* favorite subjects, Alice and the family. "It seems as if my trip home was a dream, but it was a wonderful dream, to find everything so lovely, my darling so beautiful, my children so handsome and Pete such a fine little man. I'm glad I had the furlough, even though it's hard to leave each time."

Later that day the train arrived. With plenty of time to kill before he had to report back for duty, he had prearranged to meet Jim Morrow in Los Angeles. A show business friend, Mel Shauer, an executive at RKO Pictures, had offered to conduct Ben, Jimmy, and Jim's buddy George Fender on a studio visit. "It was kind of radio business stuff to me—at that it was quite touristy—but Jim and George were goggle-eyed." They grabbed a Wimpy's glorified hamburger, took a one-hour streetcar ride to Hollywood and Vine and went right into the Brown Derby for a drink. They learned that service personnel were permitted to drink only beer before 5 p.m. and that the Brown Derby only had two cold beers, which they drank. Except for a possible sighting of Groucho Marx, they were less than impressed. They had their uniforms pressed and presented themselves at the RKO lot by 3:00 p.m., where they met up with Mel. He brought

Jimmy, George Fender and Ben

along Barbara Hale, who played opposite Frank Sinatra in his first picture, "a very beautiful, very nice gal from Chicago, and we had a lot of fun with her." After watching a few retakes of a scene from a Vera Vague comedy (without the star), Ben became convinced that a radio director could easily direct a movie, a proposition with which Mel heartily agreed. They repaired to the RKO commissary, where they were rejoined by Barbara Hale and met Jimmy Jordan, ". . . a song and dance kid who has a role in the new Fibber McGee and Molly movie which will be released Wednesday at Camp Pendleton. Bill Gordon, who wrote the story, gave Jimmy his card to be sure he gets in." While Mel took a phone call, Pat O'Brien drove by and said hello to the troops.

The rest of the day was a dazzling whirlwind of activity: "Mel took us on a Cook's tour of Hollywood (we saw Ann Miller standing at the Columbia Pictures entrance) and drove us through some of the pretty residential sections, winding up at his own home, where we met his wife, Rosetta Marino, a dancer, and his V-12 Navy son. Mel was delighted by our interest in his orchard. He had two or three each of a big variety of trees—lemon, orange, lime, avocado, plum, peach, chestnut, olive, kumquat, etc. We picked some fruit from the trees."

Leaving Mel's house, they returned to Hollywood Boulevard in search of dinner. Jimmy wanted to see Trocadero; it was much too early for such nightspots to be serving, so he conducted them through the deserted Trocadero and Mocambo clubs for a look around. After a steak dinner at Victor's, they visited Hollywood Canteen, where Alan Ladd was autographing like mad. "No other celebrities were in sight, but there were dozens of cute, lovely 18 and 19-year-old kids. I started to dance with one of the lovelies, but after she said 'Oh. You don't rhumba!' I gave up. Those kids can dance, and they really made me feel like 103 again." Despite having had time to kill, they ran for their train and barely made it. "And that's the story of 'my day in Hollywood.' We had a swell time. It was a good way to say goodbye to Jim. I don't know how often or when I'll see him."

The ride to San Diego was only 122 miles, but, as the train lumbered slowly through the southern California hills and stopped frequently, it took six hours. He paused at the Army and Navy YMCA for a shower, wrote a long letter home and still reported to Camp Pendleton with five hours to spare. Only a day later, he found himself on another milk train, this time headed for his new duty station at Mare Island Navy Yard, north of San Francisco. "Just what that means I don't know, but some 3- to 4,000 Marines are usually stationed at Mare Island—it might mean that I stay there for a long time. There are 470 Marines aboard this train, all assigned to different units: Navy prison, Navy yard, guard companies. Mare Island is considered good Marine duty. San Francisco is a good liberty town—it doesn't dislike servicemen the way San Diego and Los Angeles do, and they don't get rooked so badly—and the work is easy. Should I get moved again, it could be anywhere from Pearl Harbor to Great Lakes or from Australia to Guam. In any event, I'll see the State of California."

The rattling cars crawled north out of Los Angeles, Ben watched as the city rail yards, depots and factories gave way to gentle slopes dotted with farms and luxuriant masses of trees, all against the background of a distant mountain range. He observed his fellow travelers. Unlike the recruits he had trained with for the past two months, they were older, more subdued. They had been in the military long enough to know the score and were resigned to a life of uselessness. "It's perfectly obvious to every-one on this train that the Marines have no intention of using any ability that we may have and consequently is equally obvious that none of us should be in this service. There's a lot of hope that married men over 30 will eventually be released. But, that sort of thinking only leads to unfounded rumors like the one that had us going to Alaska this morning, before we found out where we really were going. And like the discharge rumor that apparently was hot while I was on furlough." [1]

On the bus that transported them from the train depot to the Navy Yard Ben got his first glimpse of Mare Island Strait, the inlet that separated this peninsula from the mainland, and the dark blue waters of San Pablo bay, which connects with San Francisco bay to the south. He saw ships of every description—destroyers, cruisers, tenders and, in the distance, an aircraft carrier—at the piers and drydocks which lined the naval base. He got a whiff of the brisk sea air and felt an unfamiliar penetrating chill. Palm trees, a shorter, squatter type than

Native Palm

the royal palms so common in Los Angeles, lined the main drives. "The yards themselves look like a huge factory district—kind of like the South Chicago steel mills, except that they are cleaner and neat-

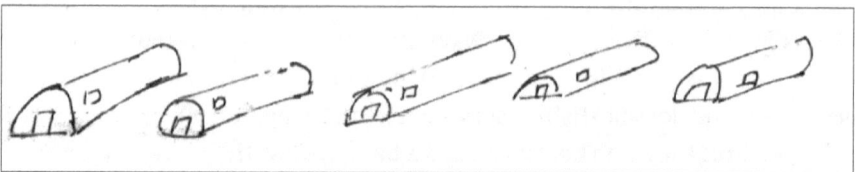

er. Noncoms get them, I think." "These little houses, which look like half a sewer pipe, are all over the base for the families of the permanent personnel. "All of the officers' quarters are white frame homes; some of them must be 12- to 14-room houses and have red tile roofs. There are lots of palm trees. And the other foliage is beautiful. Flowers thrive here and apparently there are lots of good gardeners, since a walk through the residential area of the yard is a pretty sight."

Shortly after arriving at Mare Island, on July 6th, Ben lamented the housing conditions his unit encountered: "The comfortable three-story cement block guard building at Mare Island could house a detachment of 300 men with ease and efficiency. Unhappily when our 300 arrived, 300 more appeared simultaneously from another camp in the United States owing to a clerical error." To further complicate matters, 150 members of the departing guard unit had not yet received their orders, although they were to be relieved of guard duty that day. As a result, he said, "the quarters were jam packed, which meant that the new arrivals were poured into the attic ... and our sacks are just about on top of each other."

The prospect of guard duty, which was the main shore role of Marines in the Navy, was worrisome. "A fellow could wind up standing on a

Guard post

dock at three a.m. watching the U.S.S. Portland load," he mused. "San Francisco Bay can be mighty unpleasant at those predawn hours. I'd better find out what's happening." What he had learned about guard duty during basic training was that, regardless of any danger that it might entail, it was long, boring and lonely. Here in northern California, where it was very damp and chilly, even in summer, it could be downright miserable. And Ben was never one to sit back and accept adversity. For starters, he quickly got to know his commanding officer. When he asked why all the perfunctory formations, drills and busy work that cluttered his day were necessary, the captain "gave me a song and dance on the importance of the supply and service work, all of which is perfectly true, and it is true that the Marines have discovered bombs and saboteur plants and have done much to earn a good reputation for protecting this vast yard."

He began to appreciate the mission of the 1,500-man Marine detachment in protecting the installation. Battle damaged ships lined the docks: "submarines, flattops cruisers transports, all in for repairs. Mare Island puts them in shape." He concluded, "Every kind of ship from underwater demolition unit and PT boat to the largest of the aircraft carriers put in there for overhaul and, in a few short weeks, a man comes to know and respect our Navy might."

Located 38 miles northeast of San Francisco, Mare Island Navy Yard was on the north side of the bay and considerably inland from the ocean; the "island" is really a peninsula, finger-like in shape, separated by a wide slip from Vallejo. It derived its name from a mare discovered living on the island (and expropriated) by General Mariano Guadalupe Vallejo, the northern administrator and future *commandante-general* of Spanish California. The mare had escaped from a capsized animal raft and swam ashore. The military history of Mare Island began on January 4, 1853, when the United States purchased it for $83,491. In September of 1854, Commander David Glasgow Farragut and his family arrived. Farragut, later to become a naval hero of the Civil War and the first Admiral of the U. S. Navy, had been sent west to personally oversee the building of a navy yard in support of the Pacific Squadron.[2]

By the turn of the century, the installation had become a major naval base and was famous for building submarines, from the earliest, such as the Grampus, the Pike (1900) and the Nautilus (costing $5 million in 1916) to the last of 17 nuclear-powered subs built there, the USS Drum. During World War II, the base built subs, helping to double the U. S. submarine fleet from 111 to 260. "At the height of World War II the shipyard employed over 46,000 civilian and military personnel and served as one of the most important ship repair facilities for the Pacific Fleet. By VJ Day, Mare Island workers raised over $75,697,000 in war bonds—enough to pay for all the submarines built during the war, and a tender to boot."[3]

Ben was to have a minor role in that effort as well. In the War Bond Office, he was assigned to guard a detail that daily collected and deposited receipts from the continuous war bond drive.

After a tour of the docks, he wrote: "I wish Pete had been with me yesterday. I visited the docks and saw the heavy cruisers, Baltimore and Portland. The Baltimore, considered the most beautiful ship in the fleet, has just been overhauled and painted (it's only a year old) and the scuttlebutt was that the President is going to use it and that one elevator has been installed for him.

"We went aboard the Portland, which is almost as big as the Baltimore, and climbed aboard it for a couple of hours. These ships are so intricate that they stagger the imagination. How they make these things work, even when conditions are favorable, is hard to understand—but they can operate even after they've been pounded in battle. There are miles and miles of wire and pipes, and while we were aboard the ship was undergoing a complete overhaul, so everything was torn up.

To illustrate his experience for his son, he drew a picture of the Portland, bristling with guns. He apologized: "The ships are hard to draw. I'll try to find some picture postcards for Pete." This ship, commissioned in 1929, saw action in the battle of Guadalcanal, November 12-15, 1942. In his endorsement of the Portland's action report, Fleet Admiral William F. Halsey, Jr. commented, ' the Portland's performance was most commendable, especially as regards ship and damage control, including the sinking of the enemy destroyer Yudachi by Portland, one of the highlights of this action." After participating in the Gilbert and Marshall Islands campaigns, the Portland screened carriers during air attacks against Palau, Yap, Ulithi and Woleai by April 1, and supported invasions in New Guinea, Truk and the bombardment of Satawan. Following this series of operations, Portland

Chapter 2-San Francisco Chronicles

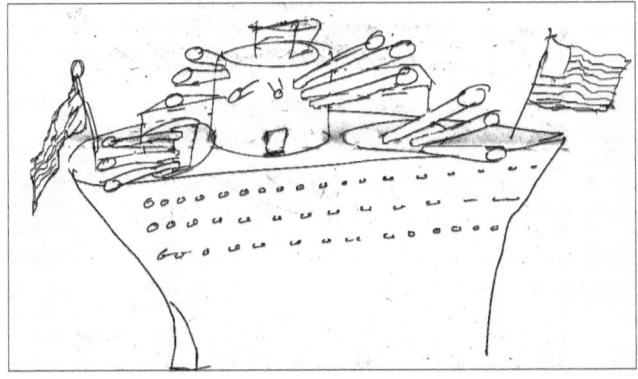

U. S. S. Portland

steamed for Mare Island to be overhauled. It was during this refitting stop that Ben toured the ship. She was ready to return to duty for pre-landing bombardments and the bloody landing at Peleliu in mid-September. The Portland was the prototype for the Portland class of heavy cruisers, which went on to serve the Navy with distinction in numerous later conflicts.

Ben soon settled into the life of a Marine guard. Reveille was at six, then chow, which was "fair, and you have to go when it opens or stand in a long line." Police call and an exercise called "troop and drill" were required of Marines when not on guard duty. The duty itself was 24 hours on and 24 hours off, standing guard for a certain number of hours, varying with the assignment, and being on call in between.

He had a new vision of his role in the military: "My philosophy about this life has changed considerably: I'm going to try to find myself a soft job and make believe I'm back in college. I'll read (there's a good library). I'll play tennis. I'll drink beer. When I can afford it, I'll take a tourist trip or two to San Francisco and find out if there's a place to fish in the ocean nearby—I'd probably be happier fishing than doing anything else on liberty. So if you hear from me that your Benny has run down a soft swivel chair job, don't be alarmed." He assured Alice that this would not be a change in his personality but rather that he had accepted and improved upon the Marine theory that men his age could not be very useful as privates. "If I'm not going to have anything to do with the war, I might just as well be comfortable. Except for wishing I were home, feeling a little silly about having wanted to be a 'hero' and passing up things I would have to fight for now (probably unsuccessfully), my spirits are good. I think I can work out a very satisfactory and reasonable life here, even though it will be pointless."[4]

His mail finally reached him on Mare Island on July 14th. He wrote Alice, "Hooray, hooray—my first mail from my baby! Gee, I'm sorry I scared you, but by now you have all the details of the transfer and know that it looks like I'll be stationed here indefinitely." Alice's sister Helen describes the women's emotions best in a July 13th letter: "Deadly dull as Benny must find guard duty, I can't help but feel great relief at hearing that he's been assigned to it—and on this side of the Pacific." His sojourn at Mare Island, while neither stimulating nor rewarding, would at least offer some shelter from the gathering storm.

Marines, he learned, were men of many faces, but basically, there were two styles of real, prewar and early war enlisted men. "From Texas, from Brooklyn, from New York's East Side, from the valley in Chicago, from Purple Gang territory in Detroit, came the disgruntled society haters who wanted a chance to get even with the world, no holds barred. They wanted to win some applause while they were letting someone have it. And there were the vain-glorious men from all over America—small town policemen, rangers, plainsmen, men who lived rough, were tough and wanted to be part of the roughest, toughest outfit there was." The rest, including him, were civilians in Marine uniforms who could hardly explain why they were there.

He could not abide stupidity nor prejudice, which some of the malcontents took pride in displaying—"the endless gab about Negroes and how much they hate them, about how lousy the Corps is, and so on." he naturally gravitated to men he could talk to, confide in and discuss issues with, most of them older. "I've met a guy name of Joe Aspley, who is an insurance broker from Louisville or Nashville—I forget which—who already shows signs of providing companionship. Dave Alpert, a bartender from Minneapolis, is another, so maybe I'll find a few gents in this outfit to buddy with." One good friend was Elwood Godsall, whom he called Duke, an insurance broker from San Francisco.

When it came to peaceful relations in their quarters, however, he could be a diplomat.

One day in mid-July Ben's housing conditions improved. The clerical error was corrected, the detained guard detachment finally left and Ben's platoon was moved from the attic to quarters on the "third deck."[5]

"Where was Joe Simpson's bunk?" Ben asked a short muscular guy with black curly hair.

"Oh he and his buddy Louie had that one over there." He pointed to a vacant double bunk in a corner.

"Joe said we could have this one, since he and Louie are shipping out."

"Oh yeah? I'm Charlie Donati. I wouldn't take it, though. Look who your neighbor is. Those jigs give me the creeps."

A black man was on his hands and knees, peering under the next bunk.

"What're you looking for?" Ben asked.

"My quarter rolled somewhere. Damn, that was my lunch."

Ben rolled his sea bag from his shoulder to Louie's upper bunk and got down on his knees to help him look. "Ah, here it is." He handed the man the coin.

"I'm Ben."

"Clarence." The man broke into a broad grin and shook his hand.

"You can bunk here, I guess," Charlie said. "You ain't no Jew-boy are you? I hate them, too."

"As a matter of fact," Ben said, "I am. But down on this deck I can shower every day. You won't even notice the difference."

When Dave Alpert offered him the bed beneath, Ben patted the upper bunk. "This one suits me fine. We've each got a locker and a locker box. Most guys haven't figured out you've got to inherit them from guys who are leaving."

"Beats that attic we've been crammed into," Dave said.

"Now I've got a place other than my sea bag to hang uniforms. At least I can put a shirt away without having it look as if I slept in it."

"I see what you mean," Charlie said. "You guys seem pretty smart."

"So Charlie, where are you from?" Ben said.

"Scranton, P.-A. I worked in the coal mines."

"That's hard work. But you look pretty strong."

"I am. In the mines, we had to move the rails for the coal cars so they'd run to other sections of the mine. Four men, two at each end, could barely manage to lift a rail and lay it on a small flat car. I did it alone," Charlie said.

"Wow, that's pretty good."

"Yeah," Charlie said, warming to his audience. "First I lifted one end and put it on the car; then I went to the other end and lifted it on the car. I was the only man who could do it alone."

Satisfied that these new guys held him in sufficiently high esteem, Charlie decided they were qualified to join his barracks and walked away.

"Now we can store our new clothing issue," Ben said. "I can send a pair of trousers to the tailor to be altered and have an extra shirt. I feel like a dude again. But I still haven't figured out a way to have my blouse altered, unless... "

Ben pulled an olive drab wool jacket out of his sea bag. "One of the boys going on sea duty gave me this blouse. It fits me perfectly."

"But it has red paint on it." Dave pointed to a blob on the back the jacket.

"I think I can fix that." Ben sat on the lower bunk and took out his K-Bar knife. Having little to do, he'd kept it sharp as a razor. Carefully, he peeled up one edge of the splotch and slowly sheared it off.

"That's great," Dave said, "almost as good as new."

"I'll take it to be cleaned, and when the pants are done I'll have a uniform that fits me."

Dressing well had always been important to Ben. He learned the men's clothing business shortly after he dropped out of the University of Chicago in his sophomore year, when his father died. He went on to work in a department store that offered quality men's wear. He learned the dos and don'ts of sales: don't pressure your customer, select well for him, let *him* decide how good he looks, and never show him an ill-fitting garment. He liked subtle styling and a good fit. When it was right you felt different—at ease, confident, pleased with your image in the mirror and ready to take on the world. Between regular exercise and learning to control his diet, he managed to appear tanned, lean and healthy in his well-fitting uniform.

In his spare time Ben got to know his fellow Marines and occasionally some of the local people. "My liberty last night consisted of a visit to a carnival and a hamburger—hot stuff. I also spent a few minutes with a 17-year-old girl at a USO dance who guessed maybe I was older— maybe even 24! She had just celebrated her 17th birthday last Saturday and was married to an Army aviation engineer. She ran away from home to get married and they had 11 days together before he was transferred. Then she

Chapter 2-San Francisco Chronicles

went home. What the war is doing to those kids frightens me. I don't think they'll ever live normal lives."

He despaired that the men he talked to had never had a civilian job, but had been in the Marines for three or four years, including two years or more in overseas service. "The number of Guadalcanal shoulder patches around here is surprising. Some have moo-moo, jungle rot, malaria, various kinds of stomach and kidney ailments and all are—not bitter—but simply unenthusiastic. They remind me of one of the middle-age failures I know, who didn't think he'd ever have a better job. They're going to head into a bitterly competitive world with no training for any job—and enough years to make an employer expect some experience, and in many cases health that is none too good."

He described the role of women on the base as drivers, taking their liberation in stride. He drew a picture for Pete of one of the military transport vehicles. "Did I tell you, Pete, that some of our buses are called elephant trains, because they're big and bulky like an elephant? They are driven by women—women do everything in this community. Tiny girls run great big machines, drive huge cranes and tractors. Many of them look and act just like men—kind of a curious sight at first. And the yard runs 24 hours a day, so the buses and ferries run all night. There are three full shifts in all shops. There's no coast blackout anymore, so the Island is a blaze of light all night long—must've been strange under blackout rules."

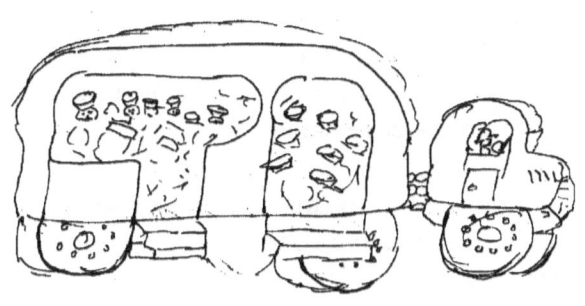

Elephant train

The base was a constant hive of activity : "I walked across the yard park yesterday just at noon and was surprised to find it filled with workers who had spread cloths and were having their lunch picnic style—mostly girls. The yard is full of canteens, open-air lunchrooms, box lunch counters and cafeterias—in most of these we can eat—but since it costs money and the chow isn't as good as ours, we never do. The women do better proportionately than the men. The men have to work long hours to make substantially more than they used to. The women of course are getting men's pay, so a good, $20-a-week gal can make $40.00 or $50.00 without any trouble."

Ben was getting to know the base well, and he had his favorite spots—Rodman Center, which had an indoor swimming pool and a library where he could read the New Yorker, Life, Time and all the other current papers and magazines; the "slop chute," an on-base canteen, where he could drink beer and was sometimes assigned to stand guard, and the tennis courts, where he was able to refine his game.

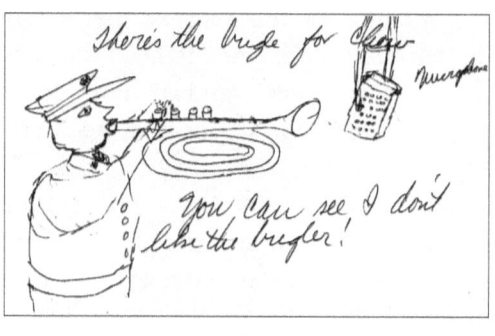

The bugler

"Maybe I'll find a few gents in this outfit to buddy with. One good friend is Elwood Godsall, called Duke, an insurance broker from San Francisco. Dave Alpert, a bartender from Minneapolis, is another." A few others he would pick up along the way had trained with him at Camp Pendleton, stayed with him at Mare Island and later remained, if not together, at least on the same island of Guam.

Jimmy Morrow, his machinist buddy from boot camp, was soon separated from him but wrote in August from Camp Pendleton, where he had been assigned to advanced amphibious training. Compared to Ben's duties, he was really working hard: "Dear, dear Ben, Oh, I was so happy to hear from you. We have just come in from tractor bivouacs and your letters were waiting for me, also about twenty others, including twelve from Jean. Ben, you are so very fortunate, in so far as your guard job goes. We here at the amphib base have a schedule that only a damned good man, or an absolute asshole, can stand up under. Compared to this, boot camp was a picnic with pink lemonade."

Jim described an arduous schedule that began at 5:55 AM and ended any time up to midnight. "And we just go and go all the time." He was

Chapter 2-San Francisco Chronicles

happy for Ben and envious of the soft duty and the good times he always seemed able to arrange, especially the tennis and other sports. "And I haven't had a midnight orgy of shrimp and boned chicken since last we shared together. I certainly miss you, Ben, much more than I can say with a few futile words on paper. I'd give anything to see you, and just sit and talk for hours. I'm still a sentimentalist, as you have probably already seen." In their barracks at Mare Island, liberty and weekend passes generous enough to get them to San Francisco and away from hated Vallejo— "at least during the war, a miserable, scrubby left-over town"—were life's one goal. "A little careful study solved the problem of the supply of regular passes, and Duke, my buddy, an insurance executive from San Francisco, and I were able to plan our trips with aplomb."⁷

With unassigned time weighing heavily on his hands and liberty permitted, Ben at first tentatively explored the immediate locality: "I've been to Benicia, Napa, Sacramento, Vallejo and soon will have to reach out for new communities. Don't ask me why I bother—it's more for the ride than anything."

But then he reported his first sally into San Francisco, which he made with his friend, Joe Aspley: "We fooled around in Vallejo until about 2:00 p.m. then all of a sudden decided to go to Frisco. It took us only an hour. I saw the Golden Gate Bridge, Treasure Island, Alcatraz and crossed the Bay bridge. I called Alfie's paper and was told Mr. Frankenstein was in. So I talked to him, and Joe and I went over to see him. We chummed for about an hour. He had something to write and something to cover, and we made a tentative arrangement for dinner and the theater at a future date."

He was happy to see his old friend from Chicago newspaper days ("the same Alfie plus a wife and two kids") and to find him so fully occupied, with "interests spread over a thousand and one activities"—as music critic for the *San Francisco Chronicle*, teaching at local universities, writing program notes for the Symphony and selecting recorded numbers for a radio program. He noted that at 47 he was "fat around the middle . . . unhealthy looking, probably very much like I looked before the Marines took over."

They made a round of the USOs and YMCAs. "Since it is against our policy to buy a meal, the best place was a Pepsi Cola serviceman's center, where hamburgers, dogs, cheese and other sandwiches are a nickel and Pepsi Cola is free. In a land of 20-cent (*minimum*) hamburgers, this makes them practically free." At 6:00 or 7:00, when the evening chill from the bay set in, they headed back to Mare Island, and managed to arrived before curfew, "luckily—because we had trouble hitchhiking and didn't arrive until 10 p.m. But I had a good night's sleep and feel fine. The trip cost us 20 cents apiece."[6]

Two days later Ben wrote that Joe Aspley was leaving, going to sea duty on the S.S. Admiral Benson, a transport ship. He noted that guarding the ship at sea was, at that time at least, considered safe duty, and that it had the big advantage of 10 days' furlough every time the ship hit the states. They had one more celebration before Joe's departure—pub crawling in Martinez. "The ride to Martinez, which is near Port Chicago, is a winding mountain road. We made it just at sunset and it was really beautiful. The bay was quiet and still—here and there a ferry boat—a blue sky and the rolling hills finishing the picture."[7]

Ben's high school friend, Chuck Mills, had introduced him by letter to friends in San Francisco; the result was several dinner invitations during his liberty visits. First he met Clemmie, the wife of Chuck's friend, Dave Barry.

"I really had a wonderful time last night—the kind I haven't had since. I've been out here. I got my "48" after I came back from my bond detail. My bus didn't leave until 12:15. That gave me time to get spruced up and ready to leave in my fancy new uniform for the first time. Your husband really looks slick. My shoes were all spit and polish and my blouse fitted me like a glove. It was just like an officer's uniform, and you know what that does for my morale. I had a grand night's sleep and felt in tiptop condition."

He purposely arrived over three hours ahead of time to do some shopping, the results of which, he hinted mysteriously, would be revealed later. "About 4:30 I got Clemmie Barry a bloom—they almost give away the most beautiful flowers out here. Huge gardenias are 25 cents and giant begonias in the most gorgeous shapes are 50 cents, which includes all the blooms on a stalk made into a corsage, sometimes three or four flowers." Then as per her instructions, he found the originating point of the cable car, the turntable in the middle of the street at Powell and Market, marveled as the conductor turned the car around by hand simply by pushing on the end of it and hopped aboard. It climbed Nob Hill and approached the old Barbary Coast region in the valley between Knob Hill and the business district. "It's like Greenwich Village or the near North Side. All the rough and tumble is gone . . . but the streets are jam-packed with all kinds of restaurants, and most of them, according to Clemmie, are good. They live in a street called August Alley, halfway up a hill . . . it's really an alley with the sidewalk and no garbage cans . . . it's one of the quickie shacks that was thrown up after the great Barbary Coast fire, and is a little shingled cottage with vines crawling all over it and a little flower garden in front, or maybe you'd say in back of it. It only has four tiny rooms."

Clemmie's husband, Dave Barry, was away in the merchant marine—a lieutenant commander. "Clemmie is about 5 feet 10 and at least 40 years old . . . she's not pretty, but misses being homely. There were two other people there . . . Gus and Dottie Matthieu. Clemmie is all wrapped up in the labor movement and works for the People's Herald, a labor paper, and next month is taking a new job with the Communist Party. But that's just her job, and she can talk about other things, and so can Gus and Dottie. Naturally, they are all poor as church mice."

After talking a mile a minute about labor and politics, their friends Chuck and Phyl and their absent spouses, the four of them went to a little French restaurant called *Normandie*, "not fancy, but good. They served a huge bowl of *potage* like the *pensions* did in the center of the table and a tasty but simple *hors d'oeuvre*. We had a bottle of wine and a very tender, aged steak, and then cheese and an apple."

There were eight girls having a birthday party at a nearby table. When they sang happy birthday, Ben, as was his custom, went over and kissed the birthday girl on the lips, while the entire restaurant cheered the Marines. "There was a little three-piece band, and it was all very Latin, very French and very gay. We left *Normandie* to go to an Italian restaurant, where they specialized in a chocolate brandy mixture made in a huge silver urn, very much like a restaurant

The Italian urn

coffee maker except that it has spigots and valves on it for hot water and steam. The procedure is very impressive and the drink, a hot one. a huge silver urn, very much like a restaurant coffee maker except that it has spigots and valves on it for hot water and steam. The procedure is very impressive and the drink, a hot one, is wonderful." With his first Italian espresso, Ben helped usher in a new era of American culture.

"Next we were off to the 'party' . . . . it turned out to be one of those fund raisers for the Party and was in honor of the third wedding anniversary of the Negro couple . . . so it was a Negro-white party. We stood around for a while, as Clemmie went around talking to all the people . . . shoved off after about an hour or so. There weren't more than about 40 or 50 people in a rather small room, and the atmosphere was a little strained, since there was a great deal of conscious liberalism present." But Clemmie informed him that that things of that sort had done a great deal to bring out Negro leadership, which is what they were trying to introduce, "instead of making it necessary for white liberals to do all the fighting for better economic and educational facilities for the Negroes," an understanding of the situation which seems prophetic today.

After a nightcap at Clemmie's Ben left at one o'clock and headed for the Pepsi cola place, where he had reserved a bed. "For 50 cents you get a bunk (just like the one I sleep in the barracks), clean sheets, about 20 men to the room. It's very nice and a good deal. All in all, it was a good evening, because I felt no necessity to get drunk and just drank lightly all evening, and, gee, it was good to talk to some real people again. It was very good for my morale, darling, especially just sitting around someone's living room having a drink."

Ben almost let the cat out of the bag with his next description. He had done some Christmas shopping for Alice in the fine stores of San Francisco; while he didn't say why he was there, he couldn't help describing the stores. "Magnin's and City of Paris and Livingston's are the fancy stores here, and for a change I saw some well-dressed gals, which was a treat. I have yet to see one that looks as good to me as my baby, and I'm an authority, because I've been from New York to Frisco now. Frisco seems to be the kind of town you could fall in love with very easily: its picturesque setting and real beauty, coupled with its very cosmopolitan air and, even in wartime, its cheap living conditions."[8]

On Sunday he called Clemmie again and "we walked up Coit Hill, being very touristy, and went up into Coit Tower, which overlooks the whole bay area." He wrote on Monday from the barracks, "I am a very well-disciplined person. I left Frisco early enough to catch the 10:15 bus and was in the sack before midnight—with the result that my first "48" didn't even cost me any sleep. No sleep and a hangover are what I expected—I missed both." His final thought on his visit was, "One thing which kept running though my mind was how much fun you and I would have showing Pete, and later Linda, all these things. I missed you even more on this weekend than usually because these were things my baby and I might do together."

There were others such nights in San Francisco, with Tom and Patsy Neblett, another couple introduced by Chuck Mills, who lived in a fashionable neighborhood with a built-in garage and a wood-burning stone fireplace, where he was treated to his first taste of California cabernet. "I needed a break from the CIO-Commie bunch," remarked Ben. They were a lovely couple with a six-year old daughter who had bad eyes and psychological problems. Ben remarked that he was relieved his own kids were so normal. Still, he was very envious of Tom, who could enjoy the comforts of home. Besides excursions planned to visit friends of his friends, Ben described the regular trips into San Francisco that he made with his fellow Marines. Jimmy Morrow, Elwood Godsall (Duke) and Ben were the threesome that most frequently went on liberty together, but occasionally they picked up another hanger-on.

"At this point our barracks-mate Charlie Donati entered our lives. Charlie thought he was the strongest man in the world. He was as gentle as Steinbeck's Lenny and loved the world, especially if it recognized his strength. He was a Marine because he thought that's where such a strong man ought to be." He would use a piece of wood to demonstrate his great strength by breaking it over his head. It was only with great difficulty that Ben restrained him on one occasion from entertaining a bored audience by running clear across the guard room at top speed to butt his head against the steel bars of the brig. Ben said, "I had a high regard for government property,"

Ben became Charlie's idol when he helped him with some long overdue correspondence and worked out an easy formula for him to use in composing letters to satisfy his loved ones at home. Charlie begged Duke and Ben to take him on liberty with them. "I won't bother you," he insisted. "I'll just walk along behind—you'll be glad you have me, you'll see." Charlie was welcomed into the fraternity. In deference to Charlie, they started visiting some of San Francisco's seamier dives. In the very first one, only minutes had passed when Charlie was suddenly marching out of the place holding a sizable sailor by the scruff of his neck and the seat of his sailor pants as if he were a kitten. Back came Charlie—alone. "Charlie, what's up?" Ben asked. "He bumped you—them guys has got to be more careful." They then moved the scene of action to the St. Francis Hotel bar, where the decorum awed Charlie and they were better able to hold him in check.

"Charlie died on the beach at Iwo Jima," Ben later wrote, "but I am sure before he went he exacted a severe penalty from the enemy for challenging his personal power."[9]

CHAPTER 3

HOME ECONOMICS

The receiver crackled and sputtered. A deep male voice boomed, "Now it's time for Lorenzo Jones and his wife, Belle." Organ music swelled with the familiar theme: "Funiculi, Funicula." I sat in my own miniature Mexican chair right next to the receiver. It was a Crosley table model, a bulky rectangular box, styled with rounded edges and the streamlined look of the 40s, horizontal wood fins covering and extending beyond the round speaker opening, its black cloth of infinite depth peeking out from beneath. Dust swirled and drifted lazily in a shaft of afternoon sunlight that fell on a corner of its cherry-stained cabinet. It sat on a bookcase in its own wall niche in the living room—actually a second sitting room behind the parlor of the Victorian house—just opposite the lounge chairs where my parents would sit in the evening and listen, talk or read.

Along the base were four cylindrical knobs, the left controlling power and volume, the next adjusting treble and bass tone, the third for tuning stations and the one on the far right offering a series of clicks, which in my experience merely turned off the program. But when Cousin Sandy, a dealer in electrical appliances, came over to visit, he showed how this knob could be used to change to the short wave band. The family was then treated to intermittent segments of a British announcer's voice, reporting the day's battles in Europe. The transmission was periodically interrupted by the roar of static, the voice first loud and clear and then attenuating to high and thin. The report was accompanied by a slowly rising and falling roar of static, which seemed to me to be the sound of the surf on the great ocean which separated the two continents.

Once a throbbing, spreading, reverberating tone emerged from the speaker, "Boom, bw-o-o-m, bw-o-o-m . . ."

"That's Big Ben in London!" Sandy exclaimed. The ability to transmit the actual sound of the clock's chimes across the sea confirmed my belief in the miracle of radio.

Before the war, Dad was Radio Director with H. W. Kastor & Sons, Advertising. In those days most radio programs were broadcast live, emanating from studios in Chicago, before New York became the nation's broadcast center. Since commercial sponsors had a major stake in the success of the program, his work involved supervision of the live broadcasts. He had varied duties, including direction, handling of writers, buying and contracting of talent and general management of programs, both packaged and agency produced. He produced network programs for such clients as Procter & Gamble. One of his unique abilities was working with writers, sometimes large numbers of them, in buying stories for programs like *Knickerbocker Playhouse*, guiding story line, contributing his own ideas for new programs and strengthening old ones.

My own favorite shows started to come on after the soap operas finished around five o'clock. First was Tom Mix, introduced by the singing cowboy himself: "When its roundup time in Texas,/ And the bloom is on the sage . . ." The jingle ended with the helpful reminder,
> Take a tip from Tom:
> Go and tell your Mom,
> Shredded Ralston can't be beat.

Next was Captain Midnight, introduced by tolling clock chimes. Stirring theme music, Reznicek's *Donna Diana Overture*, announced Sergeant Preston in the Yukon: "On King, on you huskies." My favorite, in one of the last fifteen-minute segments before dinner, began with howling winds and the words, "Look, up in the sky! Is it a bird? Is it a plane?

Chapter 3-Home Economics

It's Superman!" The adventures of this modern Robin Hood, disguised as "a mild-mannered reporter from a large metropolitan newspaper," and his girlfriend, Lois Lane, kept me glued to the set. In my absorption with radio drama, I was transfixed by the illuminated tuning dial, imprinted at intervals with "London", "Moscow" and "Berlin" and the amber eye of the operating light, which I believed could see the entire outside world.

Shows Dad produced included *Abie's Irish Rose*, the continuing tale of an urban couple, Abie, of European-Jewish origin, and Rose, his Irish-Catholic wife. Old recordings of this show reveal how both the humor and the drama of conflict were enhanced in the auditory sphere by the contrast between the heavy Yiddish accents of Abie's family and the thick Irish brogues of Rose's relatives. The situation mirrored the religious mix in Dad's own marriage, and this fact gave him a special insight into the show's production. Other shows included *Painted Dreams, Leave It to the Girls*—probably a first among media talk shows, starring Eloise McElhone and Constance Bennett, well-known personalities of the day, and radio celebrity, Irene Rich. In addition to Procter and Gamble (makers of Teel tooth-cleaning liquid, Drene shampoo, American Family bar soap and flakes), his clients included the Welch Grape Juice Company (grape juice, jams and jellies), the Lewis-Howe Company, (maker of Tums) and several others.

Dad's career had developed along a determined but erratic path. Aid from an uncle in New York made it possible for him to attend the University of Illinois at Urbana-Champaign for his freshman year. Because of his father's worsening condition and other needs to be close to home, he enrolled during his sophomore year at the University of Chicago. During this year his father, a marginally successful real estate promoter of new communities outside Chicago, succumbed to his illness and died. Soon afterward, however, he and a friend, Julian Jackson, a former fellow staffer on the *Illini* newspaper, impatient with the slow pace and routine discipline of student life, quit college and set off for Europe. They worked in New York in men's haberdashery to earn a stake for travel and then booked passage on a freighter to France. After a year of bicycle travel around France and imbibing (literally and figuratively) the continental atmosphere of the 1930s, he returned to Chicago and began to work in earnest to assist his widowed mother and three other children to make ends meet and to launch what he anticipated would be a journalism career.

But this was 1930, and jobs were scarce, especially in journalism. He got on at a weekly covering Chicago's northwest side, eventually inheriting most of the duties of running the neighborhood newspaper: reporting, editing, selling advertisements and doing whatever was required to publish this local periodical. He earned a reputation as the "Little Dynamo" and the Napoleon of the *Northwest News*—by the time he was through, the publisher of the paper was running for political office, largely due to Dad's influence.

Alice Herlihy, on the other hand, was not as economically pressed as her husband-to-be. Daughter of Francis Jeremiah Herlihy, by then a successful building contractor, she had the opportunity to graduate from the University of Chicago in 1934. But in the heart of the depression, finding no more employment offers than Dad, she tried her luck as a press agent. Her ready wit, blonde hair and sparkling personality soon earned her assignments to obtain publicity for recording and performing artists. One of her stories introduced a young engineer who had become a musician in a piece entitled "From Slide Rule to Slide Trombone." The musician was Guy Lombardo. Equally notable was a story about a barber who liked to sing in his shop and finally got a break: Perry Como.

On December 15th, 1943, Dad received notice from the draft board that he had been reclassified from 3A to 1A. With a feminine sense of the dramatic, Alice noted, their new daughter, Linda, arrived on the same day. Dad enlisted and left for boot camp in April, 1944. "Life went on as usual," Mom reported, "except for the usual commotion occasioned by a new baby in the house. Underneath the every-dayness, however, there were subtle changes. I began to keep a weather eye on the bills, and stormy weather it was. The roof over our heads and the meals we ate stopped being commonplace and became pearls of great price. The vacuum cleaner stopped picking things up; the cleaning woman raised her ante by a dollar a day. The budget grew to three pages. We took out the permanent waves and put in shoes for the baby; and then the bubble burst. It couldn't be done on my allotment." As she later wrote in the column she developed in an attempt to cure this financial

Chapter 3-Home Economics

problem, "The obvious solution was that I could go to work. Or could I?"

Mom's and Dad's broad knowledge and good contacts in the field of communications came to the aid of the family during the war. While Dad was in boot camp launching his military career, it became my mother's responsibility to stoke the home fires. Faced with the need to exist on an enlisted man's allotment check, she began actively seeking to return to work. She knew she needed to find a market for her writing talents by employing on a more practical level the skills she had cultivated at the University of Chicago in Thornton Wilder's creative writing class. Musing over her future, she had discussed her career plans with the playwright. He said, "Alice, I always imagined you pushing a baby carriage." He thought that, since she was unclear about her direction and of marriageable age, some life experience might deepen her insight and enrich her writing.

Alice reading to Linda

"My day starts at 6:30 a.m. with the baby's feeding. From then on through the day I am occupied with odd jobs. All the jobs in my household are odd because no matter how I plan my time, I never come out even. Making beds, breakfast, the preparation of formula, dressing the small-fry, the baby's bath. feeding and laundry take me up to noon . . . lunch, straightening the house, another feeding, dressing both kids for outdoors, shopping and airing combined, undressing both kids again, preparation of dinner, another feeding for the baby, dinner, dishes, taking down clothes from morning's wash while standing in for the man of the house, tuck small-fry in for the night. Then I sit down in the living room and twiddle my thumbs and try to hold my head up while waiting for the baby's night feeding to roll around. Naturally, there's a bushel basket of mending in the front hall closet, but that will have to wait until some day when the baby doesn't feel like eating every four hours. Where was I? Oh yes, I was looking for work.

"There's a labor shortage. Sure. But is it so bad that some desperate employer will pay handsomely for two hours of a frazzled females' time after a hard day? Shall we say fifty dollars a week?"[1]

Now she could wait no longer. It was time to put her talents back to work and continue her journalism career, at least to the extent that it might help pay the bills. At Dad's urging she made overtures to his contacts in Chicago and New York radio and even created a concept for a newspaper column for and about wartime wives entitled, *Between Us Girls.*

Not one of the hundreds of daily letters Mom wrote to Dad survived. After all, Dad did not have room to carry those heaps of documents around with him in his sea bag. But there was little problem in re-creating Mom's side of the story: she was eager to tell it herself. I was fortunate to have Mom's other writings, along with my own recollections, to recount what transpired at home. The tales to be told about our view of the war—from the home front—were as wrenching, painful and funny as those that were coming from across the waves. But they needed a voice. My mother, out of necessity and emotions that cried for expression, was among the first to speak.

Thornton Wilder was right: Mom's life experience did enhance her writing. In her first *Between Us* Girls column, her blunt and witty exposition of Uncle Sam's intrusion into our lives left no doubt about her feelings on the matter:

"Mr. President, Gentlemen of the Draft Board: Do you realize what you are taking from me? From us! The miracle of paid bills; the leaky faucet, magically repaired; the snow shoveled, the grass cut; the relief floorwalker during a bout of colic; the friendly shadow behind the morning paper; the strong arm around our shoulders after the guests have gone, our leaning posts, our strength. And what have I left? Two children. One son, prewar stock . . . not that he cut much ice down at the draft board; one daughter, who followed on the heels of the reclassification, just in time for a fleeting look at her old man. One ten room house, too large and

Chapter 3-Home Economics

constantly in need of repair, but it's home and it has a yard. Those are my blessings. On the debit side, there's me. Cook, housekeeper, seamstress, tender of small ills, dishwasher, laundress, hostess of sorts. Give me a ration book and I can plan well balanced meals and make the points come out even. Give me a budget, and I can stick to it. But take away the man behind the budget, and I'm flat on my face. I'll be darned if I can earn a living. The alternative, of course, is living on your allotment, $100, in my case. Food for thought, but it wouldn't feed my family. I feel more confident when he has figured it out beforehand.

"We've figured, that is, the Brain does the actual figuring. I just keep bringing up things he's forgotten, until we're blue in the face, and we're still three figures behind. It can be done. The papers were full of one girl with two children who lives nicely on it and even saves money, but I notice they discontinued the series after one shining example. Another possibility is moving out to Dead Man's Gulch, where they don't know there's a war on and they don't charge a king's ransom for a hole in the wall adjoining the glue factory. Still another way is to live on your savings, if you have any, and hope for the best when they're gone. Personally, I'd like to have something in the sock besides a hole when Johnny comes marching home."

The Green home at 5412 Blackstone Ave.

She mailed out five installments of her column to newspapers. The New York Times, to which she submitted with a cover letter in Dad's name, told her that that they had read and enjoyed her submittal: "It is better written than most of the work we receive of this kind. However due to the present circumstances, which we are sure you understand, we cannot expand at this time." The Chicago Sun also enjoyed it but "did not have a need for the work at this time." A woman editor at The Chicago Daily News, on the other hand, liked her idea but was embarrassed to tell her that "the prices we pay for such columns, $30 to $50 per piece, may not meet yours." She added, "If you decide at a later date to accept our paltry sums, please let me know." As reported in Dad's correspondence, the New York Post expressed an interest in the series and may have run the columns that she had already written later that year. There is no record of any others.

In the course of pursuing leads with editors and radio producers, she made repeated calls to Carl Wester, the gatekeeper for Irna Phillips, creator, writer and producer of *The Guiding Light*, America's first soap opera, which continued on television from 1952 until September 18, 2009, when CBS tuned it out, after a run of 72 years. She was also the author of several other daytime serials; her shows dominated daytime radio. Mom was about to give up on the hope of ever getting through to him when she received a call from the famous personality herself. Phillips wanted to know how my mother could help her with some scripts. An article on Phillips by Cary O'Dell relates her unique circumstances and creative approach: "By 1943, just over ten years from her beginning, Phillips had five programs on the air. Her yearly income was in excess of $250,000 and her writing output was around two million words a year. It was at this phase that she developed the need for assistants to create dialogue for the stories she created. To keep her scripts accurate she also kept a lawyer and doctor on retainer. Not one to put pen to paper, Phillips created her stories by acting them out as a secretary jotted down what she spoke." [2]

While Dad told Mom in his letters that attention from the successful writer-producer would primarily be of use in promoting her own *Between Us Girls* concept in New York, he did think that, if the trial scripts she was asked to write for Phillips were successful, she could earn as much as $150 per week. Her meeting with the famous author went well. She was hired to write five sample episodes of *The Road of Life*, filling in dialogue along Phillips's pre-established story line. Given about 12 minutes of copy (a minute per double spaced page) for a 15 minute program—allowing time of course for commercials—this seemingly achievalble task really could result in a stead $150per week, a serious boost to a household budget in 1944. Furthermore, there would be no need to follow the creator around and take notes: she would be permitted to work at home. Apparently, my mother was in the right place at the right time. She did not hesitate to accept this assignment and put off, for the duration anyway, attempts to write a syndicated newspaper or magazine column.

I remember sitting on the woven straw seat of one of the Mexican chairs—adorned with brightly colored Peter Hunt pineapple and pear designs my parents had painted—which served as our family's dining room furniture, watching Mom pound away at her desk model Underwood typewriter. There was a rear stair hall connecting the dining room with the second living room, a niche just big enough for a wooden desk with a disappearing typewriter well. I would sit as the afternoon sun streamed through the tall Victorian windows and watch my mother while she clattered along, fretting over mistakes as she erased them on the original and two carbon copies, years before "white-out," Xerox and, ultimately, personal computers came to the writer's rescue. The rhythmic clacking, the regular "ding" of the carriage return bell and Mom's periodic exclamations lulled me into daydreams, secure in her presence and somehow sensing the added security my mother's activity was earning for the family.

In many of his letters, Dad encouraged Mom to make it easier on herself by getting help with housework. She did have a cleaning lady one day a week. Labor was cheap, but Mom could hardly justify working long hours on writing projects for extra money, just to turn around and pay it out to a household helper. As it was, she got Dad's allotment check each month, supplemented by the extra funds he would send her from time to time, earned from his employment at Mare Island, first at the flour mill and then at the officers' club bar. Her sister Helen, whose husband was a prominent surgeon in Boston and who worked herself as a teaching psychoanalyst lecturing at Harvard, sent her supplementary checks on a regular basis as well. While her parents were well off, both she and my father were reluctant to ask for or accept assistance. In fact, Dad used to gloat in his letters as he expressed pride in sending home regular checks: "I'll bet your parents don't know how we're doing it!" Neither did he, but Mom certainly did.

Mom's domestic responsibilities included cleaning the large two-story, ten-room house, riding herd on the landlord for routine repairs of plumbing and equipment and arranging for some 40 heavy, wood-framed storm windows to be removed every spring, replaced with screens, and returned to their openings in the fall. In addition, she was responsible for keeping the car functioning—Dad made plenty of suggestions from his remote location about when to change antifreeze in the radiator and what his last impression was of the condition of the brakes in the 1940 Ford. Moreover, she had two children to feed, clothe, read to, nurture and care for, one still in diapers—the cloth kind were the only ones available in those days—and one just starting school. On top of these duties, she had to provide clean clothes, towels and bed linens for the family and me, a slightly disturbed, bed-wetting son. Fortunately, this large old house had a laundry room in the basement.

This room had grim, gray stone walls like those that surrounded the other basement spaces, lit by a single bulb in the ceiling; in post-war remodeling she had them redone in painted Portland cement plaster to make the room brighter. Two high windows facing west and south made this workspace a little more hospitable in daytime. Along the near wall was a low stove, where she could boil water over two gas burners in an oval-shaped galvanized kettle. When not boiling stained sheets or pre-washing clothes, she would put bedspreads, curtains or sometimes a dress she was tired of into this cauldron with a package of Rit dye and stir this magic brew with a stick, until her fabric was transformed with a new and different look, to create a fresh blue, green or red color scheme for one of the bedrooms or give herself a fresh start with an old outfit. On the far wall were two laundry tubs with hot and cold running water, next to which was a large, cylindrical electric washing machine on casters. She wrote in *Between Us Girls*:

Long Life to Clothes—Thanks to the Gentle, Thorough Action of the G-E Washer

The GE Electric Washer

"As washing machines go, it's nothing spectacular, I suppose. It's just a good solid, prewar product, not too old, with an open wringer which must be fed by hand. It's not fancy, not one of those that washes, wrings, dries and hangs the clothes up for you . . . for where then would be the joy of participation?

Chapter 3-Home Economics   55

But it's mine and I love it. When first I gazed upon its lovely face, it was pictured in a newspaper ad, and it was on sale. The price was attractive, and all my life I'd wanted some beautiful, big, mechanical toy to play with all by myself. The hitch was, of course, that it was a pretty expensive toy, so I set about making a necessity out of it. For two hours, I jotted down the cost of laundry, diaper service for the new baby, the cleaning of slip covers, etc. By the time I had finihsed my calulations, were we were losing money every second until we got that machine into the house.

"The next morning, as soon as the store opened, I telephoned and ordered it. When the salesman got over his initial surprise at my novel buying methods, he came to long enough to sell me a portable mangle for a 'slight additional charge', We were very poor for the next few months but very clean.

"When Paderewski sat down to a piano for the first time, he must have felt some spark of recognition, some answer to his inner self. So it was with me for the first time I filled that gleaming porcelain vessel with water and soap chips and watched the suds rise ever higher and higher. Here, indeed, was satisfaction. I had found my medium. Unfortunately, no true artist is ever really appreciated in the bosom of his own family. There were discouragements in those early days . . . the sport jacket that went into the machine fitting my husband and came out too small for the baby, the blanket for the big bed which we later used in the dog's basket . . . small payment for such great enjoyment. After all, no poet's first sonnet is perfect. True enough, our soap was beginning to cost more than our food, but look how clean we were! For three days, I washed like a woman possessed; everything washable in the house—and some not washable—had been through the mill, and then there was nothing left. So I sat down to watch and wait."

After the initial thrill wore off and as Dad's absence wore on, her enthusiasm flagged. On Mondays, Mom would sometimes boil the diapers and the sheets, especially the ones from

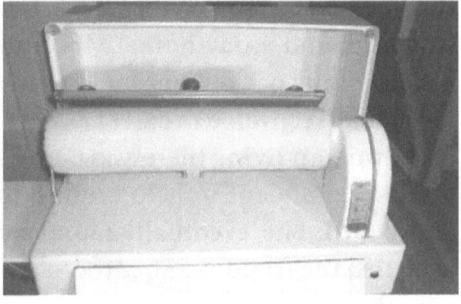

The GE Rotary Iron mangle

my wet bed, in the laundry tubs on the gas stove and then fill the machine's well from hoses leading from the faucets, put in a large load of washing and some American Family soap flakes and turn it on. The central agitator would slosh them around for a while and she would then draw them out through the wringer, which could be swung over one of the tubs to catch the water and the clothes. After filling this tub with rinse water, she would swing the wringer between the two tubs, pass the wash though the rubber rollers again and allow it to accumulate in the other tub. When she was done with the entire load, she would hang everything up to dry. In summer, she loaded them all into a bushel basket and delighted in hanging sheets, towels, and all of the clothes out on clotheslines strung across the back yard. Everyone in the family loved the fresh ozone smell of clean laundry dried outdoors. In inclement weather, she hung them in the laundry room, which she would string with several clotheslines. Between the need to wash diapers and her incontinent son, this process was sometimes repeated several times a week. My mother sat at her mangle, an electrical pressing device, and ironed sheets and the other lat laundry. I watched by the hour as she doubled each sheet and passed one side across the flat bed until it was caught by a padded roller. As she worked her foot pedal it was drawn up past a curved hot shoe and came out flat and pressed at the top. Next, she turned the folded sheet around and flattened the other half. Pillowcases could be done in one pass, or two if she took the time to do a fancy job. She also used this remarkable machine to iron pants, sleeves and fronts of shirts, her own aprons, dinner napkins and tablecloths.

In November of 1944, Mom got sick with some flu-like symptoms that seemed to hang on for weeks. Dad insisted that she seek some outside help, and a day nurse, Mrs. Perew, was called in to take care of her, do some of the household chores and tend the baby. By the time Mom had recovered in early December, she liked the idea of having another woman living there and began seriously looking for a University of Chicago student to help around the house in return for her room and board. She eventually found a young woman named Janet, who occupied the frigid rear bedroom and became a mainstay in the Green household.

When it came to managing the household budget, through all

Chapter 3-Home Economics

the sources that contributed, Mom made ends meet with a patchwork of resources. A larger problem was obtaining the goods—clothing, shoes, gasoline and meat—that she needed for the family. The war effort was on and industrial jobs were putting money in people's hands, but production was focused on war matériel, making consumer goods scarce. Recycling of waste paper and newspaper was accomplished through paper drives at the schools. My mother, along with most other families, saved fat from cooking beef, chicken and bacon, what little she had of it. Because of this scarcity, my sister Linda was pitied as a "poor little war time baby who never had any bacon." For some reason the butcher at the grocery store was the designated collector, and every week we delivered Mason jars full of solidified fat to him. He then delivered his precious hoard to the government, which somehow transformed it into explosives for our boys on the front.

The strains we were feeling at our house—and this was typical of households nationwide—were actually the result of a carefully drawn wartime economic strategy. The economy was strong during the war: the gross national product expanded tremendously. In a 1984 account of women's lives during the war, D'Ann Campbell described how government planners were challenged to channel the nation's productive capacity into military spending without radically transforming the nation's economy. The only way to do this, she explained, was first to distribute the extra income to households, and then to take back about a third of that income through compulsory taxes, voluntary bond sales, and inflation. "Income taxes were imposed that for the first time reached beyond the well-to-do and affected nearly every family. Withholding was first put into effect. Purchase of government bonds, while never

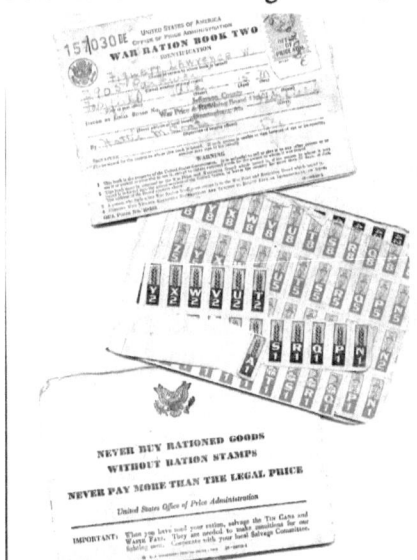

Ration book

compulsory, was made highly attractive, and found favor even in the remotest corners of the land. It was firm national policy to avoid the runaway inflation that had accompanied previous major wars. Hence the Office of Price Administration (OPA) set prices for all items (including rent) at both the retail and wholesale levels, and efforts were made to restrain wage increases."

Consequently the behavior of housewives was the target of consumer economic policy, and it was housewives who bore the brunt of the anti-inflation effort. These programs were largely successful in holding down prices. Large amounts of new family income, however, put tremendous pressure on consumer goods. Meat, coffee, sugar, housing, fuel oil, gasoline, rubber, automobile, appliances, and other commodities were in short supply because of the needs of the military, the conversion of factories, and problems in shipping. There was no problem in shutting down housing construction and the manufacture of durable goods. "The problem for the society," she said, "was how to allocate shortages of other items without inflation. Although the New Dealers were being squeezed out of power in Washington, they did manage to control the allocation process through rationing handled by the OPA. Equality was the watchword, as all men women and children were assigned the same basic set of ration coupons. A small black market did emerge . . . But on the whole, compliance was excellent and rationing worked as it was intended." [3]

Wartime scarcity governed our lives. Each family was allotted a certain number of stamps, or "ration points" of different colors. In addition to money, I recall that red points were needed to purchase meat; green, blue and black stamps were used for other scarce items, such as coffee, and separate ration books were issued for sugar. Heating fuel, gasoline and scarce items of clothing were also controlled with special ration cards. While the system was harsh, it was generally accepted, because all believed it was helping to win the war. In contrast with the self-absorbed consumerism of today's economy, in which restrictive public policy initiatives are politically difficult, the public-spirited cooperation and self-restraint of Americans during this period was simply remarkable. Because the economy then swung into a half-century of relative prosperity and plenty, such austerity and cooperation in response have not been experienced since those times.

The labor-intensive work women had to do to keep a household in those days was another daily challenge. Working wives, as personified by Rosie the Riveter, got a huge boost in income, prestige and freedom from domestic confinement during this wartime period. Simultaneously, a variety of child care experiments had to be made to accommodate the change. Nursery schools were created to absorb preschool children during the day at ever younger ages. Extended family—grandmothers, aunts and older children were pressed into service to care for infants and toddlers. Just as communities planted Victory Gardens to grow fruits and vegetables on common plots for added self-sufficiency, communal day school experiments were tried, so mothers could work to support the war effort. Since these jobs were producing money, child care for the first time had a market value, and the sparks of today' double-earner family were kindled. For housewives, the winds of change stirred in the land, fanned by the winds of war. For my mother, it was only a matter of common sense and survival. She joined the ranks of women who not only made their homes, but also managed and supported them.

It is difficult to imagine our own parents as children growing toward maturity: to see our mentors, guides and authority figures as people once like ourselves, who have to learn and grow daily to earn places in a larger world. During the war Dad made his way amidst official indifference toward his doing something useful in the military, outside employment to earn extra money for the family and duties that would allow him to serve with honor and yet permit him to return to his family. As he pursued these objectives, he grew. He cultivated his natural ability to make friends and used his contacts to make things happen. He studied his situation and discovered new opportunities. He dressed immaculately and always looked his best. And he spoke out fearlessly to his superior officers, gaining their attention and trust. These skills served him well, and long after he left military service they helped him advance in his career.

Mom was equally challenged to mature during the war. A painfully shy, retiring person by nature, further inhibited by the many social strictures placed upon women in her day, she learned to rely on her inventiveness, outgoing personality and wit to help her carry on her family's wartime existence. She kept up with domestic chores without benefit of postwar labor saving devices. She shopped wisely in a climate of scarcity. She learned to negotiate with workmen, oversee mechanical repairs to home and automobile, manage her meager finances to make ends meet and earn additional money in the workplace. Moreover, she had to lead her little brood in their daily and yearly activities. Her duties included child-rearing, arranging for home repairs, making insurance decisions and planning and carrying off all required local and long-distance travel. She learned to enlist family, friends and business advisers in these endeavors, and it brought her out of the home into a wider world.

These individual accomplishments may seem heroic, but there was nothing unusual about either of my parents' achievements during that period. Millions of troops were learning each day that they had capabilities far greater than they had ever imagined. Women held industrial jobs with good pay; they balanced these time-consuming and arduous duties with child-rearing and household management. It was the beginning of a new era, and American women would never return to the tightly restricted, socially stratified gender roles of the first half of the 20th century. For my family and for American society in general, the genie was out of the bottle, and there was no way to coax or force it back.

And yet I am getting into another story—my mother's, which I must save for another volume.

Mom got a midwinter break in her arduous routine at the beginning of 1945. She took my sister and me to stay with Granny and Grandpa for a while and boarded a train to California. Her letters to me from the train and from California were accompanied by pictures of the sights along the way, in the style Dad had devised, to make his letters understandable to a 5-year-old.

Heartwarming for the moment as it was heartbreaking, her stay of five days at Oceanside was a last joyful visit with Dad before they were torn apart. She headed back home to her challenging wartime existence, with the added stress of his overseas assignment. He was bound for distant, tropical islands, to unknown destinations and an uncertain future, for duty in the Pacific.

CHAPTER 4

THE POLITICIAN

Ben peered over the rail of the ferry. Out of the foggy murk the navy yard emerged, illuminated as bright as day. At the dry-docks sat ships with work lights glaring on decks and spilling out of portholes; others with red and green lanterns at port and starboard eased into their slips, and a cruiser draped with golden beads of light from the prow to the highest mast and down to the stern celebrated her return to port. A thousand street lamps, illuminated factories and warehouses, rows of barracks windows and the cheerful glow from hundreds of family homes, in the bustling city of 46,000 that never slept, cast a glare into the black sky, drowning out the stars. July 17th, 1944, was a typical Tuesday night in the sleepy town of Vallejo, Ben reported, and, with nothing in particular to do on liberty, he had started back to the yard to get a night's sleep. As he admired the glittering scene, the huge vessel, groaning and lurching with a series of reversing maneuvers, eased into its berth. Abruptly his tranquil mood was shattered.

"I was just getting off the ferry," he wrote, "when suddenly there were two tremendous explosions, followed by a rain of glass around the dock area. I ran toward what seemed to be the most excitement, but soon realized there was no evidence of an explosion—except the glass—anywhere at hand. Everyone was bewildered. Then I joined the crowd around the shore patrol wagon that had just pulled up. There had been an explosion in the arsenal at Benicia, some distance away." Seeing no reason to hang around, he headed for his quarters. "When I reached the barracks, no one knew much more about the situation, except that the barracks were crawling with officers, telephones were ringing madly and there was excitement in the air—but there were no orders, so I went up to my deck and began to undress.

Just as I got ready to crawl into my sack there was a call to arms—all hands out. We dressed, dashed below and found eight trucks and all the officers in the entire marine detachment, from Col. Betts on down, on hand. Our convoy started off and we learned that the Port Chicago arsenal was the scene of the disaster, about 40 miles away. In Vallejo windows were smashed, and as we tore down the road, ambulances and Navy cars packed with nurses roared past our careening trucks. As we neared the town of Port Chicago, returning ambulances raced by. Finally we reached the ammunition dump, which was pitch black. We could see that every window was destroyed in the town of Port Chicago. There were huge heaps of glass in the streets and townsfolk stood around watching the trucks and cars race through the streets.

Ben's locker

"As we pulled in the town I could see that the Navy lumber yards were a mess—piles of lumber had been thrown around like jackstraws. Pulling up alongside a barracks building that had no lights or windows and had huge hunks blown out of it, all men with rifles were detached and formed into two guard companies of 50 men each. Since I didn't carry a rifle, being on standby, I was sent back with the balance of the outfit, about 200 of us. We never did see the actual scene of the disaster and— until this morning when we learned that the first estimates place the dead at 650—we didn't even know how bad it was." [1]

Two ships were destroyed at the pier that night, the Quinault Victory, newly arrived and as yet not loaded, and the E. A. Bryan, squatting low in the water with her cargo of munitions. The main explosion had occurred

Chapter 4-The Politician

aboard the E. A. Bryan, which was completely vaporized. No identifiable part of it was ever found.

The official explanation of the explosion maintained that 1.5 kilotons of war munitions containing TNT and Torpex, placed on the pier and in the holds of the Liberty ship E. A. Bryan, were accidentally detonated all at once. It was not until the 1990s that the Napa Sentinel developed the theory that this blast had been deliberately set by the federal government—a secret test that was part of the Manhattan Project. The newspaper presented results of an extensive investigation that supported the hypothesis that the explosion was nuclear. The story seems incredible—that we would test a weapon on ourselves, especially when we lost 200 black sailors and hundreds of innocent bystanders in the blast. The articles reported that the blast was recorded on seismographs as far away as Nevada and that pilots in the air had seen a "bright white light" and "a mushroom cloud"—but of course nobody yet knew the unique significance of those phenomena. The only excuse the government might have for such a fiasco was that they did not realize this was more than just a tactical weapon and had gravely underestimated the destructive power they had unleashed, a real possibility in mid-1944. If it is true, Ben was lucky he was sent back to the barracks that night and may have received less exposure to radioactive contamination. The Napa newspaper also re- ported that the county where this occurred today has one of the highest rates of cancer in the nation; it is also a fact that Ben was to die at 69 of an aggressive pancreatic and liver cancer. He knew nothing at the time about these matters. And even if he had, with the censorship he was under as soon as he got overseas, he certainly could not have speculated on such issues in his letters.

Ben had little time to ponder the causes of the disaster; his own concerns were more immediate. The job as an officer in Marine intelligence that he originally anticipated was only his first attempt at finding a secure and meaningful assignment in the military. He learned during boot camp that this coveted position would not materialize. He had never whined nor asked for special favors. In fact, up to that time he had never relied upon the political support of friends or influential contacts to try for a choice military assignment. He always insisted he would make it on his own merits. It had only occasionally crossed his mind that prejudice might bar his way. And yet in a July 13 letter, he noted: "I see by a stray copy of Variety that Jim Stirton and Dick Smart (the *Abie's Irish Rose* substitute announcer) got Marine Corps commissions, which makes me feel that the old Jewish idea must have entered into consideration of me. Certainly, I looked better on paper than those guys did—unless, of course they had an angle, an important personal friend plugging for them." He hadn't really thought such things mattered in the results-oriented military service, at least not in the United States of America.

His anger over the treatment of Jews in Europe, on the other hand, was one of the main reasons he felt so strongly about enlisting. An avid reader of news and commentary, he was aware of the reports of holocaust that were increasingly coming out of Europe and, idealist that he was, wanted to fight for human rights against the German and Japanese oppressors who would take them away. He was a great supporter of Franklin Roosevelt and his advocacy for the working class. Like many other liberals of the time, he must have been baffled by this leader's—and America's—apparent blindness to the plight of the European Jews. He probably only understood it much later, when he read Ben Hecht's analysis of the situation in his 1954 memoir, *A Child of the Century*. His well-thumbed copy of the original 1954 edition is still in the family collection.

Ben Hecht, an early 20th-century Chicago newspaper man and screenwriter of such films as *The Front Page*, who became a reluctant advocate for the Jewish cause, argues that Roosevelt's "failure to raise one of his humanitarian fingers to prevent the extermination of the Jews, his many sullen statements about the 'Jewish situation' and his spiritual anesthesia to the greatest genocide in history" can be attributed to his mistrust of Jews, growing out of his betrayal by a prominent Jewish businessman named Goldman, who switched sides during Roosevelt's New York gubernatorial campaign and backed FDR's opponent.[2] Since the fate of millions of Jews massacred by the Nazis was beneath the official notice of many governments and ignored by the American Jews who he hoped would support the cause, Hecht struggled to understand the psychology that lay behind this mass self-delusion.[3]

According to Hecht's line of reasoning, American Jews of that period, determined to escape the ghetto and become part of mainstream American society, made a Faustian bargain to suppress their advocacy of the Jewish cause, their defense of German Jews and their very identity as Jews, lest

Chapter 4-The Politician

they risk being ignored for promotions, incur social disapproval and receive the worst duty in the military. This came home to Ben when even his own Jewish classmate from the University of Chicago, Milton Mayer, wrote apologetically about the Nazis in prewar days in a tract that he said was called, "The Case Against the Jews." Even though Mayer lived across the street from him on Kenwood Avenue, and they would wave in greeting, Ben never forgave Milt for it. Nevertheless, much as Ben Hecht had sadly concluded about American Jews, Ben Green calculated that he had little to gain and much to lose by openly crying foul in the military, or anywhere else, for that matter.

Instead he focused, not on obstacles but on his opportunities. As when he started out in the working world—poor, powerless and bored with menial jobs—he nevertheless had his wits, his engaging personality and his boundless energy to rely on, and they had never failed him. Once he accepted the fact that he was not going to get the officer post he had applied for, Ben went to work in earnest to see if he could alter his situation. While still in San Diego he had passed up a chance to go to Washington D. C. for reassignment; at the time he had been torn between the unknown risks of accepting a totally different assignment and choosing to take his chances on "the devil he knew." Eventually he came to regret his rash decision. He sent the word out to his friends across the country that he was looking for a transfer. Next he talked earnestly with Capt. Kessler, his company commander, about an office job and reported in a letter, "Gee, maybe I'll be qualified to be a clerk!" After getting a "song and a dance from the captain" every time he brought it up thereafter. he concluded, "I probably won't get the office job. If I don't, I'll probably write John Kennan (an old friend who took a position in government) and see whether, now that he's in Washington, he can work something for me." With more results, he appealed to his high school friend, Chuck Mills, then situated in Washington, who contacted a Marine personnel officer, a Captain Luxton, who suggested that he apply to First Sergeant's School or the Recruiting Service. Ben got briefly excited when he learned that this might land him a spot in Chicago, allowing him to see his family regularly. But none of these possibilities worked out. He accepted the prospect that he would stay on Mare Island for the duration and concentrated his efforts on earning extra money to send home to his family by doing such work, menial or otherwise, as he might be able to find.

Once again, his original high hopes of useful, meaningful service to his country had been dashed; he became resigned to his fate. "I think I can work out a very satisfactory, reasonable life here—even though it's pointless. There are several barriers in the way of my asking for something else," he reasoned. "In the first place, you can imagine what a public relations job for a private would be. I'd be carrying plate holders for photographers and pencils for second lieutenants who had been reporters on the Galena Gazette." Writing his own material was out, since "anything I did which someone wanted to publish would have to be interpretive or critical. Either would get me into trouble with the Marine Corps, which frowns on such writing even more than the Army." The probable consequence, he reasoned, would be a transfer to a dirty, disagreeable job or a duty station in Alaska. On the other hand, "right where I am probably offers the quickest discharge when it's over . . . But I can't do anything about it for a while, so I'll play tennis and try to think it out."

In the face of official indifference and stultifying routine, he set out to implement his new strategy of mere survival as an enlisted man in the war-time Marine Corps. He soon found that it was fairly easy to satisfy the requirements of his duty assignments and began to devise ways of reducing even those obligations.

Ben's first employment break came when an officer organizing a Mare Island tennis team noticed him playing one day and, deciding on the spot that he was pretty good, invited him to meet a Lieutenant Miller, the sponsor, who told him that if the plan was approved by the "mayor" of the base (normally the officer in charge of base affairs) and the PX Council (the sponsoring agency), he could try out. If he made the team, he would practice every day from two to four o'clock, would be placed on the per- manent standby duty and would get "complete equipment, including racquets, balls, shoes, uniforms." This also meant that he would have no guard watch. "In other words, I will be fighting the war from a tennis court, which will be more fun than standing a dog watch." If it worked out well, Miller had hopes of taking short trips to play nearby teams, and Ben had a glimpse of "a rather free life."

Tennis practice continued into August. and Ben's game improved. Equipment provided by the Marine Corps—new racquets and some long overdue new tennis shoes (he had been playing in boots and developing

Chapter 4-The Politician

blisters)—showed up, and his favorite tennis shorts and Jockey underwear finally arrived from home; there was nothing standing in the way of his enjoyment of the game.

"Now I will go out and play our first match with the Navy officers—if they show up. Yesterday I beat Fullmer (the guy who organized the thing) 6-1, 6-4, 6-3 in three straight sets, and now I'm sure none of the team can beat me..."

And by July 21st: "Maybe you're right about my tennis game. I've beaten everyone I've played so far and the game comes much more easily than ever before. My form is better, my shots steadier and my service very consistent. My game's getting harder and faster. Well, we'll see how I stand up when I meet some competition."

As they started to play matches, the team was on a roll, undefeated in several successive outings. They started to make big plans. "We have a tennis match with the swabbies tomorrow, and then I'm going to encourage Lieutenant Miller to make some out-of-town dates. I like the sound of that country club racket—or racqueting at the country clubs."

But by August 7 Ben reported: "We were beaten in six straight matches yesterday—mine, 6-4, 6-2, was as good a score as we made. Were very ashamed, but my own private guess is that we have a collection of pretty fair players, not quite good enough to go out and challenge the world. I think my first estimate was right. But we can still play tennis every day, and that's mostly what I want out of it—exercise and sunshine. Even Lieutenant Miller took a beating, which was good, because it puts him in the same boat with us."

His next big opportunity was the result of his efforts to find out how things worked on the base. He had "dug up" (as he put it) the captain who was in charge of the guard. "We found that we had common interests. He had been in the wholesale drug business. I offered to help him, should he need help, in sorting out the paper mess that was a corollary of any foul-up in the Marine Corps. He took my name, and I returned to the barracks. An hour later I was paged on the PA system: the captain wanted me. 'Go see this fellow—he's in 'B' barracks—he's shipping out tonight and someone's got to take over for him. It's good duty. Yours was the only name I knew among the new guys.'"

Ben found the evacuee.

"Boy, are you lucky," said the departing bond detail guard. "How'd you get onto this? Now do it just like I tell you.

"You're the money guard for the Navy War Bond Office on our duty days," he continued. "The post thinks it's an all-day job, and you don't have to do any regular duty. Report every duty morning at 8 A.M. to this Wave lieutenant at the bond office." He then schooled Ben on the duties of the job and how to remain inconspicuous: he should sit at the unused typewriter desk in the back of the general office, write letters, read and keep out-of the way until 10 A.M. "She'll dash through the office with the money. You fall in behind her and go to Vallejo in a station wagon driven by a little blonde civilian named Patsy. After the money's deposited, you and Patsy stay handy for a couple of hours until the Wave does her shopping or whatever she does. You'll be back at the base about noon. But don"t come back to the barracks."

He told Ben where he could swim in indoor pools, what buildings had libraries and what recreation rooms on the base were open to all personnel. "Oh, and pick up a .45 and a holster every day—carry a shell in the chamber—that's Navy regulations on the money run. But watch those .45 s," he warned, "They're old and the safeties are loose."

Ben casually announced his stroke of good luck in his July 19th letter, pleased with himself that his military schedule was beginning to fall into place: "Starting tomorrow, I have a new job—whether it's temporary or permanent I don't know—but in any event, the veterans said I got the juiciest plum in the whole guard company." [4]

The job was a breeze, and he set about organizing the remaining hours of his day. The guard company was divided into two groups, each on 24 hours and off 24 hours. His biggest problem was staying out of the way. His next report was a lot more effusive than the first: "If your husband ever does a day's work again, it will have nothing to do with his current experience in the Marine Corps. We have a kind of drill—'Troop and Drill,' they call it—every other day from 8 to 10 a.m. If it was at least good exercise, I wouldn't mind it all, but it consists of standing around 90% of the time and marching at very slow cadence the rest of the time. I got tired of it this morning and left when we had a rest period. The way this guard company is run, I could leave for a week and nobody would know the difference. If I could get my liberty card I would leave."

Chapter 4-The Politician

When he did get his liberty card, he learned that if he kept it when he returned to the post and turned it in at 7:00 AM (when he was due in), he could avoid turning out for roll call at 6 and sleep an extra hour: "See how lazy I'm getting," he remarked.

With every other day free as well, Ben had plenty of time to work and sleep, and he began to ask around about employment opportunities. While they were officially forbidden from taking outside jobs, he noted that "the management winks its eye. If we ask permission we get turned down. If we don't ask, and it doesn't interfere with our duty, nothing is said." The options were limited by the travel time to work sites at off base, the irregularity of his available hours and the scarcity of good-paying jobs. He first tried working at the Sperry flour mill in Vallejo, hauling 100-pound sacks of flour on hand carts from the plant and stacking them in rail cars, "so I'll find out if I'm qualified to be a stevedore." Working from 5 to 12 midnight at 95 cents and hour he netted about $6.00. He planned to do this as fill-in work two or three days per month to fatten his bank account, both by earning more and by cutting down the amount of liberty time he had, further reducing his financial needs. Three days later, he reported, "but I've just learned that you can do all sorts of things you don't imagine you can touch. Four of us loaded up an entire freight car in about two hours—some 800 bags or 80,000 lbs.—that's 40 tons of flour."

Loading flour sacks

Within a week of starting his arduous job at the flour mill, by the following Tues- day, he was already saying, "That's pretty rugged work. I think I'll have to look around and see if there isn't something better suited to my talents." And the scheduling was difficult because he was off on different nights each week. "A prospective employer has a hard time making use of you on that basis."

He almost landed a job with the Vallejo Times-Herald newspaper but could only work on alternate evenings, not every night as the editor required. The job at the flour mill was taking its toll. It was a long commute, it was strenuous work for relatively little pay and Ben knew he was worrying Alice, who feared that he would injure himself.

But on August 8, he reported, "I'm going to try a new job—being a waiter at the officers' club. At first, before I worked at the flour mill, I didn't like the idea, but yesterday, I went up to see Walter Lee, the Chinese boy who runs the bar, and he's going to start me Thursday night. I'll probably just get one or two nights a week at first and then as many as I want. You get $4.50 and tips, which probably brings it up to six or seven dollars, and sometimes better. Advantages are shorter hours, 5:30 to about 11—and I'm just a five-minute walk to the Marine barracks instead of a two-mile walk plus an uncertain ferry ride at midnight." He was reassured by the fact that two of his buddies, Dave Alpert, and Bob Ballantine of the tennis team, both worked there; also, the club did not take tax deductions out of his pay, so he figured he was better off all around.

Benny the waiter

"Another thing: I can work on my non-liberty nights, as well as my liberty nights, since it's in the yard. You get your dinner there too, and Dave says it's wonderful food. We'll see how it works out. Funny how you change—when I first came in here a month ago, the idea of waiting tables bothered me. Now it doesn't at all, and I regard it as a pleasant type of work. I might be able to run my income up to $20 a week above my Marine pay. Counting what you're getting from the government that would be over $200 a month, as much as an ensign gets, or a second lieutenant."

He drew a picture for Pete of "Benny the waiter" and described a party he served where the beer was free, complete with bowls of popcorn, pretzels, pig's feet, peanuts, cheese and crackers. They had bar music and an orchestra, and "lots of dressed up ladies, and but there wasn't a single one as pretty as our Mommy or nearly as nice. The Waves wore their dress whites, and that really is a uniform. I felt just like I did when I was hustling pop at the racetrack 20 years ago or thereabouts, but it's easy, pleasant work." Marines were employed as a paid staff, principally, Ben thought, to keep Navy enlisted men away from the liquor. He said that the officers seemed a little

Chapter 4-The Politician

uncomfortable about having Marines serve them: "They never say 'waiter,' but wait to catch our eye." He noted: "The women drink too much and look it. The officers do too—but they don't start to tip generously until they have a few drinks under their belts. Most of them are overspending anyway, even though drinks are 30 cents."

He actually relished his new job as a bartender and waiter, comfortable with himself for the first time in this role he had previously scorned. Here he gained his legendary skill in bartending. He took great pride after the war in being able to make any drink one could call. As a child Peter was fascinated by the drinks with mystical names his father could conjure up at the bar: Tom Collins, Old Fashioned—complete with a lump of sugar soaked in Angostura bitters, a slice of orange and a maraschino cherry (he would beg for and occasionally get to eat the bourbon-soaked orange and cherry), Highball, Sidecar (Peter envisioned a blue-uniformed Chicago policeman on his three-wheeled motorcycle with, of course, a sidecar), Screwdriver, Orange Blossom, Martini, Manhattan, Grasshopper, Stinger, Crème de Menthe Frappé and Singapore Gin Sling—or Ginapore Sin Sling, depending on how many you'd had!

In later years, as a wedding present, Ben gave his son and daughter-in-law a paperback copy of *The Bartender's Guide*, by Patrick Gavin Duffy, his bible in such matters, which he owned in its original loose-leaf format, along with exact replicas of each bartending tool in his fully equipped setup: a long stirring spoon, a martini strainer, a ¾- and 1½-ounce diabolo-shaped whisky jigger and—that classic of the 50s— an oversized Kap-King bottle opener, all still in the family collection to this day.

Now his arrangements were complete. His mornings were devoted to the bond detail, afternoons were for the tennis team and evenings were spent working at the officers' club, where indeed, he earned plenty of money, with tips sometimes bringing his total take to $20 or more per night. He wrote home to Alice, "I am widely charged with having the best enlisted man's setup in the Marine Corps. They call me 'the politician.' So while I haven't won any medals on the field of honor, at least I have made the best of the limited opportunities facing me. We probably won't ever starve to death, darling."

The news of some certainty in Ben's life, however, slight, had to be reassuring for Alice. She had charge of the family: a new baby girl scarcely more than three months old and her five-year-old son—both fatherless for the duration. Ben felt the loss terribly, and ached at his absence from the normal duties and joys of fatherhood. But as a pragmatist, he cheerfully attacked the problem head on: he *sent* a part of himself home in each letter. Ben began a custom that he carried on throughout his absence. In boot camp, he drew pictures of the tents, the canteens, his sea bag and its contents—neatly laid out for inspection—the men at the firing range, and himself, learning how to "strap in" and position himself correctly to fire a rifle. Later, in November, he expressed his pleasure that they had been well received. "I'm glad Pete enjoyed the letters so much," he wrote. "I'll write a direct one from time to time . . . he might be interested in some details . . . descriptions of ships and things . . . Also it occurs to me that I haven't been giving him much to show the kids . . . souvenirs, etc. I'll remedy that when I go to town next time."[1]

While in his first official assignment, a Marine guard company at Mare Island Navy Yard, he sketched himself doing his activities to earn extra money—loading sacks of flour at a warehouse, and later, tending bar and waiting tables at the Officers' Club; his sightseeing around the Navy Yard, including the famous warship

U.S.S. Portland, returned from sea battles in the Marshall Islands for repairs, and his rounds in his duty job, providing armed guard services to the WAC officer in charge of the War Bond collections on her daily rounds. Although they were not the work of a trained artist, these sketches delighted Peter, who at age five could understand what his daddy was doing more easily from pictures..

Alice, for her part, kept Ben informed on a daily basis: "The intimate accounts of Pete's activities are so full of detail that I feel I'm not missing as much as I might if you weren't so wonderful at telling about it," he said in August. They were first drawn together, among other things, by each other's considerable writing talent. Throughout Ben's absence, in fact, their entire correspondence was so conversational that they succeeded in minimizing the thousands of miles separating them.

In one letter Ben discussed his new-found prosperity: "I find one problem which arises out of working is loaning money. You can't very well conceal the fact that you're working, and everyone else is always so terribly broke that you can't refuse, so I normally now have about $20 outstanding among various guys, ranging from 50 cents loans to 5 dollars." He was able to collect on payday, when most men cleaned up their debts so they could be in a position to borrow again. He noted that when they repaid the money they restored the confidence their buddies had in them. He added, for his son's benefit, "It's like telling the truth: if you don't tell the truth and it causes hardship or trouble to your friends or your family, then they lose confidence in you, and they never know when to trust you. That's why, Pete, you always want to be sure that people trust you. When they trust you then you can do most anything you want that's reasonable and fair; naturally you have more fun that way."[2] Ben's transition to a lesson for his son became a normal refrain in his letters. As his mother read and re-read them to Pete, he absorbed what he could of his father's advice.

Ben used his spare time to provision the family with items that were hard to find or expensive back home. "I see high chairs advertised in the Vallejo papers, and I suppose a baby buggy will turn up one day. Also, I saw some electric trains advertised ... what do you think? You didn't tell me if you thought I ought to do more about Pete's Christmas or not and Linda's ... without your advice I won't know that ... I'll drop the electric train guy a note and see if they're still available at the time I hear from you."

Their family's separation for Christmas 1944 was particularly painful for both Alice and Ben. Neither had been especially devout in their respective religions as children. Ben was raised in an orthodox Jewish family. Alice was Irish Catholic and attended St. Thomas Apostle School in Chicago's Hyde Park neighborhood under the strict tutelage of St. Joseph nuns. Christmas, however, had become a very special part of their marriage. The first year, Alice had delighted her new husband by giving him his first real Christmas celebration. In anticipation he excitedly bought a tree that was three feet too tall for their apartment living room, eager for the chance to celebrate this formerly "forbidden" holiday. Alice had bought him toy trains, whistles, model cars and all those special surprises he was taught as a child were *not* for Jewish children on this American holiday—nor on many other holidays for Ben, since his family had been poor. In place of religious significance, the celebration had taken on emotional importance as a symbol of their love, bringing together two rich traditions that added up to more meaning in each of their lives.

Preparations for their first Christmas apart were discussed in their letters beginning in September. The first order of business was shopping in San Francisco. But to do this, he had to arrange some liberty. He described "a hectic day in which my shopping trip on Saturday was shot to pieces because, of all things, we have to parade in Benicia (a thriving burg of four houses and 30 saloons) as part of the California Admission Day, a celebration of the state's joining the Union). Consequently we have to stand by all Saturday and liberty is canceled." That was on September 6th, a Wednesday.

Undeterred, however, by Thursday he was "in the midst of what amounts to a 'big deal' here." He had decided to try to go to Frisco early to get his shopping tour in. He asked Lieutenant Miller to arrange for him to go on liberty at 11 a.m. instead of 4:30 so he could get some tennis shoes. "He said he'd speak to Captain Kessler and thought it would be all right. My tennis 'pal' could scarcely refuse so simple a request. And anyway tennis needs are 'duty' for me. Then I can go to the Emporium, get the car seat and some other things. And I may then do a very simple but luxurious thing. I think I'll check into the Chancellor, have an early dinner, have a radio sent up to the room, buy a magazine, read and listen to the radio for a couple of hours and then have an uninterrupted 10 hours of sleep with no lockers banging, no drunks rolling in, no reveille, no Marines."

On Friday, September 8th, he reported his success: "Well, I doo'd it, I got my extra liberty . . . I was in Frisco by 2:15. I hitchhiked and did my shopping and bought the car seat. It's a good one made of metal and canvas with wooden armrests and it hooks over the top of the seat. You'll have it within a week. I also found some tennis shoes. Gee, shopping is an experience which discourages you from doing it again in a hurry. The car seat cost $5.00 and tennis shoes $5.50, although a perfectly adequate kind we used to get cost about $1.25."

Again on November 17 Ben again said, "You didn't tell me if you want more of those corduroy pants for Pete—and I think those are '6.' Would you want that size or '5.' And what about the bike? I see some advertised second hand out here—this is a very transient population and

Peter, giraffe and Linda

Chapter 4-The Politician 75

people are always getting rid of hard to move things. It's a world full of electric iceboxes nobody wants."

The electric train never materialized until after the war, when Ben bought Pete a full American Flyer "HO" gauge layout for them both to play with, simultaneously fulfilling the childhood dreams of both boys. Ben set it up in the basement on a huge 5' x 10' board with a large, oval track; it featured freight cars, a passenger car, caboose, a hopper that actually loaded tiny lumps of coal into a coal car and realistic steam that poured out of the engine's smokestack. Christmas 1944 did bring Peter a Radio Flyer coaster wagon, a coat with a sheepskin lining, a clothes rack in the shape of a giraffe made by Uncle Mel and many other gifts from relatives who wanted to make up for his father's absence.

Ben concluded on November 20: "Pete's Christmas seems to be rounding out and I am impelled to remember that we both go through the very same crisis each year, worrying about whether or not he'll have enough, and then kicking ourselves because we don't have house room for what he gets. He'll certainly not be forgotten by the family. His clothes sound so grown-up and so all-boy. I remember my first Mackinaw. They were standard with kids, and I didn't get a sheepskin- lined coat until I was a freshman in college, and I wore it with my green spot on my head (the freshman stigmata of the era) and looked very college." In addition to having his military life in order, he was confident he'd done all he could to smooth over life back home.

But there was trouble in paradise. Ben reported he had a situation needing attention, which that he couldn't talk very much about. The letters became shorter and tenser in tone. A few weeks later, he explained what happened. "Because it was somewhat dangerous to carry a loaded .45 with a shell in the chamber and a loose safety, I made it a practice to clear the weapon after depositing the money, as soon as I rejoined Patsy in the station wagon. To clear a weapon you eject the shell from the chamber, press the trigger for a clearing shot to be sure and replace

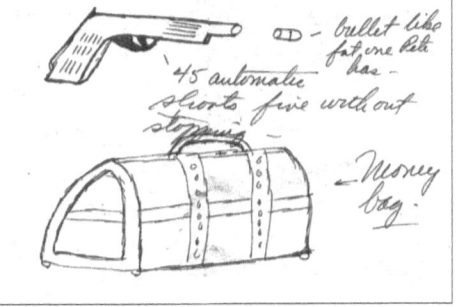

Bond detail essentials

the cartridge in the magazine."

On the eventful day, Main Street of Vallejo was quiet and lazy. Vallejo was strictly a nighttime town, coming to life when the sailors and shipyard workers streamed in from the base after 5 p.m. Suddenly the peace was shattered by what sounded like a a sonic boom. Smoke poured from the station wagon. Pedestrians stopped and gawked as little blonde Patsy screamed and jumped from the vehicle.

"Get back in," Ben ordered. She was too frightened to disobey. "Now start the motor." It started. "Just keep it running," he instructed her. He opened all the windows to get rid of the acrid odor of spent gunpowder. "By the time Lieutenant Evans returned," Ben explained, "all was in order, and we returned to the base without further incident.

"At 5 p.m., I was summoned to the captain's office."

"How did you happen to have an accidental discharge Vallejo this morning?" he queried.

"How did you happen to hear about it?" Ben asked.

"Well, after your driver dropped the wagon in the garage, the next driver found it wouldn't start. She lifted the hood and your .45 bullet had split the battery exactly in half. The battery acid sprayed all over the motor. We can't figure out how the wagon made it back to the base. By the way, you know, that's an automatic court-martial? Well, don't worry; we have a nice brig here."

Ben's work as a bartender evenings at the Navy officers club suddenly came in very handy. His chief Marine commanding officer was a colonel who love to drink and entertain his friends but was always broke. Since only a few Marine officers drank at the club, Ben and his fellow Marine waiters made it a practice to omit giving them bar checks about every other round. He said it was one way of getting even with the Navy. In the case of the colonel, they had made sure that rounds on the house were frequent and regular. "So at least," wrote Ben, "I felt the top man on the board of inquiry might feel a little friendly. There were 23 officers in the inquiry room when I was given the center stage, all spit and polish in my best Corps manner. I was told to describe the incident. I did." At this point the colonel exploded: "How could you make the mistake like that? Didn't they teach you anything about firearms at Matthews?"

"Sir, we never had training on .45s. They substituted Browning Automatic Rifle training for the .45." A lieutenant affirmed the accuracy of Ben's statement.

"Do you mean that's the first time you ever fired a .45? What if you'd had to use it? You might kill somebody." The board of inquiry broke into a roar of laughter. The colonel pursued his inquiry, but he was no longer interested in Ben. He grilled his subordinate officers:

"Do you mean, none of these men know how to handle .45's?" he persisted. "Why, half of our duty assignments call for side arms on this post. Green, you're dismissed. A man can't be expected to use a firearm he's never learned to handle. We're lucky you didn't kill a civilian or shoot your foot off. Tomorrow morning at 6," he continued, "I want .45 training to begin for every man in this detachment."

With this providential outcome and a different turn of international events, Ben's stay at Mare Island could have been the last stop on his military tour. Indeed, he was hopeful his pleasant arrangement would be the extent of his duty for the duration of the war. But the shot fired in Vallejo was a portent of many to come—shortly thereafter Ben got his orders for overseas duty in the Pacific: "And so it was. When we left for Guam a week later, the day after Christmas, our little band of warriors knew how to handle the .45's they would lay aside forever for M-1s, B.A.R.s, machine guns, flame throwers and grenade launchers." [5]

Thus it seemed in the cosmic chess game of war—nation against nation, clan against clan and man against the organization—he had been checked at every turn. When he enlisted as an officer, they studied his request to help the masterminds run the operation. Did they decide that his kind of people need not apply? When a brilliant light illuminated the sky at Benicia, hundreds of personnel were killed and debris landed many miles away. Was it a nuclear blast? Were American troops the guinea pigs, exposed at close range to risky experiments that would later be used on the enemy? We may never know the answers to these questions; but the grand planners were happy to have our troops as pawns in the game. Most interpreters agreed that the great sacrifices our troops made in the war effort were justified to preserve world order. In this light, by manipulating his assignments so cleverly, was Ben shirking his duty? He didn't think so: he frequently offered to serve in key posts and was repeatedly rebuffed. It eventually became clear to him that, under the circumstances, his own actions could have absolutely no impact on the course of events. Looking ahead toward his next career after the war, he wrote to Alice, "Our breaks haven't come in trying to serve our country, so maybe they'll come when we try to serve ourselves. Well, it's better here than working for Hitler."

But on the individual level, Ben had a world of his own to save—his family, his vision of the future and his personal legacy. Toward this purpose, he maneuvered skillfully, with all his cunning, knowledge and resources to serve, to survive and to fight another day. Nevertheless at this stage of the campaign, each of his hard-won triumphs was trumped; it was checkmate, and the board was cleared to begin the game anew.

By now his officers' club connections were leading to requests for favors. "All of a sudden my life is full of lots of clamor for help. Dr. Frantschen, the Navy commander in charge of our dispensary, told me at the club last night that his daughter is now in Chicago and would like to have some auditions, if I could arrange them. So I'm going over to see him today. I figure the more friends I can make around the yard, the better off I am. Anyway, I am a nicer guy since I have been in the service, I think. I'm nicer to everyone and more considerate and patient than I used to be. I think you'll like me." [6]

Ben bought a trench coat at the PX for $21.50 and began to put it to use. "We've had a couple of days of light rain and it looks as if our second rainy season is about to begin." He made fun of his sister Ruth's comment in a letter about how nice it would be to be out in the California sunshine. "Ha, ha—it's 8:20 now and it's still half dark outside. It's usually nine o'clock before it's light and—if there is any sun, which there isn't today— it's noon before you see it." [7]

About this time, he got a letter from Mike Wallace, in a sub squadron in Australia, who reported: "We flew down here, stopping at the logical places on the way, and then—once in Australia—managed to get bumped off the plane whenever possible, so as to see what there was to see. Got to see virtually every major city on the continent, though, of course on one or two days' stopovers only, and it was a glorious experience."

On one of his last liberty trips from Mare Island to the mainland, Ben looked out into San Pablo Bay from the deck of the ferry. A few nautical miles to the southwest lay the Golden Gate; his thoughts wandered to the open sea beyond. Its global waters lapped Australia, where

Chapter 4-The Politician

Mike was stationed; Europe, where the Allies were closing in on the Third Reich, and Japan, whose plans to dominate the Pacific threatened the world order.

As the fog lifted, he studied the sullen water. If he crossed the sea, where would it take him? Would he, Mike and his buddies who had already shipped out be able to survive, help their country and return? Would he ever see his family again? He had never been less certain of what the future held for him.

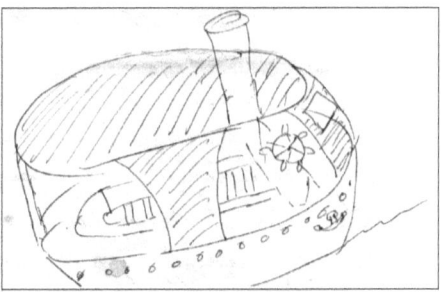

The Mare Island Ferry.

CHAPTER 5

TRANSPORTED TO GUAM

Ben clambered downstairs to the first deck of the barracks. There was Goldie with his wife and children—two darling little boys, one about Pete's age and the other about two. He was just going to guard mount. As Goldie kissed his wife and headed out the door, Ben held first one and then the other boy up to the window so they could see their father, and that was almost too much. When the youngest put his arms around his neck and asked, "Is that my daddy?" tears came to Ben's eyes.

Barracks-Mare Island

As Christmas approached, Ben checked again with Alice on presents for the children, including a wagon for Pete. He spent Christmas Eve with Lt. Burns and her fiancé, "Burnsey and Bob Ives," and arranged for a telephone call home, a process which normally took 18 hours: "The operator and I started chinning and shooting the breeze in a very friendly fashion. I think she must have put me in ahead of my turn, because it really only took 11 hours, and, when the call came through, the day operator acted as if she had known me all my life." Pete seemed so thrilled to talk. For once he had lost his "allergy to telephone conversations," and Ben admitted to singing afterwards. His holiday loneliness was also eased when he dressed and went to dinner: "It was such an elegant affair: TABLECLOTHS, and a printed menu, which I am sending you . . . free cigarettes, a bag of nuts and an orange, and a really marvelous turkey dinner." Afterwards, he went up to his bunk. "Then I had the glow of my wonderful presents all around me . The watch is positively beautiful and keeps second-perfect time. It's one of those good Swedish watches, which in case you didn't know are the only ones left that still carry Swiss movements, since they alone can get them. The wallet is slick and just right. It fits snugly, either in my inside coat pocket or in my trousers."[1]

As the year 1944 wound down, rumors had begun to circulate that a major troop deployment was in the works. Everyone on the base was jittery. To head off a transfer, Ben continued to try to improve his situation, both by petitioning for his bond detail to become a six-day-a-week assignment, to ensure a more permanent and stable position at Mare Island, and by changing from the officers' club to the warrant officers' club to improve his working conditions. In view of the troop movements planned, Col. Betts, his battalion commander, even called him at the officers club, confiding to him that he was trying to hold on to a few key men when the transfer occurred and assured him he would put in a word to try to keep him at the base. Meanwhile Ben had received through the good colonel's offices his first and only military stripe—that of a Private First Class—which he wore proudly, hoping it might spare him from the more onerous duties normally assigned to unrated recruits.

But when the hammer fell, it was a Department of the Pacific order, and it specified men by name instead of indicating that so many men be transferred in the usual manner. The colonel couldn't even take his own orderly off the list. On Friday, December 29 Ben reported: "So we are all going this afternoon at 5:00 p.m. At Pendleton we'll go through reclassification and where we go from there we don't know. Most of us will do overseas duty, but that does not necessarily make it combat duty. We'll probably do guard duty on some of the islands already taken." He hoped that both he and El (Duke) thought they might not be shipped, but soon he realized that he would feel a certain sense of guilt if 200 of their buddies went without them. "Maybe it's better this way," he reasoned. "We've had a good break and probably will continue to have it."

He rationalized that there were a lot of things to favor the transfer, in that life at Mare Island had become duller and duller by the month, and he looked forward with anticipation to something new and different. A Marine he met on liberty in San Francisco had already been to the Pacific and back on a transport and "was full of stories which made the life sound interesting and exciting, compared to Mare Island." Receiving the news in the mail three days later, especially after their cheery Christmas telephone conversation, Alice could only have been crushed. Already reeling from the illness of her father—he had ulcers, which periodically bled and put him in the hospital—she needed only the news that Ben might go overseas to complete her misery. He concluded his letter by reassuring her, "I'm depending on you to be your wonderful self . . . don't, don't feel that this transfer, means anything terribly different."[2]

Alice's sister Helen, in a letter of late February, reflected the dark mood back home. She expressed relief that Alice blew off steam in her letter, which she knew must be accumulating. "As to Benny, I know—even without your letter—just what you must be fearing in your bad moments. You mentioned Tokyo. By now it has probably taken the form of Iwo or Jima. But in case you can't quite see it, let me remind you that they're not going to throw green (no pun intended) troops without any Pacific experience into battles of such vital importance. Benny certainly has a period of training coming to him, at worst, before he would be involved in such landings." She also reassured Alice that she would not be imposing on them by joining her family for the summer: "As to the house, little sister, we need it as badly as you and couldn't rent one for ourselves anyway for less than a month and probably not for less than the season—so any expense we see fit to make is for selfish reasons." [3]

Just five days after Christmas, writing at 8:30 a.m., Ben reported they were halfway through the 550-mile trip to Los Angeles, which "on this old rattler," the same kind they came up on, "takes 25 or 30 hours." While the main pastime was poker, they had all become more philosophical about waiting. He was surrounded by his friends, including Duke, and he had put most of his cash into traveler's checks to make it impossible to lose. Looking as usual on the bright side, Ben reveled in the fact that they had left the Bay Area in a drenching rain only a day after the rainy season had started and admired the sunny day they were experiencing in pretty mountain country through the train window. Arriving at Pendleton, they learned they had all been assigned to the Fleet Marine Force, which he characterized as "the soul of the Marine Corps" and assured Alice that it included such things as guard duty. Every third man got a 72-hour liberty and Ben was one of the lucky ones. He and two of his Mare Island friends with great difficulty managed to get a train to Los Angeles, where he hooked up with a party at the home of his Hollywood friend, Gordon Hughes, and vowed to get tickets to the Rose Bowl game. The absence of a glowing play-by-play description—which Ben would most certainly have provided—is evidence, however, that he was unable to pull this off.

Fleet Marine Force was the creation of Holland M. Smith, the general who served as commander. In just four years he had built the Marine Corps into the toughest fighting unit in the U. S. military. In the spring of 1940, he emphasized that the strength of the Marine Corps was 1,410 officers and 25,070 enlisted men; equipment included five tanks you could kick your foot through. In World War II total Marine strength grew to 599,693, of whom 90 percent served abroad. Their armament included all the latest weapons, amphibious tanks and tractors and thousands of landing craft, all types of mechanized equipment, improved artillery, rockets and flame throwers, as well as carrier-based and shore-based air units. He proudly declared: "That made the Marines the best equipped troops in the world."[4]

Before the war could be fought on two oceans, Smith had to win his

Chapter 5-Transported to Guam

own battles with the Navy and the U. S. Congress. His insistence with the Navy brass and the rest of government on a dominant Marine role in amphibious warfare earned him the moniker, Howlin' Mad Smith: "But I was a bad boy, I have always been a bad boy in interservice arguments," he confessed, "and I am often amazed that I lasted so long in the Marine Corps. In this instance, I knew my arguments were sinking in, and to have stopped fighting would have been like quitting the beach when you're dug in."[5] Smith is credited with advocating the development of a new type of landing craft, creating new battle techniques and inventing a new style of warfare: the mechanized island invasion. Even though Ben didn't have contact with the genius behind the operation, he gained respect for his strategy and was willing to help realize his plans.

For the next twelve days there are no letters in the collection, for the very good reason that a flurry of phone calls and travel arrangements preceded a visit by Alice to California, her last chance to see Ben before he shipped out overseas. They spent it in a cottage at Oceanside, a town just to the north of Camp Pendleton. Family pictures attest to the joy they both felt at being reunited for this brief but happy period. Indeed, in letters for months afterward, Ben glowed from memories of their time together; they both referred to it ever afterwards as idyllic. It was also a chance for some of the wives to meet their husbands' Marine pals, and each other, gaining valuable moral support. Alice traded letters with a few of them, including Mary Terrill, Cliff's wife, in Barnsdall, Oklahoma; Dorothy Godsall, in San Francisco; Jean Morrow in Chicago, and a few others. Mary Terrill reported that, before he could get aboard ship, Cliff was sick as a dog and was held back from the 38th Replacement Draft, Ben's unit, to the 40th, although he soon followed them overseas. The next news of Ben is from aboard a troop ship. Just before they boarded ship he was thrilled

Ben and Alice at Oceanside

Peter reading.

to receive the Christmas pictures of Alice and the children, taken by his sister's husband Mel, a good amateur photographer. "Linda looks like a little butterball, and Pete, lying on the sofa reading book, looks like such a big boy." He said, "poker and craps will fill much of my time."

Once aboard ship, he and Johnny Hughes were assigned to mess duty: "I'm in the scullery—sanitary engineering, Johnny and I call it. Its sort of a weightlifting job, and we're on 24 and off 24, only we're really off, not half-off, as we were at Mare Island."[6] But the work was strenuous for 10 to 12 hours a day and included "a free dirty steam bath." He reported that being a Pfc. had moved him to the top of the duty list, such were the advantages of rank, and was thankful that he had something to pass the time, thus turning it into sort of a benefit not available to everyone on board.

He warned Alice that, since there would be nothing new to report and the mail would only be dropped off at the next port, his letter writing might be sporadic. "If there is one outstanding characteristic of the war, it is the power it has to make men stop thinking and to pull a curtain of dullness over everything it touches. We're stopped now; but for how many days and where we go from here none of us knows. All it means to me is so many more days of scullery duty and so many more days of the endless poker game." While the censor excised his careless reference to their first port of call, he later revealed it was Pearl Harbor, and that the Royal Hawaiian hotel, headquarters of the submarine fleet, and Waikiki Beach were pointed out to them as they steamed out of port.

By January 27th he wrote again, remarking that he missed writing daily, but that with "the forced absence of mail and the unvarying routine, there isn't much to write about." At last he was out of the scullery and serving food on the line. "It's just as hot, but you don't do as much hard manual labor, so you're not exhausted when you're finished." He had taken to reading books from the shipboard library and the "millions of pocket editions, especially mysteries, that the Red Cross handed out in our ditty bags," along with cigarettes and playing cards.

He looked over the rail on his world: half cloudless sky the color of a sailor's shirt, the lower half an infinite expanse of Parker's Blue-Black Quink. If only he had such an ample supply of writing materials:

Linda--butterball

it seemed he always had to scrounge. Before reaching Hawaii they had crossed the Tropic of Cancer; now they were crossing the 15th parallel. The mild tropical nights and black skies studded with billions of stars inspired him to sleep on deck: "The weather's splendid and it's permitted—I get to sleep topside every night because most of the guys in my compartment think it's too much work carrying their gear up and back. I don't. I was rained on last night, but I didn't get too wet because I had my tent half-shelter thrown over my blanket. But the water from the deck did wet the underside of my mattress, so tonight I'll do it G.I. style with the tent shelter on top and my poncho underneath—but topside I will sleep."

He noted that the war news was "certainly encouraging—in the East and the West in Europe, and the Pacific is certainly ablaze with action." His source was a ship's newspaper that "circulates in somewhat haphazard fashion, but I get to see it four or five times a week." He encouraged Alice to go ahead with her plan to join her sister's family at a cottage they planned to rent on the shore in Massachusetts for the summer, and speculated that she might even want to do some sightseeing in Boston with Pete, "since he'll be studying American history soon . . . even though it may not mean much to him now."

On February 1st Ben wrote excitedly, on Marine stationery decorated with hand-drawn Valentine hearts and greetings: "Guess what! I went on a picnic yesterday! Right in the middle of the Pacific Ocean at one of our ports of call. After 19 days at sea it was really a break. We were taken ashore in a Seabee's nightmare—a bunch of ballast tanks fastened together by iron or steel decks and powered at the stern by something with plenty of push, because this seagoing pool table got there all right. We had beer—plenty of it—they gave us a couple of cans apiece and then we were able to buy it for two dollars a case: Budweiser and Pabst in cans! Then we swam, and so far as I was concerned, it was the most wonderful swim we've ever had. It was warmer than the Mediterranean and crystal clear. We were burned to a crisp under a hot sun in a cloudless sky, but I have enough tan now so I didn't hurt. We were ashore from ten in the morning until four in the afternoon and enjoyed every minute of it. Johnny Hughes and John Greely were with me."

He asked Alice to contact their wives, since they both lived in the Chicago area. Ben later revealed that this pleasant sojourn occurred at Parry Island in the Marshalls, their second port of call. Only a year earlier, on February 22, 1944, the Marines had wrested it from Japanese control. Their next stop would be Eniwetok, another of the volcanic atolls making up the Marshalls, where they would lay up for two weeks while a defensive convoy was formed. Ben later remarked that his troop ship, being the largest of the flotilla, presented the biggest target for enemy aircraft.

Dorothy Godsall wrote Alice on February 13th, thanking her for "such an interesting letter," and continued: "The best news is that Ben and El have managed to stay together. That is a great comfort to me, so I know how much it means to them." She also expressed hope of a nice safe berth for their boys in Manila, a city already subdued. Holland Smith, however, had other plans for his troops: there were islands to be taken, battles to be won. Philip Roth, in discussing his novel *The Plot Against America* on PBS, quoted a passage: "The terror of the unforeseen is what the science of history hides. What armchair historians coolly study today as the panorama of grand events did not look that way to those about to be swept up in them." History looks awfully different to those who are about to make it.

Having plenty of time on his hands, Ben made careful observations on the management practices of the military—especially as regards the distribution of beer, a subject to which he seemed to return frequently: "We do have a lot of swimming and drinking beer, although the services certainly manage to do the simplest jobs the hardest way. Part of the trouble is that a lot of former shoe clerks want to be executives and run around with what Kay Chase used to describe as a 45-degree-angle executive air. They're full of lists and computations and maneuvers, so that by the time they've worked out a plan to give two and sell two cans of beer you'd think they had been re-planning the social structure of the world. But they're doing the best they can with what they have to work with."[7]

As the days wore on, Ben expressed reasonable contentment doing his work, playing poker, reading for recreation and sleeping topside. "I spend quite a bit of time trying to keep reasonably clean, which is a chore with salt water. Some of these lads, I am sure, haven't had a bath since we've been aboard and, unlike the French, they don't use perfume." It is not surprising that he preferred to sleep on deck.

On February 15th, Ben wrote that they were on the move again headed for a destination to be kept as a military secret, which he later reported they were told was Guam. By then he had met four journalists on the ship, Red O'Donnell and Bob Reilly of the Chicago Times, Robert Terrell, of the Chicago Sun and George Young, of the San Francisco Chronicle, who knew Ben's friend at that paper, music critic Alfie Frankenstein. Meanwhile Ben fretted about what problems Alice might be facing around the house and how Pete might be faring in his first year in school. At long last, on February 17th, they were informed that they would reach their destination the next morning: "The voyage is nearing an end. Only three more meals to serve. No matter what lies ahead, there will be a tremendous feeling of relief about getting out of that sweat hole. It's the worst job many of us have had since we've been in the Marine Corps. While we may hit worse ones, we will never forget this one."

The deck was alive with activity: luggage, sea bags and rations were brought from the hold and stacked, and the men received their debarkation orders. All was in readiness for their arrival. But Ben's biggest hope was that there would be mail awaiting them; knowing Alice's daily custom, he anticipated receiving about 38 days' worth of mail, one letter for each day he had so far been en route. But for reasons known only to the military bureaucracy, they lay in port three days waiting: their actual debarkation did not take place until the following Wednesday. Ben and his comrades in misery served a few more meals. "Today's a little cooler, and there's a good breeze, but yesterday and the day before, the official bridge temperature is supposed to have been about 120°, so you can imagine what the mess hall was like." From January 13th to February 21st, including a day at each end for loading and unloading, they had spent 43 days at sea, half of his duty days working in the scullery and half at the steam table in the mess hall. "When the order finally came to disembark on Wednesday, we cheered. We were taken off on Higgins boats, packed in like sardines. We had our packs, our full equipment load and our blankets and bed rolls, but we didn't mind: we were going ashore."[8]

Lister bag and water wagon

The long-awaited moment arrived on Friday: "Waiting for me were 37 letters from my darlings, plus one from Mother. I've done nothing all day but read and read. Tomorrow I'll read them chronologically and slowly. But right now I'm full of glow and intimacy with the family and what's happened in the last month and a half. Two hundred bags of mail were waiting for us and we've done almost nothing but answer mail calls in the two days we've been here."

Their encampment, which consisted of tents with wood floors, in addition to the permanent shelters for common functions such as mess halls and administrative support, were soon to be served by electricity and running water. Since they had no duties yet, they were put to work picking up stones, clearing and raking the area. After a few weeks of this life, Ben said it felt like an extended camping trip and wondered how long this could last. They knew little about the island. It was 30 miles long, as narrow as four miles in some places, nearly 8-1/2 miles wide at its best. They learned that the U. S. took it away from the Spaniards during the Spanish American War, held it until the Japanese took over in 1941 and recaptured it in 1944. "Other than that, we knew we had landed, were encamped for a few days on a tropical coral beach, protected by rows of royal Hawaiian palms and then had been moved into the heart of the jungle to build a new camp in a swamp.

"We put tents up on bamboo stilts, built coral roads, killed rats, and set ourselves up to live out of Lister water bags and any other water we were willing to stand in line for and tote from the once-every-other day visit of the water wagons. The camp we had deserted was never used again."

"For amusement we gave some of the thousands of toads on Guam cigarettes to puff and watched them stagger in a kind of intoxication."

Smoking toad

Chapter 5-Transported to Guam

They soon began to understand what it meant to be in the tropics. The transient company where they were first assigned was near the beach amidst groves of palms, not far from the gently breaking surf. Their activities were the typical camp functions—formations, inspections, chow, drill, and even movies at night, although they were shown outdoors, with no seating provided. "The chow is amazing. We figured on eating K-rations but instead we're eating in clean mess halls with modern equipment and getting swell meals. For breakfast we had butter—real butter, not canned, although the canned butter is a good spread . . . tastes sort of like cheese— Spam, potatoes, Cream of Wheat, tomato juice and coffee, bread and jelly. All the meals are comparable, and living in the open this way makes us ravenously hungry.

There were plenty of three-day bivouacs, and these were no fun. It never failed to rain. "Tropical rain on a South Pacific island is like a prolonged shower with all your clothes on," he said "But then the sun takes over. The red mud you've accumulated dries in minutes to a hard cake and there you are for three or four days. Caked or sodden."

Ben's first trouble on Guam developed over a letter. Although most men in the service write letters, he wrote daily, establishing a kind of communication that became almost conversational. "That one of my hundreds of letters could cause a commotion and completely change the battle field in my war came as a shock."

"The Corps was hard put to keep us busy," he noted. They were being combat-trained, but the instructors were running out of things to teach them. Having fulfilled all their training duties, the Marine Corps cadre decided to try to educate the troops with a series of indoctrination lectures. But in most cases the indoctrinator had not done his homework the night before. Finally came an officer to tell them about Guam. He had done his homework. "He told us about the original Micronesians: a strangely beautiful people who had a strong tradition and a proud way of life. Each spring, all the single males and unwed females embarked in large canoes for neighboring uninhabited islands. Here for a month, they frolicked and played and chose their mates. When they returned to Guam, they were wed. And marriage on Guam was for keeps. Infidelity after marriage was punishable by ostracism, when the tribe felt merciful, and by death in more severe cases."

"The wildlife, explained their lecturer, was peculiar. The birds had been destroyed by lizards, which ate the birds' eggs. To control the lizards, the U.S. Navy introduced giant toads which ate the lizard eggs. Then they introduced flights of doves. These were just beginning to take hold and could be observed by alert bird watchers. The rats, he explained, were an American gift. U.S. rats made their way down the Navy ships' hawsers to find a tropical paradise full of nutritive coconuts and bananas. The final answer: nail strips of tin made by flattening out five gallon food containers around the tree trunks. The rats couldn't climb over the metal. Clean up the ground, get rid of all fallen coconuts, then bait the hungry rats." Ben found the lecture to be articulate, informed and interesting. In his daily letter, he said "Today, I heard the first informed, intelligent lecture since I've been in the Marine Corps.'"

The next day he was called in to the office of Captain Jenkins, his company commander. The captain was a former gymnasium teacher from Paducah, Kentucky, who seemed to spend an inordinate amount of time standing on his hands, which he explained was an integral part of the annual graduation ceremony in his Paducah school, and he wanted to stay in condition. "Whatever the motivation," commented Ben, "the physical result may have been largely to addle his brain."

"Green, I have your letter here," said the captain. "You've said some terrible things."

"Sir, why do you have my letter?" asked Ben. "Are you the company censor?"

"I'm your captain, Green."

"Yes sir, and a fine captain sir; but sir, only the censor is authorized to read my letters. If he thinks I have violated military security, I am subject to court martial. Otherwise, he censors undesirable material and sends the letter on."

Captain Jenkins shifted uneasily. Ben considered suggesting he stand on his hands to relieve the pressure.

"Captain, sir, what have I written that's so terrible?"

"Green, you say that Col. Thomason's lecture was the first intelligent lecture you've heard in the Marine Corps. You've been in the Corps over a year. You've heard dozens and dozens of lectures. That makes us sound awfully dumb. Gosh, it would be terrible if this letter ever got published."

"Sir, I've written hundreds of letters home. My wife already has formed

Chapter 5-Transported to Guam

her opinions, good or bad. Not one letter has been published. How do you imagine this one will achieve such unusual distinction?"

"Green, you oughtn't write this stuff home."

"Well, sir, if the letter disturbs you, I'll be happy to withdraw it." The captain was silent. After a long time I reached for the letter. "No," he said. "I'll send it."

With that, he stamped it, sealed it and told Ben that he was dismissed. End of episode, he thought. But he didn't reckon with Marine Corps logic. "The man's a trouble maker," reasoned Jenkins. "I don't want trouble makers in my company." At 6 a.m. the next morning he was on a truck bound for the central supply dump on Guam, miles away from Captain Jenkins and headed for a new round of skirmishes. The Marine Corps had met another crisis with a typical solution: "Let somebody else worry about him."[9]

The ration dump proved to have its unpleasant moments, and yet it was as if Br'er Rabbit had been thrown into his own briar patch. True, the schedule shifted from days to afternoons to the graveyard shift on a regular weekly rotation. It was heavy manual labor, which involved handling huge quantities of food—"each box weighs 40 to 80 pounds, and to handle 1,000 boxes a night is not unusual"—since all the food for the entire island was routed through this depot.

Indeed there were some miserable jobs: "I finished work at 8 a. m., and we go back on at 4 p.m.—just an eight hour break, because we're changing shifts. We're on a dirty, nasty job now, which would be bad enough in the daytime, but under searchlights at night it's a bum business, and I hope we're through with it soon. We're re-stacking a mess of C-rations. We're looking for good ones—these are so old and crummy that they're being condemned. They had to be dumped in a hurry when the island was first taken, and were stacked without protection. This weather would rot the inside of a marble vault, much less an ordinary packing case. I know what

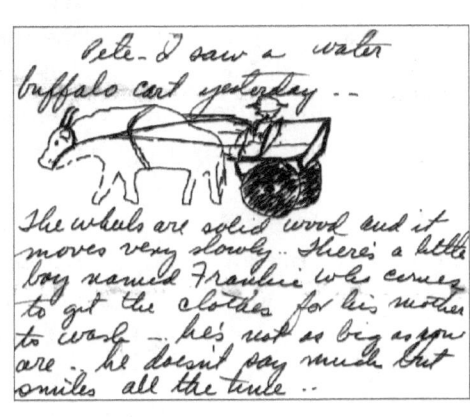

Frankie and his water buffalo cart

Native house on blocks

a gas attack is like now, after handling this stuff. It can't last forever (I keep telling myself), and the next job may be pleasanter."[10]

But there were no inspections, procedures were informal, there were only four men to a tent (at the transient center there had been eight) and the men were left alone when they were off duty. There were native women willing to do laundry for a few dollars per load, and the men were able to spend daytime hours—when on night shift—and days off at a nearby beach. The freedom afforded here was in stark contrast to conditions back at the transient center, which reminded them of boot camp. Ben had some time to relax and dream in his off-duty hours, because his letters got longer with his speculations on the war. He resumed drawing what he saaw his children.

Ben even took some pride in one of his special assignments: there was a shortage of pallets, and for a few days the men were assigned to work in the warehouse building new ones: "I worked on the pallets again last night. It wasn't bad: at least there is the satisfaction of doing something that's needed, and that's a feeling which has been rare in the Marine Corps. They need these so badly that they take them away and start using them as soon as they are made. Since I can't be useful at anything I know, it might as well be at driving nails. I can drive them straighter and faster now. There are 60 nails in each palette. I probably drove some 2,500 nails last night." When he returned from the war, Ben taught Peter good nail-driving technique. They spent many happy Saturdays in the basement workshop doing household repairs.

During the period he spent in the ration dump, their ninth wedding anniversary came and went and Ben had ample opportunity to reread the letters delivered to him upon his arrival. In his spare time he also began exploring. He visited Island Command to use the chaplain's library and to meet the public relations officers, to see what employment opportunities might be available. While in the vicinity of Agana he also visited the island radio station and CincPac headquarters on Nimitz Hill, which gave an ex-

Chapter 5-Transported to Guam

cellent view of the town and Apra Harbor on one side of the island and of the open ocean on the other. The Seabees had built many tiny houses of wood with thatched roofs.

He liked the food at his new outpost: there was a cook there who, if he had better facilities, Ben felt, would be able to prepare some outstanding dishes. He even roused himself early one day, sleeping only briefly after the 4 to midnight shift to sample a rare treat—some eggs prepared sunny-side up, the sign that they really came from shells and not a can. When his younger sister Rosalie—whom he kidded mercilessly anyway for what he called her half-baked, ideas—worried he was not getting enough eggs and offered to send him some, Ben wrote: "Time out for chow—corned beef, canned cabbage, bread and jelly, green beans, sliced pineapple, lemonade, dehydrated potatoes—which reminds me that Rosalie asked if dehydrated eggs came in shells, and would I like a box of them? Was I getting all I liked? I hope she's waiting for a reply. Can you imagine sending anyone dehydrated eggs as a present? She would have to call out the Marines to make the Army eat them, and no one can make the Marines eat them. Anyway, tell her they look just like yellow talcum powder, come in two-gallon cans and taste just like yellow talcum powder." [11]

But as soon as Ben had become comfortable with his situation at the ration dump, by April 7th, about three weeks after his banishment, he was recalled to his 38th replacement company at the transient center. Apparently the Marines wanted him back more than Capt. Jenkins wanted him gone. Happy to be reunited with his Mare Island cohorts, he was less happy, however, to return to the silly military routine of the camp—drill, inspection, bivouac, and boredom.

Then, on Friday, April 13, came the awful news: "This will have been a Black Friday the 13th indeed if the scuttlebutt about Roosevelt's death is true. It's been going the rounds all morning and seems pretty persistent, so I fear it will turn out to be true. To lose him now will be a tragedy for the whole world and may even give the Axis encouragement to fight on in the hope of a softer peace. But maybe it's scuttlebutt. I'll hope that it is until we have definite news."

But bad news had traveled fast. As the troops on Guam circulated the rumor at about 9:00 a.m. on the morning of April 13th, simultaneously on the other side of the world, which was nine minutes past 7:00 pm on April

12th back in Washington, Harry Truman was taking the oath of office at the White House. Since the moment when Franklin D. Roosevelt died in Warm Springs, Georgia, the nation had been without a president for just two-and-a-half hours.

The dull routine at the transient camp, however, was not to last much longer. The camp was abuzz with news of a move; by April 16th, it occurred: "I'm in the Ninth Marines," reported Ben, "which means Ninth Regiment, Fifth Amphibious Corps, of the Third Marine Division. They wear a three-bladed propeller as a shoulder insignia." The move took six hours, including a one hour drive in trucks to a new camp deeper in the jungle, but it had showers, a PX, decent chow, outdoor movies and the privilege of sending in all the laundry you want once a week, free. "This part of the island wasn't in the invasion—the camp is built in a thick coconut grove and is surrounded by a very pretty jungle—lots of bright green foliage and plenty of tall palm trees. It's hotter here and much more like Chicago in the summertime. If last night is a fair sample even the nights are not too cool. Mosquitoes are plentiful. Fortunately I brought my mosquito netting along and got it up . . . they attack in squadrons." [12]

The regiment was then broken into companies and platoons capable of fighting a battle: Johnny Hughes to a machine gun squad, another as a mortar man in Headquarters Company. (to hide the unit's organizational structure, the rest of the page below this point in Ben's letter was cut off by the censor). Ben was assigned to a communications unit, which included field telephone wiremen and radiomen. "I'll ask for and likely get radio, so I'll probably wind up with a walkie-talkie on my back (still producing programs!). He said it sounded interesting and was pleased with the assignment.

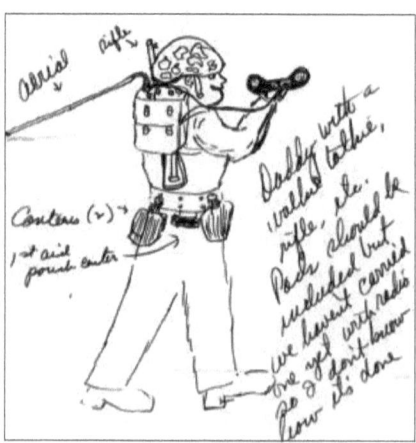

Ben with walkie talkie

"We'll train for a minimum of 13 weeks, which means you can relax until the end of the summer. Of course, conditions then will dictate what happens. And the training is intensive

Chapter 5-Transported to Guam

and vigorous but doesn't include so many of the things I don't like, most of which have to do with drill, etc." He noted, "There's much to be said for the general atmosphere—if it continues—99% of the cause my previous griping will have been removed. We are treated as if we were men instead of Boy Scouts. There are no unreasonable restrictions, and what mistakes are made are those of honest judgment. The self righteousness, the useless activity, the aimless attempts to keep us busy when there is no purposeful work are all gone."

With uncharacteristic enthusiasm for a military assignment, he wrote, "Communications are of primary importance in every campaign. At Iwo, radio was employed almost exclusively because of the difficulties of maintaining lines. You can see I have real enthusiasm for what is ahead."[13] A week earlier, men from their regiment had come back from that campaign and temporarily rejoined their unit while awaiting their return to the States. "Naturally, we have a whole new saga about the campaign and are very pleased not to have been here in time for it."[14]

Learning fundamentals and testing radio equipment were also interesting: "We had a regular CPX drill this morning. I was the colonel. We set up our radio network, and 'played' at war for about 2½ hours. It was interesting and informative and begins to give us an idea of what's expected of us and how we operate. It was followed by a session in fundamentals of radio—at last I know approximately what makes a radio set operate and learned somewhat clearly the difference between FM and AM (standard) broadcasting."[15] He remarked almost joyfully in this letter on how quickly the time had passed: "Two weeks of our 13 week program are gone already!"

But thirteen weeks in the steaming jungle with inadequate instruction in a fairly technical field was very long indeed. In Morse code, for example, instead of the intensive course he knew they followed in stateside training camps, with eight hours of instruction per day for a week or more, they merely had an hour once every week or so. As a result he despaired of "ever learning to receive code, much less sending it." He was nevertheless able to learn the phonetic alphabet: A-Able, B-Baker, C-Charlie, and so on—"it took about five minutes." Another communications skill they were expected to master was the art of using semaphore flags. He proudly proclaimed after several exposures to this training that he could spell out, "The quick brown fox jumped over the lazy dog," thus establishing that he knew the flag equivalent of every letter in the alphabet.

One morning he and two teammates were assigned to make a distance test on 300 radios. They tried to establish contact over a long-distance with some of the companies out on the field problem. "We were in the field all set up by 7:15 and found our spot wasn't very good, so we moved farther into the hills. Now we were alone in the jungle on treeless hills, where the north half of the island lay in a pattern below us. The flies and mosquitoes were gone, and the stiff ocean breeze fanned us. Here we found it easy to transmit, and soon had contact with an outfit more than five miles away, which is supposedly two miles more than the range of the instrument.

"About 10:30 I had to bring a message into camp. While I was about it I picked up the peanut butter and cheese (provided by Alice and Peter Green). I managed a loaf of bread, and when I returned we had a picnic lunch. It was pleasant and relaxing and the absence of officialdom was a great relief. About noon we came in, and I snoozed for a couple of hours in preparation for a night problem."[16]

However days like this became mere bright spots in the tedium of daily roll calls, periodic inspections—for which preparation was often interrupted by blowing dust or rainstorms, requiring all the cleaning of equipment and clothing to be started over—and guard watch, including the especially tedious "double watch," which entailed standing guard from 8 to 12 a.m. and again from 8 to 12 p.m.

Ben had begun to receive magazines and letters with news clippings, seen newsreels and heard radio updates on the progress of the war. As he had done ever since he boarded the troop ship, he read whenever he wasn't writing letters home. A library had finally been formed at his camp. He applauded efforts to bring good reading material to the troops: "Incidentally the best all-around job on the morale end of the war has been turned in by the book publishers. In an excellent pocket edition, paper cover, they've published countless titles of books new and old. It's called Council on Books In Wartime, Inc. The books are free, the Council nonprofit and the authors run from Leonard Ross and Thurber to Steinbeck and Dickens. These books always turn up in any spot where there's a chaplain or recreation room, and usually in quantity."[17] Because he was now better informed, he was able to keep up with progress of the war. He must certainly have begun to understand from his reading the strategic importance of his location on Guam.

The recapture of the Marianas island group—including the key islands, Saipan, Tinian and Guam—was the pivotal event of the war in the Pacific. Holland Smith explained: "When Guam was regained, providing the Pacific Fleet with advance facilities second in importance only to Pearl Harbor; we controlled the whole of the Marianas, a series of powerful bases from which we could carry the war to Japan proper."[18]

Washington University Professor Kevin Herbert served on a B-29 crew based at Saipan, in his critical analysis of the role of that aircraft in the war, states: "The seizure of Saipan and the others in the group was as significant for the Pacific war as the D-Day invasion was for the European." He explains why: "The import of the Saipan action, which began only days after the Normandy invasion, was not generally perceived then, nor is it now, for the far greater scale of events in Europe has overshadowed this operation in a remote and unknown area of the Pacific. But the Japanese leadership knew full well what this battle portended, as one of their numbers freely acknowledged after the war: "Hell was upon us after the loss of Saipan," Herbert concludes. "The final decisive phase of the Pacific war opened with the capture of Saipan. Direct aerial attack on the Japanese heartland was its consequence. The B-29's would deliver the crushing, fatal blows." [19]

By late May, Ben thought he would remain in his radio company. However, a reassessment was made of the qualifications and training of each man in the unit. In this reclassification, Ben fell short: he did not have the requisite training for the MOS (Military Occupational Specialty) to which he was assigned, and it looked as if he would once more be turned loose with no specific assignment related to his strong capabilities in many areas and was again in peril of landing in the infantry. He remained concerned about his fate.

The Pacific war, on the other hand, was going well and could conceivably be over before he got too deeply involved with another assignment. In fact, the opinions of the top generals bore this out. Professor Herbert describes their conclusions: "The success of the long-range aerial campaign from the Marianas was so swift and devastating, it outstripped the ability of most analysts to recognize the facts or to adjust their plans in accordance with the results. By early summer of 1945, Japan was at bay, stripped of naval power, merchant Marine, and air defenses, and with large elements of her Army cut off and withering in the South Pacific and in East Asia.

A few of our commanders correctly interpreted the situation. General Holland M. Smith, leader of the Fleet Marine Force, predicted in early June that the Japanese would submit before September, a truly brilliant assessment and one made without knowledge of the coming atomic attacks. And General Curtis E. LeMay, field commander of the superforts, was also aware of the impending enemy collapse. Despite these indications by people having day-to-day familiarity with the war, massive invasions of Kyushu and of the Kwanto Plain in Tokyo were being scheduled by others for late 1945 and early 1946. Herbert points out that the top military leaders did not realize what their siege had accomplished and ignored the evidence at hand that Japan was on her knees.[20]

Even so, Ben was again cast adrift in the Pacific war. He no doubt sensed and drew conclusions from his own reading, hoping beyond hope that the war might end soon. Nonetheless, he was subject to orders from those who were still preparing for many more years of battle. In his typical fashion, using all the techniques he had developed to cope with the whims of military officialdom, he set out to prepare himself for the worst and began actively seeking a new assignment suited to his capabilities.

Furthermore he was receiving bad news from home.

As the challenges of running the household, making ends meet and serving as both mother and father continued to mount, Alice's composure began to give way to frustration. This trend became increasingly evident to Ben through her letters. He offered such advice as he could without the advantage of observing Peter's emotional state and his behavior problems first hand. Peter must have sensed her anxiety.

Evidence of these problems had started with nightmares. Alice reported Peter dreamed about being irresistibly pulled off the platform as a train left the station, awaking in terror as he was sucked into the wake of the departing express. Another recurring nightmare was that he was falling off a cliff into an infinite abyss, his heart in his mouth, again disturbing the family with his terrified screams.

One night as she crawled into bed, exhausted from her daily routine and feeling sick, she had just dropped into a fevered sleep, when she heard a cry in the night. In her dream-like state she first blamed the haunted Victorian ruin they inhabited. On hearing another moan, and a louder scream, "Don't, no—NO-O-O!" she realized the commotion came from Peter's room. She threw off the tangled sheets and raced barefoot to his bedside. Her son lay on the floor, twisted in an edge of his blanket, flailing his arms. She shook him. "Wake up, Peter. What are you dreaming about?"

"The wolves—they're howling!" His eyes still closed, he flailed his arms, his hands tensed into claws. "They're, they're—chasing me."

"It's okay," Alice assured him, as she lifted him back on the bed and rearranged the covers. There would have to be a radio ban on Sergeant Preston in the Yukon and mystery programs for the duration. She stroked his forehead and tucked him in again, with a bear on each side.

Reassured, he dozed off again in peace. She climbed back into bed, noting it was only 2:30 a.m. by the alarm clock. She fell into a restless sleep.

He entered a period of chronic bed-wetting. While less disruptive of sleep, this added the burden of washing and replacing Peter's bed linens just about every day to the chore of doing Linda's diapers.. In self preservation Alice gathered all the pandas and teddy bears parents and relatives had given Peter and tucked them into bed with him at night. with soothing advice, which Peter accepted, and all slept a little better, if not drier. One night Alice found him—a considerate boy—curled up asleep on the tiny bedside table, with six bears neatly occupying the entire width of the bed, their heads peeking innocently from under the covers.

As Ben read, he wondered why this had worked, until Alice explained at the end of the letter. "Don't worry," she had told Peter, " wolves are afraid of teddy bears!"

But teddy bars could do only so much. It was time for Ben to devote some serious study, as he liked to call it, to the problem of getting reassigned.

CHAPTER 6

CAMBRIDGE BEACH

Ben's platoon assembles on the deck of a destroyer. The thunder and smoke of artillery guns rock the ship with each salvo. A lieutenant barks orders to sergeants, who relay them to the men.

With full packs on their backs and M-1 rifles in hand, Ben and his buddies—Duke, Charlie Newhall, Ed Golly and the rest of the Mare Island crew, somehow transformed from taxicab jockeys into warriors—scramble over the rail into a Higgins boat and are lowered into turbulent seas. A flotilla of a thousand landing craft heads toward the rocky beach. The amphibians land on the beach and debouch ten thousand men into the surf. Ben fights through crashing waves to gain footing, splashes ashore and flattens himself on the sand, trembling beneath volleys of machine gun fire emerging from the smoke of rounds hurled from the ships as they burst among pillboxes in the rocky jungle fringe.

From the rocks behind the beach, a furry head appears though the parted smoke, then another and another, until a pack of angry wolves, yellow faces snarling, narrow green eyes glowing and fangs gnashing, attacks the landing force.

Alice observes from a raft on the water, invisible as she glides landward. Stepping gingerly on the beach, she advances behind Ben, barefoot in her swimming suit, on sand that scorches her bare feet. The wolves advance in packs, so close now that their jaws snap at her. She runs back toward the roiling waters, the lesser of two evils. One creature catches up and bites her heel, sending a wave of pain coursing through her body. The waves crash higher than her head. She's inundated and can't breathe. She utters a cry of pain, but no sound comes out.

"Mommy, mommy, what is it? " Peter shook Alice awake. He must have been able to hear her cries. Dawn was peeking through the curtains.
"Oh, it's nothing," she said. "Just wolves."
"Oh," Peter said, accepting her explanation as something normal. He returned with his favorite teddy bear, a giant panda, to protect her.
She opened the drapes to a glorious sunrise, forcing the horrors of the night to recede. Ben's ship was supposed to reach its destination a week ago. Maybe today she would receive some news.
Indeed a letter arrived with the morning mail.
"The long-awaited moment, mail call, arrived on Friday," she read. "Two hundred bags of mail were waiting for us and we've done almost nothing but answer mail calls in the two days we've been here." Their encampment, which consisted of tents with wood floors, in addition to the permanent shelters for common functions such as mess halls and administrative support, were soon to be served by electricity and running water. Since they had no duties yet, they were put to work picking up stones, clearing and raking the area. Ben said it felt like an extended camping trip and wondered how long this could last.
With a surge of relief that Ben had arrived safely and looked forward to a period of resettlement and training, Alice relaxed and pitched in to the work of preparing for her family's trip to Annisquam for the summer.

When at last they were settled in their roomette on the train, Alice unpacked their special picnic supper, with all the children's favorites—fried chicken, bread and butter sandwiches with the crusts cut off, deviled eggs, home-made brownies, and lemonade from the thermos bottle. When they were finished, she gathered up the children and sat them all down in the club car of the New York Central's elegant express, The New England States.

Chapter 6-Cambridge Beach

"Mommy, why are all those men staring at us?" Peter asked.

"They're not staring," she replied. "The chairs are just a facing the middle."

Green cloth lounge chairs lined the sides and the curved round end of the parlor car in front of large windows. With Linda propped in a chair in one side and Peter on the other. she reflected on the flurry of the day's activity. She glanced again at her companions, lots of business men, smoking cigars, drinking their highballs and glancing at her every so often as they conversed. She was the only woman in the car.

A waiter in a white coat with a numbered brass button approached and took their order: a lemonade for Peter, milk for Linda in her own cup and a double scotch and soda for her. He brought them right away and poured the drink from a bottle with a mermaid on it, a White Rock lemonade, found only on the stately New York Central. She lit one of her Lucky Strikes and sighed: at last they were on their way.

"Aagh!" Peter said, holding his throat and making a face when smoke blew toward him. When he'd told her Linda was the only child in Chicago with cigarette ashes in her baby formula, she despaired that this boy was getting too big for his britches.

She'd made Peter scrub before they left. "Make sure you wash your face, neck and ears," she warned. He looked cute in his round, gold-framed glasses, which at least matched his round face, in his best brown slacks and a tan sweater. She wore her traveling outfit: a navy blue dress a white sailor collar which hung down her back, and a matching hat and white gloves. One didn't go out in public without gloves She even put a little white dress on Linda. She'd combed her own brownish-blond hair into a pompadour.

She'd told Peter her father was on bivouac in the jungle, hiking and learning to use walkie-talkies. They lived in tents, The first thing he had done was to arrange his mosquito net surrounding his bunk. They lived outdoors, with a lot of mud when it rained and dust when it didn't. Cleaning their boots and washing clothes was a full time job. But they had movies every night on a big outdoor screen, which was fine, except when it started to rain. He wrote a letter every day, and he even drew pictures for Peter and Linda. She hoped his efforts to get reassigned would pay off with a radio station assignment , so the Marines could make use of his skills in the war effort.

Her parents had driven them to the station and seen them off. Papa was big and gruff, but funny, and he loved the children. He asked Pete if he knew how to comb his hair with a washcloth, like he did when he was a kid. Tall and of "Black Irish," or Spanish, descent, he had straight, dark brown hair. Her mother, who was much shorter than he and also Irish, had given them a paper sack of mints, the round white kind with XXXX on top, for the train ride.

Alice had taught Peter to be a good citizen and always tell the truth, to speak correctly and use the right words for everything. A precocious child, he learned to say, "basket of vegetables" at age two. One day after an overnight visit, his grandmother took him on a walk over to a store in the Palmolive building and bought him a book shaped like a shoe, which he learned to lace up and tie.. He was only four but he could read it. "Peek-a-boo, I see you. Baby sees Mommy too. We have toys, Lots and lots. But we prefer to play with POTS!" Then the little boy in the book put on his shirt, shorts, socks and shoes and the book said, "Now that he is almost dressed. See if you can do the rest." This is when he was supposed to tie the shoelace that held the book closed. Peter chattered away, telling his life story to the man next to him, They strove to make Peter articulate; she hoped they hadn't overdone it.

As she smoked and sipped her drink, her worries about Ben returned. She also worried about Peter, because he teased her, got mad at her and played tricks. One day in the kitchen, when they heard on the radio that President Roosevelt had died, she had reacted in shock and sorrow; Peter started to laugh and couldn't stop, apparently because she was so upset.

They had a roomette in a sleeping car. By the time they woke up and had breakfast, she told the children, they would be in Boston. Aunt Helen and Uncle Joseph would pick them up at the station and take them to their house. On the coming weekend they would proceed to the beach at Annisquam. If only Ben could be with them it would be a real vacation. Joseph was a surgeon at a Massachusetts General Hospital in Boston, so he could obtain ration stamps to buy gas and visit the family on weekends.

The men were looking at them again.

"Mommy, those men don't have any hair!" he said.. The men all laughed, but clearly not because they were happy about their hair

Chapter 6-Cambridge Beach

"Peter that's not polite. Now sit up straight and drink your lemonade," she warned. She dropped her purse. When she reached to pick it up, the men were watching her. They had become the center of attention.

"Mommy, my penis sticks out," Peter blurted. The men roared in unison. Alice reddened and shot a glance toward the exit. She gulped down the rest of her drink, set the glass sharply on the table, picked up Linda with one arm, grabbed Peter's hand with the other and dragged them back through the train to the safety of their roomette.

In their compartment she got Linda into her "sleepy suit." Peter read the new comic books she had bought him especially for the trip—Superman, Donald Duck and Little Lulu. In her letter to Ben that night, she told about their son's behavior in the club car. She fretted about his nightmares and expressed her concern that he was disturbed by his sudden separation from his father. She hoped Helen, with her knowledge of the mind, and Joseph, with his ability to reassure his patients, could help him. She wondered if Helen could help restore he own sanity as well.

When she looked up from sealing and stamping her letter, the lights down the center aisle of the sleeping car had dimmed. Presently a Negro porter with a white jacket approached, smiled and said he was going to get them ready for the night. He asked them to get up while he slid the padded seats together until they closed up the leg space. He slid the cloth seat backs down on their tracks to the level of the seats to make a double bed. Next he reached up to a bulge in the wall above the window and stuck a crank into a socket. Down came a piece of the wall on a hinge, making a wide shelf above. He had created an upper bunk, already made up with sheets and blankets. He then took bedclothes from his cart and made up the lower berth. Almost like magic he had transformed the roomette into a bedroom. Finally he added pillows above and below, turned down the covers and unfolded a ladder, which he put next to the upper bunk. He smiled again, said good night and disappeared.

"There's your berth." Alice looked up at the upper bunk. Peter sprang up the ladder. She handed up his pajamas. He put them on as she tucked Linda in below. He climbed down one more time to their private toilet and lavatory compartment and back up into his own cozy cubbyhole. He turned off his reading light, and his mother tucked him in. As she lay reviewing the day's events, she looked forward to some much needed support from her sister and her husband and reintroducing Peter to his cousins the next day, the click-clacking rails and the gently rocking train lulled her to sleep.

At the Boston station early the next morning, Joseph and Helen gathered up their bags and drove them to their old white house near Harvard Square, a block from Cambridge Common. There they joined David, who was four and Alan, who, like Linda, was just starting to walk. They met Anna, their gray-haired housekeeper and babysitter. In their homey, carpeted living room lined with bookshelves, Alice related her adventures with the children on the long trip. Joseph listened to Alice's tale of woe. Curly black hair, graying at the edges, and rimless octagonal glasses framed his serious face When she told about the kids and the club car, he broke into a broad grin and chuckled. In his soothing, deep voice and Boston accent he asked, "Did ya reahl-ly say that, Petah?"

"Yes, because it was true!"

"Of course: that's normal for a man." He explained mysteriously that it would allow him to have babies when he grew up.

Helen reassured Alice, gave her gave her a stiff drink and laid out her ideas for a relaxed summer routine. Peter would feel safe and cozy there with them. As they made plans to shop and pack for the family's trip on the coming weekend to the cottage at Annisquam. Peter expressed his mounting excitement about their trip to the beach.

The Fairbanks Cottage sat on a low rock seawall overlooking a cove. It faced west on Ipswich Bay. Joseph pointed out Wingaersheek Beach on the left, past the opposite bank of the Annisquam River, which leads to Lobster Cove and Gloucester. Even further beyond lay a spit of land he said was the Town of Ipswich. On the right hand side of the bay behind the rocky shore, green front lawns, turned further down to wooded hills, with weathered-shingle roofs and sides of cottages peeking out. At the very end an arm of land reached out to sea. Beyond the last hill and this bar, the tiny shape of Annisquam Light, with its white shaft and black lantern, poked into the sky. It was perfect and wild, the raw edge where the sea and the land collide

Chapter 6-Cambridge Beach

The Fairbanks cottage in Annisquam, near Boston

The cottage was white with clapboard sides, split into two halves, one for the tenants and one for the Fairbanks family, the owners. who came on weekends. Peter's bedroom was in the attic. It had a dormer window peeking from the center of the roof. From there he had a view of the whole cove—and a special bay window in the pointed gable end that looked out both ways on the road. On the ground floor there was a huge screened porch—the "piazzer," Mrs. Fairbanks called it, which surrounded the house on three sides, welcoming guests and fitting right into the rocky steps of the site. Peter thought a sea captain must have built it, because all its windows and openings looked like dark eyes watching the sea.

Every day after breakfast, Alice and Helen did chores: cleaning, laundry and walked up to Lobster Cove to shop and prepare for dinner. During the afternoons they went down a few steps to the beach, where the two sisters would read, watch the kids and talk. They didn't swim much, but occasionally took a dip to cool off in the water. At dinner time they sat at a round wooden table in the dining room, where the children could hear what the grownups talked about: the news, the war (although they didn't mention the bad stuff because of the kids) and what Alice h ad had heard from Ben. They talked about manners and made Peter try new foods. Evenings were quiet. Alice and Helen read books to the children and talked. There were blackout shades which had to be kept closed at night, because enemy submarines might see and attack the seacoast.

On weekends, Joseph made the 50-mile trip to the cottage, using the gasoline ration stamps he could get as a doctor. He taught Peter what animal lived inside each seashell and made geometric shapes for him in clay—cylinders, cones, triangular and rectangular prisms, cubes and pyramids. At bedtime Peter would put on his robe and slippers and give a lecture in his "gown," naming each object as he pointed to it with a stick. "Just like a professor at Harvard," Joseph said.

Alice mending

Rationing made life hard during the war. Ration stamps were needed to buy meat, gasoline and footwear. Peter had his own problem with it. At the beginning of the summer, Mrs. Becker, their next door neighbor in Chicago, took the family's ration points which came in the mail, bought those things that were easier to get in Chicaago nd mailed them to the family at Annisquam. Among them were some new leather shoes for Peter. Shoes were scarce, requiring many ration points, because all the factories were making boots for soldiers. Over the past year he had outgrown every pair he had. Mrs. Becker promptly bought them and shipped them parcel post. Week after week, Alice checked at the post office. There were no more packages: the shoes never arrived.

At dinner they often talked about why the shoes disappeared. Helen had the post office trace the mail delivery route, and they couldn't find them. The family were finally forced to face it: someone in a post office along the way simply stole the shoes.

"I can't believe someone would just take them,"Alice said.

"Well, perhaps they needed them more than we did," Helen said.

"Yeah, but I don't have any shoes!" Peter objected. To him his

Chapter 6-Cambridge Beach

aunt's idea was ridiculous. Nobody needed the shoes more than he did: he had gone barefoot all summer. He learned this the hard way. Whenever Alice and Helen, with Linda and Alan in their strollers, with David and Peter trailing behind, walked the three blocks of gravel road from Cambridge Beach to Lobster Cove to do the shopping. For the first few weeks it was awful. The sharp stones cut, pricked and scraped his tender feet. He tried walking more slowly but fell behind the group and got even more miserable. Joseph said his feet would eventually toughen up. Meanwhile they really hurt and didn't feel much better until the middle of July.

He was always arguing with his mother and Aunt Helen. Alice called him "Little Yeah-but." She said he was argumentative and stubborn as a mule. He said it was because he was just like *them*.

Linda feeds Alan an apple.

They both went to college at the University of Chicago. Helen was a psychoanalyst. Before she was married, she studied in Vienna with Sigmund Freud, Her classmate was Anna Freud, his daughter. He was getting old but they could still have him as a teacher and visit him in his cozy house and office near Vienna's university. Helen was there for four years until 1938. To be a psychoanalyst she had to become a medical doctor first. Then the Nazis kicked Freud out of Vienna, because he was Jewish, like Joseph and Ben. Family lore held that she came back from her classes one day and found two soldiers inside her apartment, overturning furniture, emptying drawers and throwing her papers on the floor.

"Stop it this instant!"she ordered in German, which she had learned for medical school.

"We are under orders to investigate all foreigners," said their leader. Helen said he was just a boy of not more than 18.

"I'll have you know I am an American citizen," Helen said, pointing to the American flag she wore in her lapel, "And I demand that you clean up this mess and leave immediately!"

The storm troopers were so shocked they cleaned it all up. Apparently they were more afraid of Aunt Helen than they were of Adolph Hitler.

Once his feet got used to walking on the gravel, he began to notice things along the way. One Saturday, when Joseph was with them, he pointed out an unusual flower among the weeds by the side of the road, a Venus fly-trap, he explained, open and inviting its prey. On their way back, they looked for the same flower and found it had had snapped shut. They could just see the crippled wings and legs of a poor fly, crushed by the clenched petals. Peter was surprised how one living thing killed another, just to survive. Joseph said it was the law of nature.

Crowding in along the road were tiny gray-shingled cottages, with bay windows, recessed doorways, porches, or "piazzers"—made up of all different shapes: boxes, prisms and round towers with cones for roofs with shingles and boards covering them, like the clay models Uncle Joseph made for Peter at the cottage. Their size made them look like a miniature village to the adults, but to Peter. who was only three feet tall, they seemed just the right size. One block further along, the street took a turn to the left and continued on to Gloucester. But they would head straight, down a steep path that dropped to the bank of Lobster Cove. There started a long wooden walkway about a quarter of a mile long across the cove to the heart of town. It was a shortcut for walkers and it blocked off the end of the cove from seagoing boats.

On the left dinghies and small motorboats that could slip under the bridge in the walkway were moored at private docks in the narrow end of the inlet. To the right lay the busy harbor. Dozens of fishing boats were anchored in the channel, docked along the bank or moving out into the bay. Fishermen on their decks prepared their nets for the day's catch. The sturdy engines of the work boats made a loud, rhythmic "pocketa-pocketa" sound as they chugged out to sea. On the shore a dozen buildings crowded together, with docks facing the shore, reached by sloping gangplanks. At the rear side, shop windows, doorways to fishereis and small truck loading platforms faced the road. These markets were bursting with fresh fish, lobster, clams and other seafood; colorful fruit and vegetable stands; fish cleaning and packing houses;

restaurants, taverns and a grocery store.

Whenever Alice tried to get Peter to eat the lobster, he was afraid they would pinch him and refused. But he really liked his mom's wonderful chowder, with potatoes, mild onions and butter, fish and other seafood, if it had been cut up so it didn't look scary. Even though they couldn't get much meat, they were really lucky, because they could buy all the fresh seafood they wanted.

On sunny days it didn't matter that Peter had no shoes. He ran and played on the beach from sunrise to sunset wearing only swim trunks. The sun turned him dark tan and bleached his dark brown hair to blond. There were plenty of new sights, mysteries and natural wonders to explore. He watched the tides flow, on stormy days sending huge breakers crashing on the seawall and splashing spray into the air. When the tide ebbed each day, the broad beach was a new unexplored territory; the wet sand at the water's edge had breathing holes for a new crop of clams and was littered with the remains of undersea animals, shells and beautiful new stones, hinting at the secrets hidden beneath the sea.

But he loved the squalls best. As he stood facing the bay with the morning sun at his back, slate blue clouds rolled in from the west. The gale whipped up whitecaps on the water, which glowed in a bright turquoise blue, lighter than the lead gray sky. White gulls circled and mewed against a dark background as they warned of the coming storm.

One early evening at about seven o'clock he heard a cry for help to the left beyond the big rocks. People came running to the water. Soon his mother and aunt ran to the beach and made him stay back. where he couldn't see. He waited by the rocks in silence. Finally, after the longest time, the men walked slowly back up the beach in a line, heads bowed. their long shadows in front of them in the sunset.

"What happened?" Peter looked up at his mother.

Helen had been talking quietly with some of the men as they passed, and she had the grim news. Alice was in tears. Helen was the only one who could speak.

"A little boy was swimming alone beyond the rocks. He got caught in the undertow and drowned," she reported in her serious doctor's voice. He didn't need any further explanation. He had been told not to go in the water alone, not to go in over his waist and especially not to go beyond the rocks, since he didn't yet know how to swim. He knew it was bad to do this, but until now he didn't know why. He was shocked that the boy's shouts had been his last; that his life had been so fragile that it could be snatched away from one minute to the next on a beautiful summer evening.

Nothing in Alice's life went unreported to Ben. He could hardly bear not being there to play ball and teach his son all the things that a young boy should know.. From halfway around the world he had instructed Alice to buy him a softball and ask Joseph to play catch with him.

He particularly missed the opportunity to give Pete swimming lessons. When he heard about the drowning incident, he tried to make up for his absence with his customary confidence:

"There isn't very much to swimming Pete." he wrote. "There are three parts to it:

Breathing.
Use of the arms.
Use of the legs.

> *Keep the fingers together — you pull more water that way — Reach out straight*

"Most important is breathing: you simply inhale above water, exhale under water. A good way to practice is to stand in shallow water, let the air out through your <u>nose</u> and take air in through your mouth, just opposite of the way you usually breathe. The trick is to take short breaths — then you don't have to let so much out under water. Practice this slowly first — then a little faster. Then get in water up to your chest, and bob up and down, letting air out under water taking air in when you come up." Fresh from his Marine Corps swimming training, he cautioned his son to do this in the presence of a grownup, to tell him if he was doing it correctly.

"When you have the breathing down pat, so that you know how easy it is and can do it without getting a noseful or mouthful of water (you may at first—then you know you're doing it wrong). Then start on the legs—have someone hold your arms and kick straight up and down from hips without bending the knees—not too fast, but steadily—this will come easily. Now come the arms: keep the fingers together. You pull more water that way. Reach out straight ahead and pull back straight along your side, first one side, then the other—not fast—very slow and steady—have someone hold your feet while you practice this. When you take your arm out of the water to reach, take it out close to your side and don't raise it too high in the air. Swimming should be easy, and not hard work. Learn to do each thing slowly. That's about all I can do to help you, son." He expressed hope that Pete would find a swimmer to help him at the beach. "But you ought to make a real effort to learn to swim, because you can have so much more fun in the water when you know how." [2] Despite these concerted efforts, Peter didn't learn to swim until Ben had come home from the war, given him some lessons in person at the beach and enrolled him in swimming lessons at the YMCA.

Peter developed a following among the neighboring vacationers—and a reputation: "He wakes the beach up in the morning and puts it to sleep at night," said one. "He has a voice like a pebbly beach," commented another. When he learned that his father was in the war, one kindly vacationer arranged to meet him every morning and show him some new beach activity. He taught Peter how to make forts at the water's edge. Some days they filled a bucket with sand and used it as a mold to make round castle towers; at other times he would scoop up wet sand in his hands and dribble it on a mound to make a drip castle. The man showed him how to make protective moats and walls around the moats, and outer walls around the inner walls, and how to strengthen it all with rocks. Despite all these clever tricks, each day they would watch the incoming tide begin to lap at the walls, which would resist the first few waves and then be overtopped by the flow. Soon, even the tallest, stoutest castle they could build would begin to slump like melting ice cream. A half-hour later the only trace of their efforts would be lumps and dents in the firm, wet sand.

There were not many other children on this stretch of beach. But this fatherly man, like the Pied Piper, soon attracted them all. He included the three or four boys and girls that were there in the daily beach activities. A boy named Jamie, about a year or so older, joined in and became Peter's daily companion. He was fun-loving and active, with sandy-colored tousled hair. He could make Peter laugh with funny faces. One day, while Jamie's mother was enjoying the sun on the beach, she saw them playing together and invited him come to her hotel for lunch the next day with Jamie.

When he got home and told his mom about the invitation, Peter figured something was up. His mother and Aunt Helen flew into action. Alice instructed her son to go back down to the beach and make sure to thank the kind lady, ask what time to come and tell her that he would be there. He began to think that that this was no ordinary invitation. He suspected it even more the next day when the two women began at eleven o'clock to coach him, scrub his face and dress him in his best white shirt and navy blue shorts.

"You are going to meet a very famous lady," explained Aunt Helen. "She is a very great actress that performs plays on the stage," his mother added. "Be polite and say 'Please' and 'Thank you'." Promising his best behavior, he he took his mother's hand to cross the gravel road.

Jamie's mom was wearing a simple sun dress, her hair swept up in a permanent wave and pompadour. She held her head high and had a fine, pretty face that made her delicate upturned nose look even more appealing. Her warm, dark eyes twinkled as she talked to them in common speech, yet more clearly and more carefully spoken, he guessed, because she was an actress.

"Well, hello, Alice. And Peter, you look so grown up today in your fine clothes!"

She and the great lady talked, and Peter wondered why his mom was speaking in such a strange, high voice and took so long to say goodbye.

"Peter, would you like a sandwich?" Jamie's mother asked.

"Yes, Ma'am," he replied, careful to say it correctly. He and Jamie sat at a round wicker coffee table on the porch, as the actress offered them seconds on essential boy-food—more sandwiches, Kool-Aid and cookies.

Years later Alice explained that this nice mother was Helen Hayes, first lady of the American stage. She was staying at the Bryn Mere, a retreat she had discovered between summer stock engagements at the Cape Playhouse. She got her striking appearance and regal posture from pride in her English and Irish heritage and the royal stage roles she had played, including Mary of Scotland and Victoria Regina. Only then did Peter realize why his mother and his aunt were turning somersaults to prepare him to meet her. He learned that the two women also had other things in common. While Alice had long been an admirer of the great actress and was nervous and thrilled to have the chance to meet her, Helen Hayes herself had the "common touch" and was equally pleased to meet her. She had held her own in a cutthroat business into which she was introduced at age 5, because she loved her craft, loved people and had never set out to pursue fame.

Although she was 13 years older than his mother, they had similar concerns about raising their sons. They shared a common-sense outlook in an era of very self-consciousness about child-rearing. In her book of reminiscences, *A Gift of Joy* (1965), Hayes describes what conscientious parents, such as she and her husband, Charles, as well as Alice and Ben, worried about in those days:

"Charlie and I reared our young during that period of terrorization of the parent—the thirties and forties, when everything we said could be used against us, or so the book told us. One slip of action, or one word, and our offspring could be marked for life. Every child who had the means had to have a bout with a child psychologist, his teeth straightened, and his vitamins toted up daily. And schedules: everything had to be meted out—play time, meal time, sleep time, reading time. From what I'm told, the situation has not changed very much since. The reign of terror continues, and parents are just plain scared stiff of their children."[1] In fact, a couple of years later, after Peter had learned to read longer books, he used to read his mother's copy of Dr. Benjamin Spock's *Baby and Child Care* and offer suggestions on how she could do a better job of raising Linda.

Alice, also of Irish descent, loved literature and theater. Their husbands were both in the military. Charles MacArthur, the actor, writer and producer—best known for his play, written jointly with Ben Hecht, *The Front Page*—was despondent at age 45 at being left out of the war and had accepted a commission as a colonel in chemical warfare. They chatted frequently. Alice relaxed and felt more like just a neighbor than a royal subject of the queen of the American stage.

Fifty-five years later, I revisited the beach, the Fairbanks cottage and the Bryn Mere Hotel, finding the same porch where James MacArthur, her adopted son an accomplished actor himself, and I had munched our sandwiches.

As if its elderly owner had wanted to erase time altogether, he had preserved its original appearance. It had not changed in all those years: the simple wood floor, ceiling and railing of the porch, the unadorned walls and austerely furnished common rooms of the hotel recalled a simpler age. There were no noisy electronic devices, no rich designer fabrics adorning the furniture, no carpeting, magazines nor other clutter of daily living to mar the scene. The sea, the sand, the blazing light and a few white wicker chairs on plain board surfaces managed to suggest a way of life richer in 1945 than it became even in the affluent late 20th century. While we were reminiscing, a wedding party staying at the Bryn Mere arrived. I apologized for distracting them from their celebration. The bridegroom, a young actor, was pleased to learn on his wedding day that his party was staying at a favorite stopping place of Helen Hayes. Both the actor and I agreed it was a good omen for his career.

One morning near the end of July, Peter eagerly picked up the newspaper from the steps and brought it up on the porch. He liked to make out the words in big type and see how much he could understand of the stories. He stood on the screened porch of the Fairbanks Cottage, stunned in disbelief by the headline and the photograph of a damaged skyscraper, flames licking out of the 78th and 79th floor windows, the entire structure above that level shrouded in smoke. He could make out some of the words:
"A twin-engine B-25 Bomber, lost in a blinding fog, crashed into the Empire State Building today at a point 975 feet above the street level. Thirteen persons, including the three occupants of the plane, and ten persons within the building, were killed in the catastrophe and twenty six were injured. Brilliant orange flames shot as high as the observatory on the eighty-sixth floor of the building, 1,050 feet above Fifth Avenue, as the gasoline tanks of the plane exploded."[2]
Since he had read the simple children's book his grandmother bought him at four, he was able by this time to read enough of the story to know what happened, but he couldn't understand it.
"How could that happen?" he asked his aunt, who had just come out to drink her coffee and read the paper.
After she looked over the headline and the news story, Aunt Helen replied, "It seems that an experienced Army pilot got lost in a storm and thought he was over the river; instead he was in the middle of New York."
"What happened to him?" Peter asked.
"He and his crew were killed," Helen reluctantly admitted. A psychoanalyst, she was known for her tact and gentleness with patients and family alike, but she did not shrink from reality.
"Yeah, but did any people in the building get hurt?" he persisted.
"Yes, several office workers died," she replied firmly, "but many others

escaped." Concerned that he was upset, she was quick to add, "But don't worry about it: this sort of accident doesn't happen very often."

His aunt's reassurance didn't do much good. He couldn't understand how such a thing could happen. Men like Grandpa constructed huge buildings from the ground up. Airplanes were supposed to fly around them; it just couldn't be any other way. Many adults thought the same thing: how could an honored war hero make such a mistake, with such terrible consequences?

In his Chicago neighborhood, there had been reminders that these were not ordinary times. Once after a weekly air raid warning, when everyone had to stay indoors, Peter went out at the "all clear" signal and saw a boy carrying a brightly colored paper airplane with trailing streamers. His mother said, "He's not supposed to be fooling with that: it was dropped from a plane. He's supposed to take it directly to an air raid warden." These markers were reminders that ordinary people were open to attack from the sky.

Air raid drills were also a regular occurrence during his first year in kindergarten at Ray School. At the sound of the warning siren, according to plan, his teacher Miss Dickey would round up the children in her class and march them out of the school building. Following her like ducklings in a row, they would parade three blocks down 57th Street to the University of Chicago campus, where she would shelter them in presumed safety beneath a wall supporting the high seating of the football stadium at Stagg Field. Sensing the danger, Peter believed these drills were something very important the grown-ups were doing to protect them from the war.

Many years later, we learned that this structure concealed a secret laboratory for the Manhattan project, where Dr. Enrico Fermi had created the first self-sustaining nuclear fission reaction, making possible the atom bomb. The family howled with laughter at the irony of the situation: there was probably no location more strategically important for the enemy nor more vulnerable for civilians than the very spot that the dear, well-intentioned Miss Dickey had selected to shelter her precious charges.

In recent years, I was to relive the events of that Saturday in New York when I read a book carefully researched by an eyewitness to the aftermath of the skyscraper tragedy, *The Sky Is Falling*, by Arthur Weingarten. As a boy of ten the author had pleaded on that morning to accompany his father, a New York City fire marshal, when he was called to the scene. In writing his book, he interviewed families, eye witnesses and public officials and reconstructed the events leading up to the mishap with an eye to answering these questions. Not even after finishing this book did I understand my morbid fascination with this event. However, my vivid recollection of the day is one of those moments when I could recall precisely where I was—like the day Franklin D. Roosevelt died—which I would carry with me for the rest of my life.

Until now I had faced wartime bravely, as when my father sent me a birthday letter just a year earlier and asked me to help Mom and try to understand why it was important for him to be away:

> Dear Peter:
>
> I hope you have a wonderful time on your birthday–it's your fifth and a very important one because you and Mommy have to take care of things without Daddy's help. It would be great if we could celebrate your birthday together, but I know you understand that Daddy is away for a very important reason and we must never forget that. If Daddy and millions of other daddies were not away from home to fight the bullies, we might never be able to have nice homes and live happily together. So however much we miss one another, we should try to remember that things would be much worse if Daddy and other daddies if were not willing to fight the bullies.
>
> Have a wonderful birthday and Daddy will be thinking of you—and when I eat my ice cream here, I'll pretend it's your birthday ice cream.
>
> Here is a real Marine pennant for your room.
> Love, Dad. [3]

I remembered standing in the glare of the living room window as Mom read me this letter, and how proud I was of my father. But the plane crashing into the Empire State Building got me worried about people dying, and whether my dad would come home again to take care of our family. I knew Mom was worried too, about whether Dad would have to use his gun to fight, and I worried that maybe he would die.

Back in my room in Chicago, Mom pinned up the Marine pennant Dad sent home for me, maroon felt with "U. S. Marine Corps" in gold block letters. When I lay in bed, I would look at the Marine emblem, with an anchor going across the whole world. Somewhere out there Dad was helping to keep it safe for Mom and me and Linda. From the pennant I also learned my first words in Latin, *Semper Fidelis*. In high school I took second place in the Illinois State Latin Contest, freshman division. I didn't have to wait until then to know the words mean "always faithful."

CHAPTER 7

ARMED FORCES RADIO STATION WXLI

Toward the end of May, change became inevitable in Ben's field radio unit: 16 men who did not have the CP warrant—the appropriate technical training for the field radio job—had to be moved out of communications. Ben was concerned he would be thrown into another job which required no particular skills, meaning infantry.

"I decided to try to get moved to a spot where I could at least be useful," his letter reported, perhaps at PRO, the public relations office. He went to Colonel Hoyler, his battalion commander and explained the situation: "He was swell, listened and proceeded to do something about it," Ben reported. The colonel called the division headquarters and sent through a request for reassignment to the public relations office. "Meanwhile, I still had a date with the captain in charge of the radio station here. It turned out he managed a radio station in the states that we had placed business with and remembered my name and of course knew the company. Since he was a Marine captain, this changed the whole setup: he was hunting for a

Marine with administrative and radio experience. I sounded like what he needed." [1]

Ben hastened back, told the colonel about this new development and arranged a meeting between the colonel and the captain. They met and agreed that if it could be arranged he belonged with the station. Colonel Hoyler then went to see a major and a colonel, who told them how to proceed. The captain was to send a letter through to Forward Echelon, which upon approval through channels would authorize Ben's transfer to Island Command. Meanwhile, he was told to go back to his unit and wait, doing his regular duties, until news of his fate arrived. But he was cautiously optimistic, because he had learned of expansion plans for the station. Many of the station's staff, were being transferred out, leaving him to run the programming, do much of the writing and plan special events.

He tried to look at this turn of events philosophically. "I'm trying not to get too steamed up—there's so much chance for it to miss—but I have a lot of support and it may go through. I'm about ripe for something to happen to me in the Corps—the right way. Thank heaven my civilian life never followed the pattern of luck that my Marine Corps career has—we'd be eating hardtack in a garret."

Ben kept up with news, but he missed the luxuries he had enjoyed at Mare Island—the libraries, recreation centers and multiple sources of current newspapers and magazines. On May 29th he wrote, "According to Time, the problem of Russia is great and looming: the Russian attitude à la Time is very much different than I imagined it would be. Is Time giving Russia a bad deal or is that the way the news looks?" Nevertheless, Time, with all its faults, was as welcome as spring to him, compared with the other news sources he had available, especially the island radio station. Armed Forces Radio was less than satisfying: "Believe me, if I ever do make that job, there will be something worth listening to in those broadcasts. Each night's show is a weary recitation of the tactical progress on Okinawa, a few Washington notes and the more obvious headlines. I don't know what's available to them, but they do listen to any shortwave shows they care to, so it can't be as limited a choice as the broadcasts indicate. The whole station lacks color, lacks programs to interest the audience here—and the schedule isn't slanted toward the few free hours the men have. I'm temporarily out of range of any radio broadcasts, which means that the observation of the station by B. J. Green will cease for the time being." 2

Finally he got a day off to look into his transfer situation. He went to see the station manager, Captain Steven A. Cisler (Louisville, KY), to run the thing down. The captain was pleased and showed him a letter to a captain at the Forward Echelon of Fleet Marine Force, located at the other end of the island. Reaching that office, Ben caught him just as he was leaving. He read the letter, vaguely remembered the name and called a lieutenant who thought the request had been turned down. But just to make sure, all three of them marched into the colonel's office. "Just disposed of it this morning," he said. "Put it through." So far, so good! Then they went across the road to another office that had the papers, which were in the "today" pigeonhole and there it was: approved by General Erskine, his division commander, recommended by Forward Echelon and sent to Fleet Marine Force (Pearl Harbor) for action. Ben asked what "for action" meant and was told that they invariably followed the Forward Echelon's recommendations and therefore that the transfer order would come through in two to three weeks. Then, while hitchhiking back he ran into Captain Cisler on the highway, who was very pleased at news, had Ben hop into his Jeep and took him up to look at CincPac Radio, where Ben met an acquaintance from WGN radio publicity in Chicago. With this immense change in his life looming, the next two to three weeks promised to be a long wait indeed.

How he finally heard the news is a story in itself: "Actually Sunday I spent the entire morning chasing from Forward Echelon to the radio station to the division. At Forward Echelon I learned nothing, but when I got to the station, Captain Cisler asked me if I was reporting for work. From then on, it was a very fine Sunday. I chased the order down and saw it in all its glory "From the Commanding General FMF to the Commanding General [censored: Third Marine] Division..." This morning at eight a.m., I was called out of the field and told to be ready to move at 12:30. I was ready at 8:45, of course." 3 On Tuesday, June 26th, just over a month after his initial conversation with Colonel Hoyler, he officially received his orders to report to WXLI.

Once his transfer was official, Ben could hardly believe his good fortune. After months of living in hastily erected camps and doing field exercises, the opportunity to work regular hours, wear a pressed uniform (and keep it clean!), eat at one of several mess halls and organize his own work schedule was almost more than he could have hoped for. It revived a sense, now faintly remembered, of the beloved freedom of his former civilian life. When he reported to his unit and begin surveying the situation, he realized what a change he had brought about for himself. Perhaps his skills in making friends, sizing up situations rapidly and speaking up for himself and his buddies had some uses in the military after all!

To expedite his transfer, instead of being assigned to Armed Forces Radio Service—the unit that ran broadcast operations in the Pacific—he had been attached to Island Command, which operated two radio stations. One was K2XO, CincPac Radio, a short wave channel used for official communications, which connected Guam with other headquarters throughout the Pacific theater, San Diego and San Francisco. It was situated at Commander in Chief Pacific Fleet-Pacific Ocean Area (CincPac/ CincPoa) headquarters on the top of Nimitz Hill, a vantage point just south of Agana overlooking Apra Harbor. A short distance away was the AM Armed Forces Radio Station. He was assigned a bunk in a collection of Quonset huts not far away, and a desk at the station. The AM station was housed in a standard Quonset hut originally set up for offices, intersected by another hut, which formed "wings" at the far end, and topped by a large painted sign: "Armed Forces Radio Station" and the call letters, WXLI. Continuous shutters along each of the curving side walls were permanently propped open, giving this awkward cruciform-plan complex the impression of a huge goose preparing to take off. The building was entered through a door next to a picture window in the semicircular front end.

Once inside, makeshift as the physical set up was, Ben immediately recognized it as a radio station. A control room, with its consoles of glowing dials, knobs, switches and turntables, was curiously located at the center of the building and accessed by a door in each of its four walls—making what should more properly be a quiet nerve center it into a busy traffic way. Nevertheless, through large glass openings in the partitions, it overlooked rooms of different sizes on two sides, each of which, he could tell by the presence of standing and desktop microphones, was used as a broadcast studio. Small offices, with filing cabinets, telephones and desk model typewriters lined the perimeter of the building on both sides. Furnishings were of standard Government Issue: green metal tables, desks and

Chapter 7-Armed Forces Radio Station WXLI

chairs. A few men in various states of uniform from different branches of the service could be found working at their duties: the engineer in the control room, a copy writer clacking and dinging away at his typewriter and a couple of officers conferring in a larger office.

One of them was Captain Cisler, the man in charge of the station, the *Marine* captain who had interviewed Ben about the assignment, and an army corporal, discussing the day's schedule. "The station is virtually stateside in its equipment," he wrote. "It's brand-new has a large studio and two smaller ones. I'm in an office with the captain. I gather I can do anything I take a shine to, for example, an anniversary program July 21 on the

The WXLI Building.

invasion of this Island, which I have already started thinking about." The station will soon be operating on a 1,000-watt basis (it's 300 now) and is going to run from 6:00 AM to 10:00 PM starting July 8. We're off the air for three hours in the morning at the present time."[3]

He began by making the daily broadcast schedule and a transcription log: "Naturally, we use scads of transcriptions. They arrive in one huge package and when we're through with them we send them on to another station." On the second day, he reported, "I've forgotten as much about radio as I ever knew... and the technique of holding a hundred things in my mind is (momentarily, I hope) rusty."

By the third day, he had mastered the routine tasks and was looking 
...te his first radio script in fifteen months, a one-hour show for the Dick Jurgens Band. "I also tossed together two fifteen minute segments of programs which we will record and give to the AFRS to make pressings and distribute on a show called Melody Roundup—corn and all."

Things were going much more smoothly now, including his typing: "This typewriter is no longer my Public Enemy No. 1, and I am beginning to master it. Incidentally, it's a Spanish typewriter with a tilde over the Ñ and an accent mark 'é' and this gizmo 'º', also an upside down question mark to precede questions '¿'. Everything is in the wrong place, especially punctuation, particularly the exclamation point, which is where the comma ought to be."[4] Although he complained as if he were a topnotch stenographer hampered by poor equipment, Ben had acquired his two-finger typing technique as a Chicago reporter and publicist: to adapt to the foreign keyboard it was merely necessary for him to direct these digits to different keys.

Ben's typing technique

He was amazed at the sedentary life style and the absolute lack of physical activity of his new job. He feared, after his rigorous routine of the past year, he would become "fat as a pig." He was happy to learn that he would be working with Norman at CincPac, a nice guy he had known as a reporter from the Chicago Tribune, who was now in Navy public relations.

"Incidentally, the sharp cleavage between enlisted men and officers disappears when there's work to do; apparently, everyone respects everyone else for what they can do, and there's general good feeling between all concerned. It's quite a good atmosphere to be working in." "This is a peculiar setup. There are Army, Navy, Seabee and Marine Corps all mixed. Wayne

Chapter 7-Armed Forces Radio Station WXLI   129

Center is Navy; Don Davis is Seabee; Kani Evans is Army, as are Dick Stern and Jimmy Shaw. Center is the youngster who was an office boy at NBC and is announcing. Davis is pick of the lot and a swell guy about 25 years old, but mature and currently my companion. He is a single guy, West Coast, and was just getting going in radio. Kani Evans is more Hollywood than anyone else, full of ambition and pretensions and a pretty fair announcer. Everyone is a jack of all trades and the announcers all handle the control board too." [5]

Don Davis was to become another of his life-long friends from his wartime experience. "We've received reinforcement from a new direction: a new man, Russell Beggs, arrived. He's a mild-mannered, well-informed, reasonable person. His job will be Program Director. Mine will be Production Manager." Ben's job would involve smoothing out their handling of transcriptions, "which is lousy now," refining live programs, producing new ones and working on new ideas and promotional schemes. "I will now be able to stop doing the daily program schedule, abandon the announcers' schedule and the tiresome daily typing grind that I don't relish. In other words, I'm getting rid of the worst features of the work I've been doing and keeping the best." [6]

After just one week of working together, Russ and Ben had their plan of reorganization in place: "Today Russ and I began to lay out an entirely new program schedule for the station, arranged on conventional lines, and with more attention to the show hours, to types of programs which are easy to listen to under conditions out here (distractions are numerous; drama is hard to follow), and in a few days, should have it in shape for presentation to Captain Cisler." Once that was settled he planned to turn full attention to the mechanical difficulties at the station—bad announcing, fluffs, poor record transitions, and inadequate planning in station breaks. "Once those things are grooved, Russ and I will concentrate almost entirely on development of show ideas and new programs to build up the station's importance."

By the 13th of July, Ben was receiving letters from the family at Annisquam. He was cheered that Alice and her sister Helen and settled their differences on child-rearing and were starting to enjoy life at the beach. He noted that when he finally had five letters forwarded to his new location, he had already received two more recent ones directly at Armed Forces Radio. They filled in the gap: "The arrangement was perfect, because in the last two, you had completely regained your equilibrium, which made the [earlier] tale of woe amusing instead of heart-rending." He was also very pleased with some sketches Peter included. "And Pete's very cleverly drawn letter gave me a wonderful picture of the life you're leading...I can just see those gulls and ships and rocks now ... he was very smart to draw such a complete picture..."

He was also very enthusiastic about his work at the station: "All of a sudden I feel a very gratifying surge of confidence ... things that seemed difficult at first ... incomprehensible or confusing ... .are becoming simple, easy to understand and easy to unravel. The problems of the station have been arranged in my mind ... I know just how I plan to attack each of them, in what order, and with what method. I'm learning how to get Captain Cisler interested in my ideas and seeing more clearly what ought to be done first and how to do it."

Ben had several new programs in the works: one called *Blind Date*, a *GI Forum*, which he felt would stimulate plenty of interest, more news features, such as *Pacific War Extra*, a documentary called *Here's Guam*, on the life and culture of the island, and several quiz shows, including one called *Sporting Chance*. "I find my greatest pleasure lies in developing the new stuff ... I'm not too concerned about actual production, writing, etc ... and would rather assign that to others .... which fits in perfectly with the continuation of my postwar radio work." He expressed his belief that returning to his former job or any other position would more likely lead to administrative and management functions, rather than actual on the spot production. However, since he was the most qualified to do it at WXLI, he said he would continue to write, produce all of the main shows and watch production techniques.

With an initial push from Ben, program development for 'Here's Guam' took on a life of its own. By mid-July, he wrote: "The boys in the station are getting more and more enthusiastic about the new shows. I sold the Captain another one yesterday ... my 'Here's Guam' idea. I made very careful preparations; saw a lot of people before I talked to him, including the director of education and welfare for the island ... some Navy people who have similar ideas in the way of printed word and photographs.

All in all my timing happened to be just perfect, since there has been a reversal in policy, and Guam will begin to get some rather broad publicity. Also there is a desire, now that some groups of men will be returning to the states, to see that they have a proper understanding of the natives and the island. I shall begin the show within two weeks and have Kani Evans do it."[7]

The new policy was evident in the fifteen page spread on Guam, which Ben alerted Alice to in the July 2, 1945 issue of *Life* magazine. It includes pictures of Admiral Nimitz and staff, Island Commander General Henry Larsen, Apra harbor, scenic Marine Drive (constructed in a tremendous push by Seabees along the coast of the island), a model village reconstructed for the Guamanians, scenes of native life and views of the recreational centers available to the troops. One photo shows Specialist First Class Bobby Riggs firing a serve at Vice Admiral John Hoover on one of the tennis courts whose construction had been highly criticized by Air Force General Curtis LeMay. Ben noted on the following Sunday that he "watched [Don] Budge and [Frank A.] Parker play" tennis on those courts: "Gee, they're good!" Another photo shows service men and women in a large audience before a stage and band shell at the Gab Gab Bowl, "Guam's open-air theater", where they were entertained by traveling USO troupes and jazz bands. Actually there were 150 such amphitheaters, where nightly movies and occasional live shows were presented, 90 of which had covered stages. This was perhaps an intentional omission by an over-zealous public relations officer sensitive to General LeMay's expressed disdain for such non-strategic recreational facilities.[8]

On the following Saturday night, *Sporting Chance* had its debut, which Ben proudly described: "We finally put *Sporting Chance* on the air, and it was a smash hit. We didn't have a large audience at the theater, just five or six hundred men at the most, but they yelled at cheered like they do for a Kay Kaiser show. Russ Beggs thought it was the best we had done so far of any of the new shows. This boy Bud

Robert G. "Bud" Blattner

Blattner, who worked with our announcer Dick Stern, is a real find. He's an interesting fellow too." He was the world's champion table tennis player and traveled all over Europe, playing exhibition games, Ben noted. Then he came back to the U.S. and went into baseball; he was with the New York Yankees when he went into the service. "He's with Islands Welfare here, and has been doing a sportscast for us. He has a real style—genuine enthusiasm—and lots of initiative. He's the kind of guy who could be built up into a radio personality without any difficulty at all. The job he did last night would compare favorably with a Ralph Edwards performance."

Robert "Bud" Blattner's job in the Navy was to developed athletic programs, as a First Class Petty Officer. He described how he attended school at Bainbridge (Maryland) for a couple of months. In a September 2000 interview, Bud explained: "They turned us out as 'Athletic Specialists.' That was my job on Guam, stationed above Agana, to set up athletic programs. I worked with battle-scarred Marines. They could fight better than they could field. They wanted to play baseball to get out of patrol duty. These guys were American heroes—they were the guys that secured the islands—with purple hearts, Legions of Merit."

Bud said the job took him on tours of the forward areas. The Third Fleet baseball team played against the Fifth Fleet. He played exhibition tennis matches with Bobby Riggs, and table tennis matches. "We hit these hot, coral windswept islands, played tennis in the morning and conducted the Gene Tunney program and a swimming program in the afternoon." His work with the Tunney program, named after the champion boxer, led to the Marianas boxing championships, a competition among those troops stalled on Guam, Saipan and Tinian, the islands where the atom bomb was assembled. "The Third Marines would compete. Peewee Reese and I would describe the action and Georgie Abrams would sit with me and analyze the bouts."[9]

Ben's vantage point at the nerve center of the Pacific war fed his keen interest in keeping up with the news. Moreover, his job at the radio station gave him the responsibility and the opportunity to keep the island's populace up to date. On July 28 he reported: "News of the world and the war is the exciting business of the day, and for once I am grateful that my spot here at the station enables me to keep fully and well-informed, if I make the effort. I listened to half a dozen shortwave broadcasts yesterday and watched the wire services all day long (we get the news off the CincPac wires by picking up their sheets)."

His top realization from reporting world news was that the Allies were now in the same position relative to Japan that they had been in regarding Germany six months earlier and were starting to consider means of her disposal. "Ultimatums of the character issued yesterday could only be issued if the situation in Japan were known to be so grave as to give such demands completely serious consideration. He relished the prospect that the president would hold out for complete and final victory: "Truman seems to be ignoring the [Col. Robert R.] McCormicks and [Charles A.] Lindberghs..." Ben made a scornful reference to Lindbergh: "I see our fascist flyer was in Chicago visiting the tower of infamy" (the Tribune Tower) "and making speeches for Henry Ford again." [11] Ben could not abide Lindbergh's and Ford's isolationist harangues, and was pleased to see President Truman ignoring them.

He noted that the result there on Guam was to begin a "welter of speculation on the probable end of the war and a strong hope that we will be home by Christmas, which I think is impossible, even if the war were to end tomorrow."

CHAPTER 8

HERE'S GUAM

"Quiet, please. Thirty seconds," Ben called to the announcers and the band assembled on the stage of the open-air theater. He counted down the last ten seconds by curling each finger of his upraised hands. He pointed a forefinger to cue the leader of the CincPac band, who launched them into a rousing chorus of "The Stars and Stripes Forever." He then cued Don Davis, who began a voiceover introduction.

"Good evening, soldiers, sailors, Marines, the Army Air Corps and Americans and allies everywhere." Davis stood tall at the WXLI microphone, in his pressed Seabee uniform, his dark hair peeking out of his sailor cap. "Welcome to the first anniversary celebration of the United States recapture of Guam. It was just a year ago today, on July 21, 1944, that the U.S. Marines of the First Provisional Brigade and the Third Division and soldiers of the 77th Division invaded Guam, which was our final objective in the Marianas."

After his Friday rehearsal, Ben had written home, "It was just like Knickerbocker Playhouse days. Paquette, who leads the CincPac band, is as clever almost as Bob Trendler and did a marvelous job on music for me. The cast was professional enough to make the job pleasant. The show is written without sound effects, heavily scored for music, mostly original arrangements…and ought to run very smoothly. I have seen the two generals' speeches and they are short and to the point…. the admiral's will be recorded for us this morning, and this evening we will transcribe the native chorus, which has just one spot and will be easier to handle separately."

The show itself reflected a change in military policy toward Guam, which the government began to implement in mid-1945. Officials reasoned that the liberated citizens of Guam, celebrating their reborn relationship with the United States, wanted to be recognized as part of the American alliance. Moreover, concerned that returning soldiers knew very little about history and culture of the place where they had spent their time during the war, the military government reversed its course of wartime secrecy and began to speak openly and proudly about the island, its people and their ties with America.

"Guam is an island of 225 square miles," Davis continued. "It was discovered by Magellan in 1521. The United States got possession of it by the Treaty of Paris in 1898 at the close of the Spanish-American War. Guam is in the heart of Micronesia, a group of 1,400 islands, measuring some 1,300 miles north and south and 3,000 miles east and west, reaching within 2,000 miles of the Hawaiian Islands and 500 miles of the Philippines. It is the largest land mass between the Hawaiian Islands and the Philippines, a distance of 5,000 miles, as well as the largest between Japan and New Guinea, a distance of 2,200 miles. Its position is most strategic and the key to the Pacific.

"Situated on Guam," he continued, "are the Fleet Headquarters of Admiral Chester W. Nimitz, headquarters of Vice Admiral John H. Hoover, Commander of the Marianas, headquarters of Lieutenant General Barney Giles, Deputy Commander of the 20th Army Air Force, and Marine Major General Henry L. Larsen, Island Commander.

"Let's listen now to a recorded message from the Admiral."

From his control console on one side of the stage, Jimmy Coleman flicked on his wire recorder and fed it into the loudspeakers. "Good evening troops. This is Chester Nimitz, Admiral of the Fleet. Admiral Hoover and I want to congratulate you and the many others who fought alongside you on your success, and to remember the thousands injured or lost in order to win this hard-fought campaign. The island of Guam was declared

Chapter 8-Here's Guam

'secured' on August 10, 1944. American casualties totaled 1,358 killed, 5,636 wounded and 37 missing. Japanese totals were much greater. It was the first American-populated Territory recaptured from the Japanese. Its 23,000 natives, American nationals, expressed great gratitude and relief to be liberated from two-and-a-half years of so-called 'Asiatic prosperity.'"

The troops greeted the recorded voice with polite, sporadic applause.

"Now I'm proud to introduce Lieutenant General Barney Giles," the announcer continued, "Deputy Commander of the 20th Army Air Force, to describe the effort."

General Giles stepped to the podium and began: "The retaking and reconstruction of this most powerful bastion in the Pacific under the direction of General Larsen was a story of American ingenuity and perseverance. He'll tell you about it in a minute, but, I thought I'd better describe his achievements for you first, since he's so modest."

The crowd of 15,000 Seabees, sailors, airmen and Marines roared as one.

"It was the monsoon season when U. S. troops invaded Guam; the heavy rains left the island's few dirt roads a quagmire and turned beaches, into nothing but a mud-filled swampland. The Seabees no sooner got a roadbed laid when the torrential rains washed it out. It looked like a long, arduous and impossible task to keep up with the construction blueprint laid down for the island. But the Seabees, driven on by the determined Captain, now Commodore, William O. Hiltabidle, worked seven days a week day and night to break many records and to make Guam the nerve and supply center of the Pacific war. Today, the island teems with military and construction activity. It boasts large shore batteries, hundreds of anti-aircraft guns, machine guns and radio outposts. At night, many huge searchlights can be thrown up to scan the skies. It is a nigh impregnable fortress. Here, I'll let General Henry Larsen tell you the details of this major achievement."

The troops stood and clapped, whistled and cheered their popular Island Commander.

"Thank you General Giles," Larsen said. "A beehive of activity has been created on Guam in just one year: a 4,900-foot breakwater, the reconstruction of Agana harbor. Some 3,600 jeeps, 28,000 trucks and 3,000 trailers, run on 150 miles of newly built highway, of which 40 miles are paved, 24 hours a day. We've built five first class air bases with eight completed airstrips including three large B-29 fields, from which hundreds of Superfortresses are hurled against Japanese mainland targets day and night."

The general described the relocation and reconstruction of native villages necessary to create these facilities, along with massive efforts to restore livestock and natural species, establishment of fifteen schools and his plans "to rebuild the once-beautiful city of Agana, which housed more than 12,000 of the island's 23,000 residents, but which was badly wrecked by U.S. planes and bombs in recapturing the island."[1]

In Sunday morning's letter Ben reported, "It was a most unusual Saturday night, with lots of excitement. The program with the generals was smooth as silk... both generals showed well ahead of time. We had finished a rehearsal, or all we were going to have time for... Paquette's CincPac band did a beautiful job on the music. The actors were fine and Davis and Evans did excellent narrator jobs. In between I put Baltazar Bordallo, a prominent native, on for a five-minute talk, and during the course of this made arrangements to visit a private party at his home to make our first *Here's Guam* recording."

Ben and Kani Evans had dashed off immediately after the show and made their appearance at Mr. Bordallo's home.

Army Corporal Kani Evans "was Hollywood enough to be a complete egomaniac," Ben wrote. But Kani would meet success, he felt, by banging away at it and bumping his head on many sharp corners. He was willing to try anything. He had all the nerve in the world, although not all the judgment and good taste. But he predicted Kani would get on; he had talent and enough aggressiveness to make it pay off.

"Some party!" Ben said to Kani.

"Look at the long buffet table with a white tablecloth— roast pork, fish-in-aspic, rolls, punch, potato salad—all in our honor!"

"Don't flatter yourself, Kani. Look who else is here." He nodded toward the roomful of military brass and distinguished Guamanians.

"Welcome Señor Green." Baltazar Bordallo bowed, greeting Ben as a civilian, not by his military rank, and introduced his family. The girls were very pretty, very cute and very young, sixteen to twenty-one. Mrs. Bordallo was in her forties and looked quite young, despite bearing sixteen children, fourteen living. After his network radio debut, their host was most cordial

Chapter 8-Here's Guam 139

to Ben and his group. A July 1944 photograph taken at a refugee center shortly after their release from the Japanese concentration camp shows Mr. and Mrs. Bordallo and twelve of the children—all tall, handsome people, and despite their detention by the Japanese, well fed, neatly clad and looking robust and healthy.

Kani Evans set up the wire recorder and a microphone so the interview could begin. He welcomed listeners to the debut broadcast of Here's Guam and introduced their prominent guest.

"We Bordallos are mostly Spanish," their host said into the microphone. "We used to own the taxi and trucking business here and now operate a restaurant. Sadly, this represents most of what is left of commercial activity on Guam. There is only one other public restaurant.

"You see," continued Baltazar Jeronimo "B.J." Bardallo, "we were among several prominent families of Chamorros, whose roots go back to the old mestizo families of Guam. Our family, our Bordallo relatives and two other families were forced to provide weekly quotas of beef from our ranches to the invading Japanese. Then we were interned during the period of occupation in a concentration camp near Agat.

"Late on the afternoon of July 30th," Bordallo continued, "army patrols reached the edge of the concentration camps in the Manengon Valley. A group of Chamorros, including our family, followed the patrol back to the mountains above Agat, from where we moved behind the American lines the next day."

They made their recording and played it back for the crowd. The youngsters expressed delight at their instant celebrity. The commanders and others from military government present at the party congratulated Ben and Kani on their skill.

"We were producers, engineers and announcers," Ben wrote, "using one of those tricky little wire recorders, which I had borrowed from CincPac for our use.

"The only dampener on the night's show, "Ben commented, "was the aftermath back at the station with Captain Cisler, who didn't like the results, although he had accepted the general program idea.

"Oh I know, you told me all about it. But I didn't think it was a good show."

"But the big brass at the party congratulated us profusely—that's to your credit!"

"Oh, I like the idea alright," he said. "After all, I approved it."

After all, it wasn't the captain's own idea. This was his typical reaction to anyone else's efforts. "The captain often disagrees with us," Ben wrote. "Unfortunately, he's all 250-watts-Louisville-minded. As a result he frequently misses the entire point of what we're doing, or what we're driving at, besides having a somewhat haywire conception of what should be done for the men out here. But I don't really care, just so we can go ahead and do the jobs, even if we meet some opposition."

Ben, Russ and Kani went back to town the next night to talk to Mr. Bordallo. He was helping them to arrange a show on a banana plantation, to introduce the industry of the island. Afterward, his daughter Barbara opened up and told them a lot about "life under the Nips," as Ben called it.

"We were devastated by the invasion," she said, "and under their domination we had to feed and provide for huge numbers of the occupying army. We and other families among the principalia, spent a good part of our fortunes fulfilling their demands."

"Really?" Kani said, "What else did you have to do for them?"

"In addition to the quotas of beef from their ranches, the owner of the ice plant had to keep it cold, and my father's trucking business was pressed into service to deliver the meat and supplies."

"You mentioned their fortunes. Who else on this island has major businesses?"

"Besides the banana plantation and my uncles' ranches, there's Joseph Ada, who runs the soap factory where you're doing your remote broadcast next week. He works out of tents to make about 2,000 bars of soap a week. The American government is now obtaining new equipment for him.

"What kind of equipment?" Kani asked.

"It's some kind of machinery that will enable him to supply 35,000 bars of soap a week for servicemen and native families. Another Chamorro family has the Coca-Cola license. And once Apra Harbor reopens, the shipping business will be re-established."

"After the invasion and what your father described, who can afford to do that?"

"There's plenty of money for investment. Some families here still have fortunes running into the hundreds of thousands of dollars."

Kani kept firing questions like a District Attorney. Finally, Ben felt obligated to extricate the three of them and leave the Bordallos in peace.

Robert F. Rogers's 1995 history of Guam fills in more about this unusual family. The Bordallos were among several prominent families of Chamorros, whose roots went back to the old mestizo families of Guam. While they were educated in the Spanish language, they continue to speak Chamorro at home. Under their heavy-handed rule during the eighteenth century, Spaniards introduced the concept of land ownership into the communal clans of the Chamorros. Certain prominent indigenous families, the principalia, evolved into an elite class called manak'kilo, or "high people," who lived in the center of Agana in houses of coral masonry; they adopted Spanish and Filipino manners and clothing.

As a member of the Guam Council, B. J. had made a 1936 trip with F. B. Leon Guerrero to Washington, and even met with President Roosevelt, to lobby for U. S. citizenship for the people of Guam. Although he was unsuccessful in this attempt, in 1949 he returned (taking along his teenage children Barbara, Paul and Riccardo—or Ricky, pictured at the extreme right of the photograph), to petition for formal transfer the administration of Guam to the U. S. Department of the Interior. This was accomplished by President Truman's Executive Order, followed on August 1 of the next year

Bordallo family after fleeing concentration camp. This photograph was taken about 31 July 1944 at the Fineli refugee

The B. J. Bordallo Family, shortly after their release

by his signing of the Organic Act of 1950, making Guamanians U. S. citizens and establishing the civilian rule in effect today, which will continue until Guamanians adopt their own constitution.

Throughout the postwar period, until the Organic Act, B. J. Bordallo served as President of the House Council. While his son Ricky went on to become Governor of the newly enfranchised Guam in succeeding years, his administration was blemished with scandal. But B. J., whom Ben had the privilege to meet, had served with honor and distinction, winning a large measure of independence for his fellow Guamanians.[2]

Ben took a great interest in describing native life and culture, as witnessed by his pleasure to be able to mail home a pamphlet, which "does a fair job giving you some idea of the people here."

Later that week Ben took Here's Guam on location to the soap factory owned by a non-English-speaking Chamorran, Joseph M. Ada, "about half the supply necessary for the natives," Ben said. He was expecting soon to receive modern machinery the U. S. Government was providing for him, which would enable him to make enough to supply the servicemen as well. "His 'factory' is in a canvas structure—a Jerry-built affair, which was pieced together and was working 90 days after D-Day. We took along a girl from one of the government offices and an officer from the economics department of the military government to talk on the program."

He and Kani Evans visited another location for their remote broadcast of 'Here's Guam:' a banana plantation. After picking up the native in charge of the Agriculture Department at eight, they took off for one of the towns. "It was a 'fur piece' and into pretty rough terrain, but we found ourselves in the heart of the banana country and with plenty of local color." They found the village exactly as it was before the war. It had none of the new wooden houses that the government was constructing. Houses were built of bamboo and palm fronds. "They're on stilts and are surprisingly cool. Floors are dirt. There's no recreation space indoors... they have just enough space for beds and a little space for eating purposes." All cooking was done over open grates. "These people are called *poblanos* by the kind of people we visited Saturday night," he explained. "They speak little English, wear the most limited clothing—no shoes, of course—and are quite shy."

Ben expressed his delight with the wire recorder—especially its ease of operation and flexibility as compared with recording on a platter—"since

Chapter 8-Here's Guam

you can erase anything you don't like and go on from the point at which you erase. It plays back instantly if you want it to. It times the show and stops at any designated time." 6

In his off-duty hours Ben did his best to enjoy the island scenery, swim in the languid tropical waters and make his remaining time on Guam meaningful for himself and troops listening to the station. He even started playing tennis again, since Russ Beggs liked the game, on the officers' courts, when the officers were not using them. He also kept in touch with his friends on the island. On Sunday he wrote, "Now it's raining again, and it looks like the beginning of the deluge. I'd hate to be in the boondocks now...must be really hard to live in during this weather." But he experienced real life back home vicariously through Alice's letters. "I'd like Annisquam. I think that cove sounds like ideal ocean swimming, and the nearness of the fishing all sounds ideal."

Alice wrote him about introducing Helen and Joseph to a new drink. She had watched as Joseph finished an entire pitcher of daiquiris, shaking his head and repeating, "I can't place that taste." She gleefully, informed him one quart later that the mystery flavor was the rum. Ben wrote back offering his best bartender's advice. "Tell Joseph to mix those daiquiris in an electric shaker, mixer or Waring blender, and he'll really have something, especially if he uses shaved or chipped ice. It's a drink that's better for being frigid."

Despite Ben's best efforts to encourage her, in her last letters Alice seemed downhearted. He suspected that things weren't all rosy at Annisquam. To him her fun seemed simulated rather than real. Peter's pickiness about food, his foul moods and temper tantrums persisted. "Pete's problem is an odd one." Ben said. "I had a feeling it was all gone, and that his ready acceptance of change indicated complete adjustment to his new environment. I hope you get more than a suntan before you leave, and that you do really get a rest. Helen ought to know the answer if anyone does, so it seems all you can do is to try your best and wait."

He tried to keep her spirits up and sympathized with her boredom: "But you sound reasonably cheerful, and boredom is just what goes with war. Keep your chin up, honey chile. This is really the last lap...and it won't be too much longer. We're three-fourths of the way through now. By the time you have Pete settled in school and are back in the house, it will only be four months to the time when I will be eligible for discharge on the grounds that I'll soon be 38, and you know how quickly time passes. Then we can start living again. And the war does look good. Despite pessimistic statements about its length, by the time you get this Russia will probably be declared 'in'—that's my guess—and from then on the Japs should be even easier pickings. Certainly they are taking a terrible licking every day now, and only the method and date of their surrender is in doubt.

"I feel for you baby. We won't be bored when I get home. If we're bored we'll go out and buy a yacht or a Superfortress or whatever it's fashionable to buy to relieve boredom…and when it's gone we'll get a new toy, if we need any… but I'll bet on account of you're Alice and I'm Ben we won't… huh? Love and more… Ben."

CHAPTER 9

THE HIGHEST RANKING PRIVATE ON GUAM

Luther Billis and Tony Frey were a pair! Luther was what we call in the Navy a "big dealer." Ten minutes after he arrived at the station, he knew where to buy illicit beer, how to finagle extra desserts, what would be playing at the movies three weeks hence, and how to avoid night duty...

Big dealers knew that the best way for an enlisted man to get ahead was to leech on to an officer. Do things for him. Butter him up. Kid him along. Because then you had a friend at court. Maybe you could even borrow his Jeep!
—James A. Michener, Tales of the South Pacific, 1947

Monday, July 30th, the rains came and settled in for the day. It was almost the first time since Ben had been on Guam they had experienced such steady rain, confirming his suspicions that the rainy season had begun. It wasn't uncomfortable, though, where paved roads and areas covered with coral concealed the mud, but he still pitied the poor Marines in the boondocks. The rain ended today's plans for recording more *Here's Guam* episodes in the field. Because a special meeting was planned for Tuesday foreshadowed many changes, Ben didn't expect to return to the project all week.

"At least this'll give us time to get ready for the AFRS boys," Russ Beggs said as he flopped down in a chair beside Ben's desk, now relocated from the captain's office to his own.

"The captain mentioned it to me briefly last week. Do you know who's coming?" Ben studied Russ, marveling that this boy had landed at his radio station. With balding, blondish hair and a reddish face, his slight build and glasses gave him a pixie look. This whimsical 24-year-old was full of good comedy and wise beyond his years.

"It's a big delegation from Armed Forces Radio Service, all officers, including a major from Los Angeles, which is AFRS headquarters."

"Hmm," Ben said, "sounds mildly interesting." Although his main concern was how soon he'd be able to go home, here was an opportunity to meet the men who made this outfit tick.

"Oh, you'll love this, Ben. I'm pretty sure I'll know most of them. I've been in the radio service in the Pacific longer than anyone."

Word had preceded Russ that he was very well thought of, as Ben thought he should be. He was fine to have at your side on any occasion, even at a dull movie. The other night in the film, "Slightly Dangerous," a telegram was delivered. Says Russ, "Gee, I didn't realize they could afford telegrams at Monogram Pictures."

"He's a super top gent, honest, smart and fun," Ben wrote, "definitely one of our kind of people, and one whom I'm sure we shall count among our friends for many, many years. He is 'the man I'd most like to buy a show from' after the war."

As they stared out the window the conversation lapsed into companionable silence. The downpour drummed on the Quonset hut and reduced visibility to 50 feet.

Captain Cisler appeared at Ben's doorway in the gloom, snapping them out of their trance.

"Ah, glad to find both of you together. Saves time. Look, we've got to organize the men to clean this place up tonight for the big boys tomorrow. We need to repaint the offices. And I want this place clean. You hear me? Clean."

"Yes sir," they chimed in unison, straightening in their chairs.

Chapter 9-The Highest Ranking Private on Guam

"Very well, then." He turned on his heel and marched out.

"This place is only three months old, for God's sake," Ben observed.

Russ examined the walls of the office. "Seems okay to me. Maybe I should go and spend the next four hours, broom in hand, sweeping out my office." He didn't budge from his chair.

"Cisler's mind runs to sweeping and painting. He thinks it will impress the visiting firemen."

"That's his error. AFRS management thinks these stations should be used to provide entertainment for the men. They aren't much interested in the policing details."

"Ah well, in Louisville, it was probably different. Meanwhile the SAC wants this place shipshape."

"The sack?"

"That's S-A-C, for Steven A. Cisler. You know, like the Sad Sack in in the GI Joe comic strips? That's his nickname around here."

Russ chuckled. The rain drumming on the roof, the slow whirl of a ceiling fan and the persistent gloom set just the right mood for a story.

"You know how Armed Forces Radio Service began?"

"Not really," Ben said. "I first stumbled on it when I was trying to figure out how to get out of the infantry. There's not much else going on around here today. Why don't you tell me?"

"The Armed Forces Radio Service was formed in 1942," Russ began. "During this war the brass concluded that military morale activities are essential for an efficient, fully functional force. Even in the first war, General John J. Pershing had recognized this, but found that the mish-mash of volunteer and private agencies offering to help the troops was uncoordinated and often resulted in a duplication of effort. By making it a function of the military, it could remain non-sectarian and focused on its primary purpose—maintenance of troop morale.

"I had no idea," Ben said. "So what did they do about it?"

"It went something like this. As the U.S. geared up for the next great conflict, Secretary of War Henry Stimson appointed Frederick Osborn, then chairman of the Rockefeller Foundation and a good friend of President Roosevelt, as Committee Chairman for morale activities. Osborn soon retitled the morale function as the Special Services Branch. Next, Secretary of the Army General George C. Marshall ordered Academy Award winning director Frank Capra, recently commissioned in into the Signal Corps, to report to the information services section of the new branch."

"Isn't that when he produced the documentary, 'Why We Fight?'"

"Right. It's well done."

"Although it's a bit jingoistic."

"Very true, but it has been one of the most powerful morale building films of the war. Then somebody asked Capra if he knew Tom Lewis, then vice president in charge of radio production at Young and Rubicam."

"Really? That's one of the nation's largest advertising agencies. Everyone in the industry knows of him. Isn't he married to screen star Loretta Young?"

"That's him. They met, and Capra liked him and urged his selection as head of Armed Forces Radio Service. Lewis was known to have a genius for getting things done. When asked by his boss if Lewis also was lucky—he'd need to be to launch this huge enterprise—Capra replied, 'I don't know about Tom Lewis being lucky, but I know damn well that you, the Army, and the country will be lucky. You got your man, fellows—a man who asks God for help. And gets it.'

"Lewis got a civilian colleague from Young and Rubicam, Al Scalpone," Russ went on, "to work in Washington to secure his initial funds from the Army—which was already competing with demands from all the other branches. To get a huge volume of programming produced in a short time, he called in favors from all the networks he had bought advertising time from, especially CBS and NBC, and got the use of their studios and equipment. For management, in addition to Scalpone, he called on his top colleagues in the industry, including Sylvester 'Pat' Weaver, who joined the AFRS just last year."

Pat Weaver went on in later years to become President of NBC, invent the "special," create the *Today* and *Tonight* shows, and was considered one of the geniuses of the business.

"To secure source material, Capra located the headquarters of AFRS in Hollywood, the greatest reservoir of national talent. To distribute the shows, when short wave radio proved to be too unreliable in signal strength and constancy, and too low in fidelity, he pioneered the use of a new 'vinylite' recording medium, which had closer grooves and longer play, more durability in preserving recorded sound and more resistance to breakage in transit than the old lacquered phonograph records. Vinylite program transcriptions numbering in the millions were eventually distributed worldwide on a weekly basis."

"So that's how we got these stacks of recordings every week!"

"That's in essence how we got where we are today."[1]

"Wow, great story. So how did you break into Armed Forces Radio?"

"You ever heard of the Kwaj Lodge?"

"Sure. But we can't get it here—we're too far away from Kwajalein Island."

"Sometime I'll play you a record of one of my shows. In my previous AFRS assignment, at WXLG Kwajalein, we figured a show was needed that reflected how the poor guys marooned on the rock felt—about the war, the military and the folks back home. We wanted to spoof the conditions, obstacles and absurdities that the troops face every day."

"I've heard it was the most popular show in the Pacific," Ben said. "What was it like?"

"We did a daily DJ show. My byline was 'Rock Happy Roger' and I called myself 'maitre d'hotel of the Kwaj Lodge.' My two-hour show was broadcast every weekday just after the world news at noon. We touched on all the laughable or sad daily goof-ups on the huge bases at Kwajalein and Roi-Namur, much to the delight of the Army, Navy and Marine Corps personnel. There were no holds barred, and I would lament about the dull daily life on the rock."

As today's readers might recognize, his show became the prototype for the show Adrian Kronauer later developed and Robin Williams depicted in the film, Good Morning Vietnam.

"So who are the guys coming out here tomorrow?" Ben asked.

"Some major from AFRS Headquarters in Los Angeles—I don't know him. But Lewis's deputy True Boardman, might be along. He's the one who did some island-hopping in the Pacific to convince the various commanders and the top brass of the necessity for providing a radio service. Supposedly we'll see Ted Sherdeman, a top-notch radio executive who runs the Pacific Ocean network. We call ourselves the Mosquito Network in Admiral Nimitz's Central Pacific area. They're called the Jungle Network in General MacArthur's South Pacific area."

"They're not really networks at all," Ben said, "more like struggling little 500-watt stations, often understaffed, always overworked and more often than not living in deplorable conditions."

"But the fighting men, our audience, are under much greater stress. The main principle we follow is to consider *them* first in programming. We try to entertain and divert the troops through periods of alternating tension and boredom. They have little to occupy themselves with, other than a few tattered paperback books and radio. There aren't any towns, and certainly no clubs. Food is generally terrible and monotonous.'

"That's for sure! They show the movies outdoors, rain or shine. They're often years old and in terrible condition."

"Mail from home out there is a chancy thing," Russ said, "and it's not uncommon to have Mommy send a picture of the baby's six-month birthday party, which arrives before the recipient knows he's a daddy. These guys are not happy—they just want to get this thing over with, get out of the slime and muck and go home. That's what Sherdeman knew when he wrote to Tom Lewis back in Hollywood about programming from AFRS: 'Don't to the slightest degree wave the flag. It's sure death…Only those who've lived in it and gone through the loving and hating it can tell whether what's written as honest or not.' He put the station operations under control of the enlisted men. He wants it to be a rule followed by AFRS stations everywhere. In the future officers may manage stations, but enlisted personnel will run them."

"Boy, these are men after my own heart. That's exactly what we've been shooting for here at the station."[2]

Ben and the men housecleaned until 10:30 Monday night and hit the hay, exhausted.

Tuesday morning when Ben arrived at the station, Captain Cisler called them together and announced, "I woke up this morning to receive word that the big meeting scheduled for today has been canceled."

It seemed someone failed to go through proper channels in calling the meeting, and some general or other was annoyed and canceled it. Ben, commented to Russ, "Big deal. It makes a lot of difference one way or the other. We just need to do our regular jobs."

Despite his professed lack of concern, Ben had to be disappointed. He'd been looking forward to meeting Ted Sherdeman, the man who had reformed Armed Forces Radio Services to appeal to the troops. He'd hoped

Chapter 9-The Highest Ranking Private on Guam

to communicate to headquarters in LA their hopes for WXLI.

"By the way," the captain added, "I'm going to the hospital tomorrow for surgery and am expected to be out for ten days to two weeks."

Now *there* was some news. Although he tried not to show it, Ben was thrilled.

"During the captain's absence, Russ Beggs, as the highest ranking guy," Ben wrote, "except for Jimmy Coleman who, obviously, being our engineer, couldn't be running the station, was left in charge, with me second in command. Russ has five stripes. That's the Army for you. But it promises to be a very unpleasant two weeks for SAC and a very pleasant two weeks for us. We will continue to go our merry way. We cleared everything we want to do in the next couple of weeks and will be free to work out our ideas as we see them, we think."

As soon as Ben's comfortable rug was laid down, however, it was yanked out from under him. The big news of Wednesday, August 1st, was: Russ Beggs was leaving. He was stateside-bound to take a special training course given by the information and education department at Washington and Lee University, Lexington, Virginia. Ben cheered Russ's luck and cursed his own. It threw back in his lap everything he was doing before Russ came and maybe more, because now, due to their own efforts, the jobs had expanded and the activity had increased.

Ben pinned his hopes on three new men coming in. He thought one of them ought to be of some help in partially fulfilling Cisler's obsessive requirements: he could type and sweep. According to the description forwarded from AFRS, one of them had taken a college course in radio, but had no experience. He sounded just right for the job Ben wanted filled in the office—answering the phone, writing the logs and doing Cisler's odds and ends, freeing up Ben to do his real job.

The very next day, Thursday, August 2nd, Russ was told he had to move out by Saturday, which meant that Ben would be in charge of the station while Cisler was in the hospital. Since Russ had to make preparations to leave, Ben took over immediately.

Ben was hot and dirty and needed a shower. But he wouldn't be able to take one until after chow. He had driven Russ Beggs all over the island, arranging for transportation for him and getting him set for his takeoff. He would be leaving Saturday at 2 p.m. Ben was now running the station single-handed and thus spent the morning answering telephones, handling callers and getting no work done.

"Our *Answers Aweigh* quiz show was swell last night," he wrote Friday at noon, "but the payoff was, it didn't go out on the air. We were off the air for 40 minutes. The captain managed that, as his last contribution before he took off for the hospital. He changed the patch cord on the board, which succeeded in patching our transmitter output into a CincPac line so that we only fed that line and didn't feed to the air." Early on Friday he went to visit Capt. Cisler in the hospital. He was feeling pretty punk and probably wouldn't be around for eight or nine more days. Even adversity had its blessings.

"I have drill this afternoon," he said in his daily letter home, "which louses up the rest of the day. Friday night we'll have a little party for Russ and say farewell in the usual manner. He's the first person in a long time that I've felt really close to. It's not like Duke, who is certainly a good and warm friend. But you know how I feel about our really close friends back home, the people we really care for. He's one of those.

"Incidentally, it seems that Phil Edwards, who shares a news program with Kani Evans and is still in the public relations office, will be jumped to warrant officer from sergeant so he can succeed the captain, who for all practical purposes has already left. It's a very refreshing thing to see a deserving guy get a break in the Marine Corps." Webley Edwards was known to the men as Phil for obvious reasons—what do you call a guy with a name like that for short? "He's the man for the job. He can write, handles himself well and knows the work of the office thoroughly. Although it hardly ever happens that way, barring hitches, he'll make it."

When General Larsen, who no doubt had been visited by Boardman and Sherdeman, saw some initiative and talent at the enlisted level of a type which would enable him to implement the adopted policy, he was surely pleased, and, it is apparent from his approval of Ben's new ideas, he encouraged them.

Ben was in the right place at the right time. By comparison with other outposts in the Mosquito Network, WXLI, on the same island with the Pacific Fleet Commander, both in facilities and command support, was a luxury hotel. But Ben, having suffered in the boondocks right along with the troops, knew what they wanted. "As I wrote, we stayed on the air all night last night . . . piling news on news, and at five o'clock in the morning,

Chapter 9-The Highest Ranking Private on Guam 153

General Larsen, Island Commander called to congratulate us on the job we were doing and tell us, 'If you want early chow or anything, just tell them General Larsen said it was all right.' At 6:30 AM we did a special *Pacific War Extra*, the second of the night, and at 9:30 AM, a Don Davis news followed by another at 1:30 p.m. These were locally written shows in addition to the hourly short wave news we were carrying from San Francisco."

Thus encouraged, Ben and his crew redoubled their efforts to report the building news of developments in the world's biggest war.

CHAPTER 10

THE SCOOP

The war news kept getting more encouraging. On August 2, B-29s dropped 6,600 pounds of bombs on five Japanese cities. The naval blockade of Japan was complete: nothing got in and nothing got out. Burma had been almost completely retaken from the Japanese, and Chinese troops were advancing on their mainland with little opposition from the retreating Japanese.

On August 6th, a 9,000-pound atomic bomb was dropped on the city of Hiroshima, killing 80,000 and injuring many more. Russia declared war on Japan on August 8th and Russian troops, massed on the Manchurian border, began their invasion. On August 9th, a second atomic bomb was dropped on Nagasaki, killing 30,000 people. On August 12th the Japanese leaders offered to surrender unconditionally if the emperor's status were left unchanged. The world waited anxiously to learn how the U. S would respond to the Japanese offer.

Saturday night August 11th, the news started to die down. Ben decided to run the station until midnight, and then post a watch in case something broke. He hit the sack at 11.

"At about one a.m.," he wrote, "the boys woke me up. I had only gotten two hours' sleep. The United States had replied to Japan. The only thing this could mean was we had accepted their surrender offer. I dashed back and put the station on the air again, repeating the flash bulletin every two minutes. Then I scooted up to CincPac to get some wire stuff . . . it was just starting to come in . . . so once more we were first on Guam with the news. Incidentally the Saipan AFRS station didn't come on until more than an hour after we did. I waited for enough wire stuff to make a broadcast . . . . put one of the boys to work on it and then went back to the barracks to wake up Kani Evans and Phil Edwards, because I want them to do a 6:30 a.m. Pacific War Extra . . . . they're at work on that now, and soon I'll roust Don Davis out of the sack to start work on 9:30 and 1:30 roundup."

Ben reviews a news flash

His excitement continued to build: "The news is piling up so fast now that I wouldn't be at all surprised if we got a reply from Japan before noon our time Sunday. Our answer is tough, but gives them an emperor even if he won't mean anything . . . and I can't see how Japan . . . after admitting to her people that surrender is the only way out, can possibly turn around and start fighting again. The whole ghastly thing is over, and like you, I feel that the insistence of the people of the United States that unconditional surrender was the only answer, the quick participation in the new world setup . . . Atlee in England . . . . all may add up to something good."

His letter goes on to say that Captain Cisler returned from the hospital after his surgery that afternoon, staying long enough "to write a beautiful letter for the bulletin board praising us to the skies for our work . . . He told me that Admiral [Chester W.] Nimitz had passed along some very complimentary remarks via one of his aides . . . it was all-in-all an hour of success for everyone connected with the station.

Chapter 10-The Scoop

We worked hard to bring the guys on this island the news and we did bring them every bit of it swiftly and interestingly. Every guy in the station worked hard."[1]

In the midst of this, they had to do Sporting Chance. "We had a very successful show . . . a big, wildly cheering audience ,. . . good contestants and lots of excitement. Earlier in the day I tried to do some G. I. Joes, which is what we call man-on-the-street gizmos with the service personnel, but I didn't get what I wanted, so we didn't use it. I did manage to get long quotes from two Marine generals, which I cleared with CincPac and put on the air just a little while ago, If I'm alive in the morning I'll go after some more. Gen. Spaatz's office said they'll get me one and so did Larsen's. Then all I'll need is Nimitz and Admiral Murray of COM Marianas, for a complete roundup of official opinion. I'm dog tired and in an hour will be in the sack slumbering peacefully. But I had to tell you how much I love you, how wonderful I think the world and our country is and how generally happy I feel . . . you're an angel . . . angel. Ben 1

On August 14, 1945, as the world awaited word of the Japanese emperor's acceptance of the final surrender terms, Ben kept the station on full alert. He got a call from Kani Evans at CincPac, who reported a cable had just arrived from Domei, the Japanese national news agency. Its dispatches got careful scrutiny at CincPac headquarters. The one that excited Evans was quoted later in the St. Louis Post-Dispatch and across the wire services: "An imperial message accepting the Potsdam proclamation will be forthcoming soon."

Ben instantly grasped the import of the Domei dispatch. His letter of Tuesday, August 14th, "a little after midnight" (Guam Time). appropriately enough, was typed all in caps, as a result of the news typewriter that happened to be available to him at that moment:

> AT LONG LAST...THREE YEARS EIGHT MONTHS AND ONE WEEK...AND NOW IT'S REALLY OVER...OUR FIRST FLASH WAS ON THE AIR AT 3:58 P.M. WHICH IS REALLY ABOUT 2 A.M. YOUR TIME...FROM THEN ON THE STORY STARTED TO BUILD...I WAS IN OUR OFFICE... KANI AT CINCPAC...HE HAD JUST GIVEN ME A

> STORY ABOUT A B-29 ATTACK, AND I WAS PREPARING TO PUT IT ON THE AIR, WHEN THE PHONE RANG AGAIN. IT WAS KANI OUT OF BREATH WITH THE DOMEI FLASH...WE SLAPPED IT ON THE AIR AND THEN AT 4 P.M. TWO MINUTES LATER TOOK SHORT WAVE FROM SAN FRANCISCO POINTING OUT TO OUR LISTENERS THAT SAN FRANCISCO DIDN'T HAVE THE STORY THEY HAD JUST HEARD OVER WXLI.
>
> LITTLE CONFIRMING THINGS KEPT COMING UP ALL DAY...THE BERN SWITZERLAND STORY...THE REUTERS DISPATCH AND FINALLY JUST A WHILE AGO THE WHITE HOUSE STATEMENT CONFIRMING THE FACT THAT A REPLY WAS ON ITS WAY FROM SWITZERLAND. AP CREDITED THE GUAM RADIO WITH MAKING A FLASH ANNOUNCEMENT HERE, WHICH YOU MAY HAVE READ OR HEARD REPEATED IN THE STATES...THAT WAS US![2]

What Ben's letter proves is that he was the first in the world to broadcast the news of Japan's acceptance of the surrender: this fact was acknowledged by the news center in San Francisco, and the story was fed directly to the stateside networks.

Some hours later, CBS reporter Webley Edwards made the broadcast the world remembers, over the short wave channel K2XO radio at CincPac. It was "Phil" Edwards whom Ben kept alerted of the news and called in to the station on August 12th to make the announcement of the first Japanese surrender offer. Webley Edwards also made the August 14th broadcast at WXLI, which broke news of Japan's acceptance of the peace terms. In his golden but war-weary tenor, Edwards reported:

> A wild shout was our first knowledge that something had happened. Domei had just announced that an official announcement would be made shortly, and some men here held their breaths almost in hope that there was no possibility that this could be another false one. It was amazing how quickly word spread through this Island of Guam. A truck full of Seabees came hurtling down the highway, all yelling. Workmen dropped their tools and stopped their

Chapter 10-The Scoop

bulldozers to find out what this news might be. Out of a building here at CincPac came a long, shrill whistle and a bustle of running, and all turned and looked at one another; and the question came quickly, "Can this be it? Can this be the one we're waiting for? But men looked at one another and smiled wanly.

It was mid-afternoon here, just after four o'clock. We're very tired; we have been up for many, many hours. And we were slightly incredulous. I still can't think it through. And just as I say that, I know it's being said by all men who've been considering this thing here today. If the Japanese have accepted our final surrender terms, and I'm pinching myself to see if I'm awake, this long, dreary war could be over. And even as I speak, the air is filled with messages passing information and instructions to ships of the Pacific fleet and subs and airplanes in flight.

The long-awaited word was received here almost casually. Its impact was terrific; we were stunned. We've not had time for any general tumult. There have been so many alerts and false alarms in the past few days that this is a sort of anticlimax. There are plenty of skeptics who just can't bring themselves around to believing it's all over. We're holding ourselves here with bated breath. This is Webley Edwards at Guam. I return you to CBS in the United States. [3]

The war was over. But Ben's endless wait for news that he could go home continued.

Ben had written on Sunday morning, August 12th: "My darlings: On this most wonderful day I must begin by saying I love you dearly, and every hour I worked since the grand news started coming in at 10:18 Friday night was an hour that seemed to bring me closer you and Pete and Linda and that long dreamed of day when we can be together again. You're a family that any one in the world would be thrilled to have, and I am the luckiest fellow in the world to have you all for my own."

Ben's duties on a distant island outpost in the Pacific were not over. As the staff of the radio station was dispersed for other duties, Ben felt the strain of filling the gaps. At least Bud Blattner, an able collaborator. was still here to run Sporting Chance.

Bud explained how he and Ben first got together. "We were in the Island Command, assigned to WXLI. I told him how, when I was recovering from an emergency appendectomy, sitting under a tree, I got talking to a pastor who was quite a tennis fan. We talked about all the athletes that were on the island and the tremendous appeal sports had among the troops. Couldn't we somehow put the two groups together to improve everyone's spirits? On our island radio station, time was plentiful and scheduling wasn't stringent. Perhaps we could do something once or twice a week. The athletes available included baseball figures, such as Pee Wee Reese and Gene Woodling; in tennis, Bobby Riggs and Don Budge, and Fred Postole and Georgie Abrams in boxing. We developed a format in which I kept score, kept things moving--there were no time constraints – breaks for commercials. We had a revolving panel, with 20 to 30 athletes who would ask me questions: 'What was so-and-so like? What was his record?'

"This led to another idea. Quiz shows like 'Double or Nothing' were becoming popular back in the states. Perhaps we could give away beer. Whether the show was any good or not, we would be giving away the nectar of the gods. To do this on a military base, we figured, we were going to have to have permission from headquarters. After running the idea for the show up through channels, finally General Larsen from Island Command thought it would be okay, and we were on our way. The show was called, 'Sporting Chance.'"

The program was written by Bud Blattner and produced by Ben, who arranged for broadcast before a live audience, with a band for musical background; he even auditioned a barbershop quartet for the program. Back on July 15 he wrote: "I had a disappointment last night. No audience appeared for Sporting Chance, so I had to cancel it . . . none of the stateside gimmicks work out here, apparently . . . I thought free beer would be enough to bring a crowd . . . but apparently not . . . so, two weeks from last night, I'll take the show to the audience and do it remote from a theater. It's an easy show to move around. So maybe we'll make it travel. . . nothing has

Chapter 10-The Scoop

been tried here . . . there's no other experience to work from . . . I'll just have to use trial and error to find out what can be done and what can't . . ."

They took it out on location to the various units on Guam. "I remember one large compound," Bud Blattner said. "It had 2,000 to 3,000 in the audience. We would get beer from the island storeroom and bring it to the site of the broadcast. Ben produced, I wrote. The production was quite elaborate: complete with music, drum rolls and such. A group, such as the 23rd Seabees, would request that we come to their unit and would select their best contestants: those that knew the most about football, basketball, and baseball. "I would labor for two or three weeks beforehand to come up with questions of increasing difficulty," Bud noted, "as the tension heightened over who would win the stash of beer for their unit." They made sure that even the losers, when they came backstage, got a consolation prize of a case or two of beer for their part in creating the entertainment.

"It became the most popular doggone show on the island," Bud related. "Requests came in from every installation. It got difficult to write week after week—there wasn't exactly a research library or panel of experts to ask on these questions. I was strong on baseball and knew quite a bit about basketball and football, plus a few facts like best times for the mile run and so on."

After the show, their hosts had a special jeep waiting for them, with eight cases of beer concealed under a tarp. Ben knew what to do with one of them. By the time they got back to the barracks, the lights were out. He shoved a case onto the floor of the room inside, and soon they heard the "p-s-s-t" of bottles opening in the darkness. They hid another case behind the Quonset hut and buried another before they drove on to their next destination. "I'll bet if I went to Guam today," said Bud, shaking his head in wonderment, "I could lead you to beer stashed in hundreds of underground locations all over the island."4

With the captain still gone and without Russ, Ben and Bud carried on. Personnel seemed to be the only essential ingredient in short supply. Due to the station's broadcasting success, Ben walked on water with the top brass. They were so successful that his exuberance spilled over, if you'll pardon the expression, into their work style. In a postwar essay,

Beer for the Troops, Ben explained how this came about.

"Invite a man for a beer," Ben wrote, "and he'll go where you take him without question; enjoy a second round, and chances are you can't make him take a third one. Tell a man he can only have two beers twice a week—that that must be Tuesday and Thursday at 4:30 P.M. at a designated place—and he'll hate you for it. Such was the Standard Order of Procedure for Beer Drinking in the Pacific." The call of duty, social preference and resentment of authority thus prevented the 18 WXLI staff men, composed of Army, Army Air Corps, Navy, Seabees and Marines from claiming their just ration; none would deign to fall into line to get their beer on assigned dates.

Ben took a direct approach to the problem. "I reported directly to Marine Island Command," he wrote, "where my beloved-to-be Colonel Downes took a personal interest in my affairs, his curiosity aroused by the presence of a Pfc. in such an august role."

"I described my plan for running the station: to make it sound like home—Jack Benny at 6:30 on Sunday night, National Barn Dance at Saturday at 8—everything in its accustomed place—and I kept the station spotless. This was the key to the esteem in which Colonel Downes held me; I ran things Marine Corps style, he told me." They were free agents serving 200,000 men on the island with their only escape from Class C and D movies. "One of the innovations we introduced was an audience participation program like Kay Kyser's College of Musical Knowledge. The Army Signal Corps had a $35,000 remote field unit for which it had no further use. They gladly loaned it to us. We were able to relay a program from any point on Guam back to the station for broadcast.' He said Colonel Downes liked the plan. He was easily pleased.

Ben didn't stop there.

"Recreation officers at each camp," he wrote, "were delighted to have a live show in their outdoor theatre and showered us with free merchandise from the PX for prizes. The Seabees, as always, were lavish. One night we did a show from their theatre and they provided the means for our 18 thirsty, beer-starved men to see beer flow in a steady stream. When we finished our show we found our jeeps loaded with beer, artfully concealed under tarpaulins, the load complete with passes and escort to get us back to the station."

Chapter 10-The Scoop

The next morning the recreation officer from the Seabee unit was on the phone. "We've been worrying about you fellows at the station: how do you cool that beer?" Ben confessed that although on rare occasions they were able to steal some ice from the mess hall, they usually drank what beer they could get, warm.

"Aha—that's what we thought," he said. "We've got a refrigerator for you. It's kinda big—bring a work party and a truck with a hoist." The work party was a cinch. Japanese prisoners were available for any job and they frequently were used to help clean up the station. They loved getting out and, once they became prisoners and had satisfied their need to serve the Emperor, they were happy, amiable and anxious to make friends. Even the Marines who had hunted them in the jungles liked them. The truck with a hoist was a knottier problem. "Trucks were the transport line on the Guam and they rolled night and day. You had to need one badly to get it away from the truck pool. I decided this was a matter for Colonel Downes."

With great dignity, he explained to Colonel Downes that their staff was unable to take advantage of his generous beer garden plan. "Because we had to keep the radio station on the air from 6 a.m. to 10 p.m., seven days a week, we had to go without. I told him the Sea Bees had offered us a refrigerator and I needed a truck to get it."

But, where will you get the beer?" he asked. Ben admitted this was a problem. "Ah, I have it," he countered. "How many men do you have?" Eighteen, Ben responded. "Hmmmmm—18 x 4—that's 3 cases a week. I'll issue you a ration order to withdraw 3 cases of beer a week from the warehouse. Your men do a good job. They deserve their beer." Forthwith, my colonel, as he shall always remain in my memory, issued both orders, the beer ration order and the hoist truck order. We picked up the refrigerator and only then did we understand why it needed a truck with a hoist. It was a 24-cubic foot restaurant style gadget, with four large doors, each equipped with a padlock."

They were in business, especially since Colonel Downes had inspired an idea. Ben next dispatched the proper representative of each service to see his recreational officer, tell their beer starvation story and ask for relief. "Our weekly ration rose to five times three cases and our only problem was storage. An underground pit in back of the station

Staff Meeting at WXLI, by Leonard L. Rogers

(dug by a Japanese work party, of course) covered with coconut leaves solved the problem. WXLI had become the best beer joint on the Island of Guam." Only one problem remained. To drink beer, they had to stay up late at night. The 10 PM. lights out rule on the island was a rigid Marine order. Only officers' clubs remained lighted after ten. "I appealed to Colonel Downes," said Ben. "We were on the air until 10 P. M. We needed two more hours to choose musical numbers and arrange our programming."

"By God, that's essential," he responded, "and I'll arrange for the mess hall to feed your men whenever they're hungry. "If you're going to work you have to eat."

"Our beer joint now had new closing hours and plenty of food. We even worked on the next day's programming each night to relieve our consciences," Ben affirmed. "Life on Guam had turned the corner. This post-surrender duty, if you had to do it, wasn't so bad." [5]

CHAPTER 11

WAITING FOR B. J. DAY

God doth not need
Either man's work or his own gifts: who best
Bear his mild yoke, they serve him best. His state
Is kingly; thousands at his bidding speed
And post o'er land and ocean without rest:
They also serve who only stand and wait.
    —*John Milton, On his Blindness, 1655*

On the day of the Japanese surrender, arrangements began at Island Command for press coverage of the surrender meeting in Tokyo. "But the big news of the day," Ben reported on Friday, August 17th, "is that the captain and Kani are going to the surrender meeting . . . Kani is agog about it as I would be . . . It will be quite an excursion. This puts me in charge of the station again as of tomorrow with a million details to handle and a lot of work if we're going to cover properly. Also, we have an extra job. Every radio and newspaper correspondent who has shoes will go . . . which leaves Guam virtually uncovered. We are to have the job of helping the networks out, it seems...details tomorrow." He observed that if he were younger and unmarried with no children, he would put in a big pitch to go to Japan for AFRS. "I could I'm sure . . . but I'm equally sure that it would mean an extra six months or so overseas, and that's definitely out . . . I'll get my Japanese experience vicariously." [1]

In fact, all of his subsequent actions on Guam were directed toward minimizing his stay and speeding his return. He had previously wanted to get transferred from Island Command to a more permanent status with AFRS, but he learned that this could mean that the duration of his service might be extended. And even though the job he was doing merited the six stripes of a staff sergeant, he merely took his satisfaction from that fact and abandoned all attempts to get a rating leading to an increase in rank, and hence lengthen his obligation to the Corps

Ben spent that Friday "loafing," as he called it, "or nearly so, to do a lot of little things and to set the stage for the beginning of a new show." He drove around the island collecting his friends from Mare Island, including "Duke" (Elwood Godsall), and then Johnny Hughes, whom he found at a transient center. Johnny was classified "B" and was thus taken out of combat status and had the hope of going home. Another whom they saw along the way, Dave Alpert, was classified "A" again and wasn't going home after all.

About those at the transient center, he said, "A lot of those boys will wind up in Tokyo or China . . . and some may be lucky and go right back to the states." Because of all the uncertainty and rumor that prevailed on the island, he was attempting to put together a new show featuring an Army, a Marine and a Navy officer and a master of ceremonies on a panel to answer questions about readjustment: points, jobs, education, bonuses, discharge pay and all the other problems of returning to civilian life. "I think it would be hot. With thousands and thousands of guys listening, who are interested in just one thing, I'd have the station's top audience for it. I wasn't going to do any new shows, but this one is such a natural that I can't resist putting it together. I may get stopped on it somewhere, but so far I have a favorable Army reaction, consideration from the Marine Corps and won't make my Navy approach until tomorrow. And with no opposition here in the station to a new idea, it makes the task easier." [2]

He mentioned a couple of amusing experiences he had in making his

Chapter 11-Waiting for B. J. Day

rounds. A colonel he talked with showed up later at the station and mentioned that Lieutenant Green had said it was alright for him to look around. Later in the day, "a major I saw reduced my rank to sergeant. They can't quite get used to the idea of a Pfc. having any kind of a job, I guess, so they unconsciously ascribe rank to me."

Ben was was all caught up on his sleep and not the least bit tired from the exertions of the peace story. "I don't look for any more such sieges. Guam will no longer be a great news center. Its day is done. MacArthur's headquarters in Tokyo will make all the datelines now. Ours will be a routine news job, taking the wire stories and the short wave as it comes." Thinking ahead to his return, he surmised that he should take advantage of the Soldiers' and Sailors' Relief Act and return to his former job at the Kastor advertising agency. Even though he felt that broadcasting would continue its flight from Chicago to New York and, with the advent of television, to Hollywood, he thought he could more quickly get back in the groove in his previous job, taking advantage of a lot of prerogatives there that he might have to earn back if he worked elsewhere. "But I'm not out yet, and not terribly concerned about it. The more I see of people, the more I'm convinced that it's very easy to get along financially in this world . . . and we haven't had any real trouble for a long time. Since I'm at least as smart as I was, we ought to do as well or better. (Don't tell a soul, but I think it will be even better.)

"I have a wonderful idea for making money anyway, Ben continued. I'm going to open a "Make-believe War Room," a regular nightclub where former officers can rent uniforms with bars, stars, stripes, etc. And where we'll dress all the waiters like privates, seamen, etc . . . Then when things get too depressing in the civilian world, they can come there to reminisce about the good old days when they were in the service. Only hitch is that they probably won't have enough money to afford our high prices."

When the Eddie Bracken show came to one of the outdoor theaters, he wrote, two empty rows of seats near the front had been reserved for officers. Bracken would not start the show until they were filled. When he heard they were reserved for officers, he insisted that the rule be changed before he would perform. The top brass refused. Although he finished that show, Bracken refused to give three other scheduled performances, and was cheered by the troops across the island. Ben wondered then how these officers, some of them very petty, small men, would get along later in the rough and tumble competition of civilian life without their special privileges and perquisites.

It was a time of celebration. Ben made it a point to find every one of his former Marine buddies that he knew was on Guam. He located his former barracks mate from Mare Island, Al Englert, in charge of the bar at the Third Medical Battalion: "He made us each a tall, frosty Tom Collins, and they were wonderful . . . then back to CincPac for chow and ran into a couple of rum and Cokes . . . and then a quick dash to meet Colonel Morris to help him to cut a record at 20th Air Force . . . and we had a couple of snorts there. By that time I was feeling wonderful. I went back to the station, and then decided to get a good night's sleep. I hit the sack 8:30 and slept until six."

It was getting hotter, and the heat was making work unpleasant. "There are some air-conditioned buildings—we had an air-conditioning machine, but they wouldn't let us put it in at first because it wasn't essential. The 'brain' traded it for three tiny electric fans—it was worth $1000." Speaking of their commander, he estimated that Captain Cisler and Kani Evans would not return for weeks; they still were floating around, not getting near Manila, but waiting to cover the formal signing in Tokyo, which was delayed. But even if he did get back, the boys at the station were looking forward to his replacement, who was due to arrive soon; they figured a new man could only be an improvement.

As he received Alice's mid-August letters reporting that the summer at Annisquam was going quite nicely—everyone there had finally relaxed and started to enjoy the peaceful rhythm of life on the beach—his thoughts, never far away, turned again toward home. "I'm terribly lonesome for all of you . . . more than ever before. It's hard to imagine all the things we used to do . . . coming home in the evening . . . our almost ceremonial drinks before dinner . . . Pete's adult-like participation in our conversation and pre-dinner activity . . . our Saturday night dinners, which to Pete must be like Sunday dinners were in my day: those huge T-bones, cottage fried potatoes, the bottle of wine and the wonderful bowl salad or artichokes or avocados, strawberry shortcake for dessert; the anniversary occasions; our New Year's eves with theater, champagne and cold turkey as a must."[3]

Russ Beggs, who had left the station for the States at the end of July, had written and said he was going to visit Alice, probably on his way back

Chapter 11-Waiting for B. J. Day   169

from Washington D. C. to his new duty station in Hollywood.

On Sunday, August 26, Ben took Al Englert to an early breakfast with him at CincPac and brought him to the station "with all of the necessities for a fitting observance of a reunion." They had a picnic. Present were Bud Blattner, Don Davis, Wayne Center, Dick Stern, Duke, Paul Davidson and Johnny van Sant, sitting around spinning yarns until noon chow. "We hadn't laughed so much in months." After chow they went swimming, attended a barbecue in Al's area and returned to the station, topping off their holiday with a movie. "The frenzied activity is partly an attempt to cover up the loneliness and homesickness we all feel now . . . it was certain to be this way . . . but maybe Congress will hasten the day . . . pressure ought to be terrific to change the rules, and it doesn't seem as if the military authorities will be holding the whip hand very much longer. There is an election next November, and too many politicians will be seeking favor with the Armed Forces. Bills in Congress will fall faster than leaves from the trees and we're certain to get a lot of 'hurry home' legislation. I think we need some. The point systems are cumbersome, slow, and in too many cases, manifestly unfair."[4]

Meanwhile his efforts to run the station and keep up good programming continued. He described a show called *Sack Rat Serenade*, which was a terrific hit. It had been recently lengthened to 25 minutes, ending at 10:10 p.m., at the end of the broadcast day: "Durwood Hyde does it in a whispery voice . . . it is somewhat salty, very suggestive and quite clever. His opening deals with the business of undressing . . . he describes the pulling off of the boondockers, the dropping of that sweaty sock He winds up with a verse, Dorothy Parker or Ogden Nash style. It's very rugged, virile stuff, and everywhere we go, they ask for the Sack Rat. It's becoming our top mail program, and it's easily the most talked about show on the station. It's a big thing.[5]

"Then I had to arrange for a celebratory show from the new naval supply depot mess hall," he continued, "It will accommodate 7,000 men, and apparently is a hangover from when they thought the war was going to last 10 years, because now they hardly know what to do with it . . . but need it or not, it's the largest Navy mess hall in the world . We're going to open it with music and do *Sporting Chance* from there. We have so many bids to do Sporting Chance that we are lined up weeks in advance . . . and more come in all the time . . . it's a good audience show and the areas are tickled to death to get it. It's swell public relations for the station.

On August 30 Ben wrote that that he'd been busier than he would like to be: "too many callers, to much detail and too much activity . . . I'd like to let it simmer down now. Maybe when the exodus from this island begins—it will, sooner or later—we'll have to knock off most of our special shows anyway, because the bands will be broken up, and there won't be any remotes without decent music."

Then a special opportunity presented itself: "There are some all-star ball teams coming here next week, which Bud Blattner says will be full of names bigger than those that will be seen in the World Series . . . So we'll carry lots of baseball for a while."

They were beginning to get some stuff back from Tokyo by shortwave: "Had one show from Kani and one from Cisler . . . Kani's was pretty fair. Cisler's was sort of a travelogue about the skyline and the water. . . just like a hillbilly's view of the place." However Captain Cisler distinguished himself a couple of days later: "We heard from Cisler when he got an interview with Boyington. So far we haven't been able to catch it. CincPac is trying to get it recorded for us tonight. Boyington is a Marine, Cisler is a Marine . . . so he got a big break. I wouldn't be surprised if you heard that one, I understand it was big stuff.".6

Colonel Gregory "Pappy" Boyington, a Marine Corps ace, who was credited with the destruction of 28 Japanese aircraft, was ultimately awarded the Medal of Honor "for extraordinary heroism above and beyond the call of duty" while in command of a Marine Fighting Squadron in the Central Solomons Area from September 12, 1943 to January 3, 1944. He was shot down over Rabaul on the latter date, and his capture by the Japanese was followed by 20 months as a prisoner of war.

Ben also commented on the aftermath of Pearl Harbor : "The Army certainly took a licking . . . but I think the responsible parties got off very lightly . . . after all, an enlisted man goes to the brig for having his sleeves rolled up. And all a general or admiral gets for losing a fleet through negligence and bad thinking is a "naughty boy" admonition . . . If it's going to be military for enlisted men it ought to be military for officers too, even when they have stars. Democracy is a very fascinating subject. The idea should be given an opportunity to percolate in military circles. Incidentally, the

Chapter 11-Waiting for B. J. Day

Army is making a very revolutionary gesture. They're opening a restaurant for enlisted men *and* officers ... an experiment ... I guess they want to find out if there's anything to this democracy gag they've been hearing so much about for the last 2000 years."

Finally the day they were all waiting for arrived. "The VJ Day program came through here at 11:30 this morning ... we're repeating it again at 7:15 tonight.. I thought it was a terrific eyewitness account that the unidentified narrator gave ... he really saw it ... but a wonderful day for the world ... for Wainwright ... for the Dutch. For China ... for you and me ... and Pete and Linda ... I was moved deeply by the bigness of the occasion. I liked MacArthur's smooth handling, Truman's sincere speech ... the strong indication that the Japs are up to no tricks ... within a few days they won't be able to pull any ... we'll be in control of all waterways, communications, harbors, and will be busily disarming the entire nation. Then comes the hard job of making human beings out of them." 7

As WXLI reports from the surrender ceremonies went, the captain got the last laugh. His dispatch made it through and his interview with "Pappy" Boyington, the Navy flying ace who'd been freed from a Japanese prison, had been widely aired. A half-hour piece that Kani Evans was beaming back to CincPac was aborted in the first few minutes when the wire on his recorder broke, got completely fouled and ruined the show. The men at CincPac reported to Ben that Kani was heartbroken. This was to have been his hour in the sun: he had fought with the captain even to get air time, had been upstaged by his commander at every step of the way and then had suffered this mishap. While he surely shared Kani's disappointment, Ben must have felt particularly fortunate that he had not been selected to make that trip.

With the major event over, broadcasting was winding down into a very predictable routine. In fact, Phil Edwards suggested they ought to get a giant record changer with enough records to play all day. Ben commented, "Phil has a good idea." He mused about Labor Day, and the fact that "Pete must be getting to bed early so that he can go to school tomorrow," and looked forward to hearing about school instead of seashells. "It must be nice to know that the season is going to change. One day is just like the last one here, and just like the next one is going to be; after six months of it, I'm ready to quit. Incidentally, it will be wonderful to have a job I can quit if I want to." The next day, Tuesday, September 4th, was the first day Ben could speak freely in his letters. "This is a funny feeling. It makes the war really seem to be over . . . no one but you and I is going to read this letter . . . no one . . . unless you ask them to. Censorship ended today for us. That means I can tell you what we really think about things without thinking about possible consequences in the attitudes of those around me. I can tell you something of the war that just ended as it looked to me on Guam. It's a good freedom that foretells the greater freedom that will be mine when I'm out of uniform."

The following three paragraphs in his letter are a detailed description of some of the feelings that he and the men had with regard to their commanding officer, the good captain. Ben said that he had first started off trying out ideas, which the captain rejected, "but I found ways to do them . . . then he tried to balk me by complete non-cooperation, refusing the jeeps for necessary trips, etc. Finally I had a showdown in which he first said: cut all remotes and all special shows . . . next morning he backed down completely." Without going into too much detail, it may be sufficient to say that the words "square head," "heel," "miserable, small and ungenerous" are mentioned in Ben's letter, not uncommon enlisted men's views of their "superior" officers in those (or any) times. The captain, he said, "was born with a broom in his hand and talks about nothing but sweeping." But his most unforgivable act was that he had involved the radio station staff in a general weekly island-wide exercise, a one-hour drill, as a "punishment measure," a "disciplinary thing," that the men felt could have been totally skipped on the captain's say-so (Ben noted that he had done away with this requirement as soon as the captain absented himself).

Nevertheless, Ben had been very patient in dealing with his boss. The key to his success was that he started off very even-handedly, reserving judgment about the captain for a couple of months, while still showing a good deal of respect for him as his superior officer. He said Russ Beggs, quickly observing this situation, had promptly done a sit-down strike. He simply sat and read books all day long, doing just the specific things Cisler told him to, and that was absolutely all. Ben was unable to sit still that way, so he kept on trying and was glad. When Cisler went to the hospital and subsequently to Tokyo, he had made enough contacts and acquaintanceships around the island to enable him to carry on successfully. As recently as

Chapter 11-Waiting for B. J. Day 173

the past week, Ben had taken a big chance, changing the scheduling for the station to what he had wanted to do from the start; he had submitted the entire revised master schedule to headquarters at Oahu. "However," he said, "we're now sure Cisler is really being relieved within the next two weeks, which is a great relief to all of *us.*"[8]

Now that activities on Guam were winding down and it no longer mattered, success was heaped upon success. Captain Cisler's relief arrived. He was Army Captain Tom Smith, former program director at WPEN Philadelphia. He turned out to be in total sympathy with Ben's and Russ's programming concepts. "Phil Edwards once worked for him and is highly laudatory about him, and two of our guys know him from before and think he's swell." Not only that: he seemed like "a good Joe."

As his people continued to leave, Ben put in for and received three new personnel: a good announcer, an engineer—who actually was competent, compared with the one he had put up with for the past several months—and a new writer, who could relieve him of most of those duties he had shouldered himself. The icebox arrived. They obtained from the Signal Corps—and the new engineer figured out how to use—the aforementioned field transmitter to beam remotes from anywhere on the island back to the huge receiver at CincPac for wire transmission to the station, thus avoiding the many technical glitches that the use of delayed recordings had caused in broadcasting the shows.

Ben delegated more and more duties: Bud Blattner was carrying the sports shows, Don Davis was writing and producing *Answers Aweigh*, and Captain Smith was preparing to take over Ben's duties in operation of the station.

Ben found that, so excellent was the reputation of WXLI radio by this time, almost any request he made of a military command was immediately granted. As CincPac prepared to break up and leave the island, it appeared that the Marianas commander would soon occupy Admiral Nimitz's "cottage," Ben noted "as Life magazine so coyly described it." General Larsen would move up to the home previously occupied by the Marianas commander, and WXLI might soon be offered the sumptuous broadcasting studios that had been built for CincPac. But Ben had no interest; he was impatient and bored. Finding the means to go home was his sole preoccupation 24 hours a day.

In the course of radio station business, he made the rounds of his contacts on the island, seeking transportation home and news of a change in the rules for discharge. He also constantly monitored the news wires. But nothing could happen until he held the discharge order in his hand. On September 5 he wrote: "Hooray for Congressman Savage of Illinois... that's a vurra foin idee he has ... to release all men over 26 with overseas service immediately ... I hope he gets hot on it ... I was sure Congress would open for business with every housewife, mother and sweetheart sitting on its doorstep, and that within a few days, solid legislation will be on its way to bring some of us home faster than present plans provide."

He was also seeking the labor of some Japanese prisoners to do some landscaping outside the station. The Japanese prison was within sight of their barracks. "They work under armed guard all around and look sleek, well fed and happy. They ought to be: they're not only eating, but they make more money than they'll ever make in Japan." He noted that they had only partially believed the surrender, "but by now most of them are convinced... While I was in the Ninth Marines, there was a general roundup in which they sent out Japs to bring in Japs, and we picked up a party of 43 one morning on their way to surrender." [9]

Bud Blattner also had some observations to contribute about Japanese prisoners: "Half the guys in the service didn't know what they were fighting for. We'd go on patrol. There were Japanese hidden in trees. We'd shoot and they'd shoot back. We were trading two of them for one of our own. Finally we patrolled the perimeter only, just to contain them." He recalled that one day Bob Klinger, the great pitcher for the Pittsburgh Pirates, was stationed at a hospital at the edge of impenetrable jungle, seemingly peaceful, but actually quite dangerous. He went to the outhouse one night and was surprised by a Japanese soldier who had been hiding in there. "One time we rounded up a bunch of them, charging through the jungle with bull horns telling them in Japanese to come out. They appeared, marching out in military fashion. They were the most tattered, beat-up bunch—like something out of a shipwreck movie. We herded them into 20 or 30 trucks and drove them to the Japanese stockade. The general had to have a little house of his own, even in captivity. We could see them going through the chow line behind the barbed wire fence." [10]

Ben wondered whether there was a fast way to send his camera to

Chapter 11-Waiting for B. J. Day

him; cameras then cost over $100 on Guam (compare that to about $1000 in today's currency), and he would not pay it. His thoughts again turned to home: "My son by now is full of chatter about school. I saw the little Guamanian boys and girls go to school on their first day, which was Tuesday. They wear their very best clothes and for all the world looked very much like your classmates, Pete . . . except of course their skins are brown . . . and usually the boys are barefoot . . . the littlest boys walk barefoot on the sharp coral and never seem to mind it: their feet are tough from going barefoot all the time. Recalling the summer's earlier problems with the delivery of shoes for Peter, Ben was particularly careful to describe how the local boys managed without shoes, toughening the soles of their feet until they were not bothered by the sharp coral used in surfacing roads and walks.

"Once in a while you see a marble game; they try to play a lot of baseball since that's what they see the Marines and sailors playing most . . . and of course the only toys they have now are what they can make themselves, which isn't very much . . . They make little kites and sail those quite a bit . . . but mostly, they wander around and don't play as much or as hard as American boys do."

They had met and overcome every challenge at the Guam radio station. On Thursday, September 13, he wrote on new stationery, which bore in the upper right hand corner his own photograph, standing at the WXLI microphone. "Now you really have seen everything! Personalized stationery from the front lines. Lieutenant Downey did that for me, and the pictures, which are traveling under separate cover."

Ben at WXLI's microphone

He received a letter from Alice describing some very real problems. "But it wasn't enough to depress me after the news of this morning, that men over 35 and those with more than 70 points in the USMC were to be released immediately! I was in the clouds, and even to be a man over 35 without a job, but with a discharge, wouldn't be too bad."

He commiserated with Alice on Peter's latest problem: on his first visit the ophthalmologist had discovered a lazy left eye that would require him to wear glasses. This eye doctor was a medical school classmate of Alice's sister, Helen, who was also a pioneer woman in the field of medicine. Although Ben shared Alice's disappointment at another setback for their son, his typical optimistic reaction was to remind her that the eye doctor had been reassuring and felt that early care would result in correction of the problem. He quickly returned to his happy mood: "I can't help going back to the one thing that keeps running through my head . . . you're going home . . . you're going home. So far, there is no official order on it, although you can bet I was in the Sergeant Major's office at the crack of dawn to find out if there was. As soon as the order comes through, there will probably be a routine set up for handling it. I suppose it will start with a letter and take the usual length of time . . . but I ought to be home by Christmas, and that alone will be compensation. I can't hope to make it any sooner than that, although the miraculous could happen . . . anything could happen . . . this ought to be easy now, dear."

"As to us and the future, yes it does look like New York or the coast. Logic dictates New York, although I think we'd like Hollywood better. It's healthier, easier, more friendly and full of more things we like in life. We can come closer to having the kind of house we want and the physical life we want. Friends are where you make them and we can make them anywhere." What he did not take into account in his musings was that Alice's parents were in Chicago, and that she was the youngest daughter—the one who felt responsible for them. The family's exodus to warmer and more prosperous climes was not to be—at least not until many years later.

The party atmosphere continued. On September 15th, Ben apologized for not writing, with the excuse that he had "hung one on last night." They had completed their beer deal, and acquired 17 ½ cases from their navy ration, which was in addition to their army ration. "And then, because beer is loosening up all over the island, somebody dropped two cases off for us this morning, and this evening at *Sporting Chance* they gave us three cases to take home . . . we're really living the life of Riley . . . we have the run of the island, eat where we please . . . drink what comes our way . . . and don't do too much work." The scuttlebutt of the day was that all outfits were making up lists of men over 35 to comply with the order. While he hadn't seen it yet, he knew that a captain at communications would give him a copy of it in the morning. "Then I'll know what to do. I understand that the Marine Corps is anxious to make a showing and there seems to be some healthy competition developing among the Armed Forces to make an impression on the folks back home and upon Congress. Hurray, Hurray, Hurray!"

Ben felt a strong impulse to drink up everything in sight and couldn't get enough beer into himself. "Incidentally, Duke came down this afternoon and discovered that he's an old school chum of Smith's and they are Duke and Tommy to each other, which makes everything swell. We went to a Seabee outfit and did the best *Sporting Chance* we've ever done." Since they had new engineers that now responded to his suggestions, "our engineering problems have been greatly simplified. A couple of USO girls gave a party atmosphere to the scene."

"After the girls were taken home, we settled down to some serious drinking, and I haven't any idea what time we actually broke up. Nobody bothered us: we were very noisy, and two liberated prisoners of war spent the evening with us. One was a fascinating guy named Gabby Kohl, who talked and talked and told us all about what had happened, where they'd been how they had reacted and filled us full of details that were tremendously absorbing. Gabby was back tonight, and he's coming up again tomorrow night. He was in radio in a mild sort of way before he joined the Marine Corps and now he thinks he may return to Shanghai, where he knows lots of people, and which he likes very much. They were prisoners for four years. Pictures showing him before and after liberation are very sobering evidence."[11]

I confirmed the identity of the other former prisoner, the artist, in an e-mail from Edwin Smyth's son, Terry, who read my October, 2009, blog post and recognized the drawing style and the signature as the same as that of his father's fellow prisoner. Based on the date of the beer sketch, the younger Smyth explained that other prisoner in the room with Gabby Kohl and Dad was Leonard L. Rogers. Too bad my father didn't write down those details, but I understand why: this was the type of information he kept out of his upbeat reports to us at home. They would have been too sad. Terry Smyth told me those details in his e-mail message:

"In September 1939 Edwin Smyth left his sign writing business in Clacton-on-Sea, a picturesque Essex village on the English Channel, for duty to his country in the Royal Artillery. After serving in England and Sumatra, he was captured by the Japanese in Java on March 4, 1942 and sent back to Japan to Hiroshima #6 Omine-Machi (Sanyo prison camp) to work in a coal mine. When he came down with dysentery, his sign painting talents earned him a special duty job at the prison camp. But after six weeks, presumably because he showed signs of recovery, he was sent back to the mine.

"At the hospital," he explains, "Smyth met another artist, Leonard L. Rogers, a U. S. Marine sergeant. After the liberation, when it was time to sail for home, Rogers sketched an elaborate plaque for him as a farewell souvenir." The part with Smyth's portrait is shown here.

"I have one letter from Leonard to my father dated 7 December 1945," wrote Terry Smyth. "At that time he was living in Tacoma, Washington. Over the years, I have tried to discover whether I could contact any relatives but to no avail. I still hanker after making that connection. In the letter he says that he has a job awaiting him in 'advertising layout'. While the letter is generally upbeat in tone, for me the most poignant passage is this:

"'We shall always have many memories of the past to reflect upon and no one will be able to share them because they will never know how we prisoners spent months rotting in hell'."

Edwin G. C. Smyth by Leonard L. Rogers

CHAPTER 12

LIBERTY SHIPS: THE PRIVATEER

The wait for news of Ben's release from the military continued. He even expressed annoyance at the confidence Captain Smith showed in him by "dragging me around with him on his numerous errands, which is very inconvenient, because he uses up a lot of time and it makes me work at times when I should be doing some serious loafing. If I had me around at this stage of the game, I'd be very discouraged. I'm not interested in what we're doing and can't work up any enthusiasm for anything except going home."

Once he had some concrete evidence about his status he would look for ways of getting transported separately: "I'm in good with the USASTAF people (a couple of colonels and a captain). USASTAF is General Spaatz's setup, United States Army Strategic Air Force—and I told Captain Weiner that I was going home and hoped I could fly. He said they'd certainly do anything they could for me, if the need arose. The real trouble would be getting released by the Marine Corps so I could make such a flight. We're handling the USASTAF games, and I've been very nice to them." There was also a luxury plane that CincPac sent back to the states every day. "I met Commander Brown, the executive officer, today and helped him considerably on a problem. I'll follow that contact and, who knows, maybe I can swing something when the time comes, but even a ship won't be too bad: there won't be any 41 day trips going home . . . did I ever tell you it took that long coming over? That was a censorable item, I recall, since most of the delay was lying 14 days at Eniwetok, and four at Pearl Harbor."[1]

Meanwhile Ben began delegating more of his duties, including breaking in Wayne Center to do his job so he would have time to work on his discharge, which "may mean getting out to see lots of the right people, and especially working on the remotes, which is the place to make friends. I've given radios to everybody and his brother and picked up quite a few friends that way. But I may not be able to take care of anything any better than the Marine Corps's own plan, which is undoubtedly designed as a public relations gesture."

As his wait continued, he went to work helping his friends. He wrote to Mel Shauer, the studio executive in California, and (at Alice's suggestion) Stan Baer, creator of *The Toodles* comic strip—who with Ben's guidance had syndicated a show called *The Nebbs*—about finding outside work for Russ Beggs to do in addition to his California Army job.[2] These contacts soon resulted in an assignment to write for *The Nebbs*. Russ thanked Alice for her hospitality in a letter he wrote shortly after he visited her and the children in Chicago, and especially for hers and Ben's help in landing an assignment to write the radio show.

A few more days of boredom ensued. Responding to a letter in which Alice complained of problems in dealing with her family, Ben wrote, "Gee, honey bun, I wish I was there to make things go more easily . . . but it won't be long now despite the fact that the Marine Corps, after cashing in on the publicity attending the most liberal discharge plan to date, still has received no official dispatch here on Guam which will permit action favorable to B. J. DAY."[3]

Kani Evans returned, but the captain stayed on in Tokyo. "He ought to get along well with the Japs," noted Ben. "It will be nice to see Kani again, although it's going to be hard to live up to his idea of how a returning hero should be treated. Kani will undoubtedly feel and act as if MacArthur never would have pulled it off without him. Ben also coun-

Chapter 12-Liberty Ships-The Privateer

seled Alice not to get her father riled up by asking him for money to pay garage rent on the car, reminding her that he probably couldn't figure out how they were surviving anyway, how they could afford the trip to Annisquam and why they hadn't asked for help before this—the secret being Ben's supplementary checks from overseas, Alice's earnings from writing and help from her sister Helen and her husband. He also warned in a handwritten note that he might have to skip a day or two of writing letters, adding mysteriously, "It will be because until I know something. I can't possibly say anything—two or three days of digging and working should be productive."[4]

His next few days' work were indeed just that, because at noon on Monday, October 1, he sent a hand written letter: "Darling and my very fine son Pete (and pretty little Linda, who I am going to see much sooner than I ever hoped): Isn't it amazing? Wait until you hear the whole story." He had put his letter of request for discharge in at 8 a.m. the previous Monday, the minute it was permissible. Then he took the Jeep and rode out to see Wayne Thomas—the former aviation editor of the Chicago Tribune and the Navy commander in charge of CASU 12—a Combat Aviation Supply Unit. He asked him if he could provide any help flying home. He couldn't, and just had a suggestion—there was a B-24 outfit breaking up at Agana Field. Why didn't he go out there and talk to some of the flight captains? "It didn't sound like much," wrote Ben, "but it was a lead, so off I went . . . Agana Field is a monstrous thing with all sorts of side strips, and it took me almost two hours to find the planes I wanted."

There was a lieutenant standing alongside the first aircraft. He drove over and asked if this was the outfit stripping down to go to the states "Yup," he said. Did they have any room? Well, there were about 60 guys who wanted to go with them and there were two places still open, but he wasn't going to fuss with it. Brady, his flight captain, (an enlisted man) would take over. And with that the lieutenant drove off, leaving Ben with Brady and a couple of other guys. One of them wanted a ride too. Brady said he didn't know one man from another on his list of 60 and didn't know what to do. Ben said, "Why not just settle it now—here are two men—you have two places."

"Okay," said Brady. "Have your bag aboard by 4 p.m." It was already

12:30. Ben dashed back. "I got hold of Tommy Smith, our captain, and went over to see the colonel. He called in the sergeant major, and he finally said all right . . . told me to get the letter of request from the company office, bring it to him and he'd get my papers started." While he was on his way to the company office, the sergeant major called and told them not to send any more discharge papers over that day! Ben went back to see him and was practically thrown out . . . so back he went to get Smith. "We saw the colonel again," Ben reported, "and he was somewhat more than irritated by the sergeant major's maneuvers—told him to get going on my orders—I dashed to the plane with my bag, came back during chow time and checked the battalion office. A friend of mine was there and told me my letter of request had been approved by the colonel but that it had been labeled "Clear this man in the morning' by this character. Since the takeoff was for 7 a.m. Tuesday that would have queered me."

After chow he saw the colonel sitting in his office alone. He went in, apologized for the irregularity and told him what had happened. The colonel said one of the sergeants would be in and that he himself was going to be there late. He thought they could still clear Ben. "I took no chances. I went over and got hold of the office sergeant, whom I knew, got him into the Jeep, told him the story, and soon he was at work on my orders. It was already 8:30 p.m. At 10:30 he finished them. I dashed to the health office to get a clearance, got a few more signatures, and then took the whole mess to the colonel's tent . . . he signed it, wished me good luck, and I was off." Ben went back to the station, where the boys sat with him until one AM drinking beer. He had a short sleep, a shower at 4:30 a.m., and Don Davis and Dick Stern took him out to see him off. He got aboard the plane.

The aircraft was a *Privateer*—the Navy-Marine Corps version of the B-24 *Liberator*, as distinguished by its single tail fin. For Ben, it was a liberator anyway, but, traveling as a civilian again, serving only his own cause, he was the privateer.

"We sat down at Tinian for three nights and two days, hopped to Kwajalein, then to Johnston Island, and then to Kaneoke Field here on Oahu, arriving here Saturday. Everyone is amazed at my escapade—23 hours between filing my request for discharge and my takeoff for the

Chapter 12-Liberty Ships-The Privateer

states. It's unheard-of. Besides, I'm carrying my own orders, my record book and my health record. I haven't any time or place to report, and I'm strictly on my own."[5]

But never one to be without contacts, Ben quickly located his high school chum Chuck Mills at Pearl Harbor and spent Saturday night and most of Sunday with him. Since he was literally penniless by this time, he borrowed $100 from Chuck and asked Alice to send a check to his military address right away to reimburse him. He wasn't sure how badly Chuck needed it, "though he assured me he could spare it. Of course, I was flat broke—had ten dollars, which is gone. I've 'seen' Waikiki, the Royal Hawaiian, had two steak dinners, a luncheon at a private home (a la Chuck) and toured the island partially. I feel like a farmer—although I bought some unclaimed laundry this morning, and therefore can at least appear in starched khaki today, even though it probably won't fit." He was the only Marine in this giant Navy barracks, which amused everyone, and he had become fast friends with the crew of the "Punkie," the plane he had been flying on. He was also careful to stay away from the Marine barracks to make sure Marine red tape did not foul him up. He wasn't sure how he would arrange transportation when he hit the states, but assured Alice he would not hang around any longer than he had to "Of course I'll telephone immediately. Aren't we lucky? Don't get too excited and don't be impatient. Figure another month to be safe—I love you so much. Ben."[6]

The next day he reported that the base at Pearl Harbor was just like those in the States. In his uniform of starched khaki, except for the shoes (he wore his boondockers) he said he looked "something like a Marine now—anyway as good as Chuck, and he's a lieutenant." They had dinner the previous night at the privately operated Maniwana Hotel, next to the Royal Hawaiian. They had "a very ordinary meal, but it was *served*—there were tablecloths, ice water, napkins, and waiters—all pleasant reminders that soon life won't be chow lines, G.I. sacks and uniforms."

There was no news on the trip home; he reported he would not know anything till the end of the week and planned to relax, take it easy and catch up on "some of that sleep I lost, but I don't sleep as much as I dream about being home so soon." He found Oahu to be more honky-tonk than he had expected, and the beaches disappoint

The B-24 Privateer "Punkie" (right). Ben is shown above, with crew members J. W. "Mickey" Mickle, John W. "Johnny" Pollman, Jr. and W. R. Brady. There were ten passengers in addition to "Hub" Baskin, Carlton W. Stallworth, L. G. Wack, Richard Ogden, J. M. Frink and "Doc" Wilde, the crew members not pictured.

ing. While he suspected that the other islands were beautiful and worth seeing, he was "not much tempted right now" to go sightseeing. The climate was perfect after Guam, "although the men who have been no further think it is hot." He was happy to report that Chuck would be out by Christmas. With time on his hands waiting for transportation, Ben continued to jockey for improved status, consciously avoiding the Marine Corps, and going to the 109th Bomb Squadron for a liberty card. "After trying to understand

> my status, the executive officer gave up and gave me a permanent card, whereas they just issue overnight cards to their own men. At that I'm never questioned: I eat in any mess hall I choose—the others have to eat in the one they are assigned—no one ever questions my goings and comings, and the Marine guards never ask me for my identification. Maybe I'll be spoiled rotten when you get me, but I love you just the same."

On Wednesday, Ben felt like the life of the party, because Chuck had been introducing him to various people, "who expect me to tell them anecdotes about the war and be generally amusing. Actually, there have been no parties—Chuck's life has been somewhat dull. Limited financially, he has taken to doing mostly Navy things . . . consequently, he's enjoying my dragging him around to restaurants." He took Chuck to a new one he hadn't ever been to. "It was Chinese—very elaborate, in an unusual setting—a huge covered garden open on the sides where water cascaded down rocky cliffs. The food was good and I ordered about a dozen different dishes for us—which Chuck and Dick protested we'd never eat half of. We finished it and, amazingly enough, the bill only came to $2.00 apiece, which is the most inexpensive lavish meal I've seen since prewar."[7]

Ben spent his days exploring the island and looked for interesting activities, even borrowing Chuck's Jeep to make his rounds. "Chuck and I may go deep-sea fishing tomorrow. It costs $10, all tackle provided, and ought to be good here. I'm being good to Ben, you see! But I'm being very careful to be on hand every morning to get the latest dope—so far there hasn't been any." He was also careful, as always, to look good in his newly acquired uniform: "I'm a Marine dude now. All my khaki is starched stiff and, except that I'm still wearing boondockers. I'm in Honolulu uniform, which makes it easy to navigate, because all the guards are Marines; and since they are a very small detachment (100) they are very friendly and helpful to a fellow Marine."

On Friday, the day when he had hoped to rejoin the crew of the B-24 "Punkie" for the final leg of his trip home, he got the news: "Well, I'm back in the Marine Corps. It was a nice vacation and I hope the letdown isn't too sharp. I finally was bumped from my airplane ride, and after trying other airfields and seeing a Wing Commander at Kaneoke Field, I decided I'd have to turn in for surface transportation.

First, I went to Fleet Marine Force headquarters, told my story to a major, who in

Ben and Chuck Mills in Pearl Harbor

turn called transient center and told them I was to be placed at the top of the transportation list. I then got hold of Chuck for one last pleasant evening." They went to dinner and then drove across the island for his gear. He reported in about 9:30 that night and was billeted in the casual battalion. "So once more I'm in a tent. This morning I reported to Lt. Bishop, who said I would be placed at the head of the list—whether they will follow through or not, I don't know—but I ought to be out of here in a week at the worst, in 24 hours at the best. This should get me to the states no later than October 20. I'm still way ahead on the whole deal, and we ought to be together by the first week in November, which is more than we ever dared hope for."

It would be dull time, with nothing to do but wait. A list went up almost daily, at 11 a.m. He had to draw a lot of gear that he had discarded at Guam, because he was going by ship. "Seems silly, but Marines must *look* like Marines. There is the usual here—lousy chow, 'recreation rooms,' dirt and movies. I'll try to relax and take it easy until I get the word. There are only about 300 men in the transient camp, so maybe it won't be too tough. Also the Third Fleet is in and may clean out the whole camp. I'm very much in love darling and dream, dream, dream of you. Ben."[8]

There was one last letter: a single page, on which was jotted: "Sunday, 11 a.m. Darling: Change signals—I go aboard ship at two o'clock this afternoon! Love, Ben." It was enclosed in an envelope with 6 cents postage due, postmarked October 14, 1945. He was on his way. He no doubt made it to back to San Francisco in ten days or less, called one of his California friends to help arrange for the three-day train ride home and arrived in Chicago on October 28, 1945, as he predicted, exactly one month after his remarkable escape from Guam, and just a year and a half after he had set out so confidently for the war. As unconventionally as it began, his Pacific odyssey had ended.

CHAPTER 13

HOMECOMING: SCRAMBLED EGGS

When the boys come home,
We'll all be as merry
As merry as May,
We'll all be as merry as May.
—1940s popular song

Dad arrived back in Chicago on October 28, 1945, owing to his skill and to serendipity. He rode the Punkie from Guam to Pearl Harbor, boarded the Liberty ship Walter B. Cobb to San Diego and took a three-day train ride home. No doubt there was as moving a scene at Great Lakes Naval Center near Chicago when he returned as at the train station on the day of his departure. I don't remember.

I wasn't anxious to have this strange man reenter my life. After all, I had been "man of the house" during all that time. I had handled my mother well; I had things under control. For example, one summer afternoon, I was feeling neglected, bored and in need of some excitement. I dropped my shorts and underpants and relieved myself in the middle of my parents' bedroom floor. I was pleased to see the golden arc cascade into a big pool on the hardwood surface. When Mom discovered the puddle, she demanded, "How did this happen?"

"It just bubbled up, while I was standing here," I lied, eying my mother for signs of stress.

"Oh dear!" she exclaimed, as she added one more worry to her long list.

A week later, I was thrilled to see a big truck, hauling a trailer that belched smoke and roared with internal fire, pull up to the front of the house. This standard roofer's rig was what the neighborhood boys called a "tar burner." It was always exciting when a new kind of vehicle came: there was the traditional milk wagon, drawn by a horse that obeyed his driver's commands and advanced house by house as the driver made deliveries (on hot days, when we begged him, the milkman would give us chunks of ice); the ice truck, with a man in a leather apron, who carried huge blocks of ice with steel tongs to the iceboxes of homes that had no electric refrigerator, and the coal truck, whose bed would rise up and dump its load on the street for men to shovel into wheelbarrows, roll up the curb on a plank and pour through a window, down a chute and into the coal bin in the basement of the neighbors' house. When the roofers arrived I watched with fascination, first from the bedroom window—at the scene of the crime—and later from outside, as they placed in their ladders against the tall, two-story Victorian house, climbed with their buckets of tar to the roof and attempted to correct the mysterious leakage problem. They lifted the edges of the shingled surface, applied new strips of roofing felt to the valleys where the many gables intersected and mopped them in with coal tar pitch before laying the shingles down again over the black, sticky goo.

If my active brain weren't constantly inventing ways to torment my mother, her wartime experience might have been considerably more bearable. I later felt guilty over the fact that she could ill afford the expense of calling in the roofers on the off chance that a roof leak was the problem. My guilt was somewhat assuaged when I realized that no doubt she had immediately called her father, a general contractor, and he had sent out the roofers at his expense. But it was not just the cost: it was

Chapter 13-Homecoming--Scrambled Eggs

the aggravation, stress and disruption I caused that added constantly to her wartime worries. I felt more guilt when I realized how hard she would try to please me to make up in some way for my father's absence, and how many times I rebuffed her efforts, just to see her reaction. One hot summer day, long before ice cream was kept available in home freezer compartments, she carried an ice cream cone all the way home for me from the "little store," which was a long block away. "I didn't want an ice cream cone!" I screamed, and I began to bawl and make a scene. With no one to hand it off to, in utter frustration she stood it in a drinking glass on the kitchen counter. Now I really wanted the ice cream, but, realizing I was out of options, I watched it melt into a pool at the bottom of the glass.

The drafty old Victorian house was scary for a six-year-old. In particular, the basement was dark and forbidding. It was reached through a door in the kitchen from which one stepped down to a landing, turned left for a few steps, and then began to wind back 180 degrees to a long run of steep stairs down to the basement level. Since this was just a utility stair, not for show, as in the rest of the house, the 1890s carpenter had made treads of 2-inch-thick boards, no risers and a simple board handrail on each side, except on the winding turn, where special curved woodwork would have been necessary, so there was no railing.

Each time I descended the stairs, which I dared do only in the company of an adult, I was stricken with dread of the unknown. On the left, like the limbs of an ancient oak, huge warm air ducts branched out from a large cylindrical furnace which had been converted from coal to gas. I would watch as Dad went down there to fill a receptacle near the furnace door with water, intended to increase humidity in the house. Through the peephole and at cracks around the edges of this door I could see the blue and yellow flames and hear the roar as the fire-breathing monster poured heat upward into the house to counter the bitter Chicago winter. Up in my room I would often crouch over the ornate brass floor register which delivered warm air before getting dressed in the morning, and let the life-restoring warmth flood upward on my small, underwear-clad body.

Beyond the furnace a few bare light bulbs hung from the ceiling, making pools of light on the cement floor. But past these warm and inviting zones, visibility dropped off and I could just make out the rubble stone exterior walls, occasionally pierced by the glare of small high windows. When I was small I imagined that monsters and other spirits were hidden there, ready to pounce on me from the gothic, cavernous gloom. At the foot of the stair on the right was the laundry room, where Mom spent so much of her time.

In the rear of the basement, opposite the laundry room, was the water heater. Because of the large quantities of hot water we used and the age of the mechanical equipment in the house, Mom was advised by her contractor father to get a new and larger capacity water heater. After the new one was installed, she put an ad in the neighborhood newspaper offering the old water heater for sale. I remember following Mom early one Saturday morning to the basement as she showed the used tank to a man who needed one. As she was pointing out its features I said, "Oh, that old thing? It doesn't work anymore!" Despite Mom's protestations to the contrary, this ended the discussion and killed the sale. The next day, I was again following Mom as she trooped back up the steep stairs. When I reached the winder treads where the stair began to reverse, I stared with fascination at the open side where there was no handrail. I peered into the mysterious and inviting darkness down below. Inexplicably, I gathered my nerve and leapt into the void.

What possessed me at that instant I have often wondered and only recently begun to understand.

How easily I could manipulate my mother's emotions, discomfort with my power to destabilize the only person I had to guide me and the hidden hurt I bore from the absence of my father were apparently taking their toll in self-loathing and pain. The darkness promised peace, and relief from these heartaches. I was later shocked at how easily and painlessly the oblivion had come. Fortunately for me, it was short-lived.

"My, my!" said Mrs. Becker, our kindly gray-haired next-door neighbor, who sat in our living room, balancing a teacup and saucer on her lap. "He's stirring."

"Oh, thank God!" exclaimed Mom. I looked around and two other neighbor ladies were also sitting there, consoling my mother.

When I awoke, I was stretched out on the couch. Shaking off grogginess, I asked, "How did I get here?"

Chapter 13-Homecoming--Scrambled Eggs

Peter riding in Bluey

My mother was speechless. Mrs. Becker spoke: "You fell off the steps and hit your head. Here's your bedroom slipper—it flew off as you fell and punched a hole right through a screen!"

I felt a new bump on the back of my head. It hurt. I suddenly recognized that I had attempted to fling myself out of my house, perhaps even out of my life. A new awareness dawned. I hadn't realized I had the power of life and death in my own hands, in my own leg muscles, and I was terrified. Sensing I would be in big trouble if I confessed, I played along with the adults' explanation of what had happened. To her dying day, I never told Mom I had jumped.

The following week, my grandfather sent over a carpenter to build a handrail at the open turn on the basement stairs. He built a strong one, with three wide rails that would completely prevent even a small person from falling over the edge. While I had no plans to have another "accident" at that location, I felt reassured every time I came up the stairs and looked past the new railing into the fathomless dark.

Mom was relieved and overjoyed to have Dad back. Their letters had kept them close and in tune with each others' daily experiences, although they were half a world apart. This almost conversational correspondence, carried on by two articulate and talented writers, had smoothed over what could have been a rocky reunion; it probably allowed them to avoid some of the difficult misunderstandings and disappointments that many reunited couples faced in readjusting to each other after the war.

My parents were able to resume some comfortable family traditions: their quiet time at home before dinner, with a drink—in summer, rum and Coke or beer; in winter, Scotch and soda—good conversation and a rundown of the events of the day. Dad was thrilled to be able to go once again to the delicatessen on Saturdays and buy corned beef, salami, Swiss cheese and Jewish rye, topped off with a big kosher pickle. He would slice through the hard crust, pile his sandwich high, smear on plenty of dark spiced mustard, tune to the ballgame on the radio, pour a beer and settle in his chair for a great lunch. On Saturday nights Ben could again enjoy doing the cooking. He loved to broil thick steaks, rub them with garlic cloves and season them with salt and pepper. He would peel potatoes, cut them into round, thin slices and deep-fry them in Crisco. He would get excited when the fat reached just the right temperature to cause the rounds to puff up, just as he had seen in Paris. "Look, they're starting to soufflé!" he would exclaim. As each batch reached golden perfection, he would take them out of the cast-iron skillet with a spatula, put them into a brown paper bag, pour in salt, grab the bag by its neck and shake it up until the crisp chips were drained dry and seasoned. In summer, he topped off the meal with corn on the cob for a very special feast. Mom always taught me, "A man who can cook will never go hungry." In this, after Dad returned, I had an ideal role model.

Pete in sailor suit

The inevitable first clash between father and son developed, in fact, over Dad's cooking. Mom enjoyed sleeping late on weekends, and on this particular Sunday morning so did my sister, Linda. Always an early riser, Dad often prepared his own breakfast. On this occasion, a ham was left over from a family dinner; he sliced it off the bone, minced it, browned it in the pan, cooked it into scrambled eggs, put them on plates and placed them before us on the kitchen table. He began to eat.

"Uggh," I said.

"What's the matter? That's my special ham and eggs."

"It smells funny!"

"It smells good. Now eat your breakfast," Dad insisted, getting a little

Chapter 13--Homecoming--Scrambled Eggs

upset that his special offering was being rejected.

"No. I don't want it.!" I shouted angrily. I picked up my plate and dumped the eggs on the floor.

Ben had taken guff from officers, sergeants and his own reluctant fellow soldiers for too long; he wasn't going to take any from an ungrateful six-year-old, especially not a son of his. In fury he grabbed me, laid me across his knee and gave me several sound wallops on the behind. Terrified as well as hurt, I wailed in mortal agony.

Dad scraped the ham and eggs off the floor, put them back on the plate and commanded: "Now shut up and eat!"

Too frightened to disobey this unaccustomed order from this unfamiliar source, I suppressed my howls and, whimpering, choked down the detested breakfast. By this time, the whole household was awake. Mom appeared in robe and slippers, trailed by my 2-year-old sister, who was all eyes and ears. "What on earth are you doing to that child?" Mom demanded, to my utter relief.

"He threw his food on the floor. I taught him a lesson," he retorted. I don't know what happened next, but I suspect that the harmonious homecoming was over. Mom and Dad probably had their first fight in a year and a half; re-entry of the original man of the house had begun in earnest. I was never spanked again—Mom must have seen to that—and Dad regretted his impulsive reaction.

But some much needed Marine Corps discipline was asserting itself back home. Mom's tenure as both mother and father, which had stretched her to the limit of human endurance, was drawing to a close, and Dad was finally able to reassert his role, *in person*. I never forgot this incident. It has always flashed through my mind whenever I was about to take advantage of someone or trying to get away with something just because no one was watching. The memory that wrong behavior has consequences stuck with me.

As of that day, the readjustment process began.

The Green household headed back to normal. While I resented my loss of status as top dog, I felt a huge weight lift from me, as my sense of inadequacy to deal with things I didn't understand began to slip away. Now there was a boss, someone to ask, someone to rely on besides Mom. There was even someone to help me fight off evil spirits. While it would be years before I exorcised all the ghosts that haunted me during the war in that big, scary house, I had at least made a beginning.

Learning how Dad related to the outside world was my next initiation. A couple of years later, I went out with him on his Saturday errands. I vividly remember a scene he made in the Porges hardware store on 53rd Street one snowy December Saturday morning. I was about 12, and we were picking up some necessities to finish decorating for Christmas; we were on a simple quest for replacement bulbs for our tree. Back then, they were not sold in individual packages. Dad found the red, green, blue and gold bulbs he sought and began unscrewing them from the sockets in the 7- and 15-light strings. The clerk approached. "I'm sorry, you can't do that, sir!"

"What do you mean?" Dad fired back. "Where am I supposed to get replacement bulbs for my tree?"

"They come with the sets, sir."

As an expert in retail marketing and merchandising, Dad regarded this as an unforgivable mistake in merchandise distribution, a gaffe in customer courtesy and inadequate retail service; he scorned this clerk for evading his perfectly logical customer question. Besides, he wanted what he wanted and usually got it.

"I'm buying them anyway," Dad insisted as he continued unscrewing the brightly colored lamps and collected them in a pile on the counter.

"I'm sorry, I can't let you do that, sir. They come with the sets. How can I sell that string of lights without bulbs?" He began screwing them back in their sockets at the other end of the wire.

"Don't tell me your problems," he snapped. "I'm the customer."

I became uneasy. Now we had a situation on our hands, and I simply hated conflict. Why couldn't people agree and work things out? I wanted to sink into the floor with embarrassment.

"Get me the manager," Dad persisted. The manager arrived and was made aware of the issue, first by the clerk and then by Dad, in no uncertain terms. The manager stood firmly behind his clerk.

"They come with the sets, sir," he said in a cold and steely voice. He gathered up the bulbs and what by now was a tangle of green wire and mostly empty sockets and walked away. Dad's face reddened, the veins on his head stood out and he clenched his teeth. A triangular ivory shape

Chapter 13-Homecoming--Scrambled Eggs

popped out of his mouth fell on the floor.

"Dammit," he said. "My pivot tooth!" The clerk, who had been standing open-mouthed, his head moving back and forth as if watching a tennis match, just grinned. Dad bent over, picked up his tooth, turned on his heel and said, "C'mon, Pete, let's go." As we stormed out of the store, he ranted, loud enough for all to hear, "That's the last time I'll ever shop at Georgie Porgie's Hardware!"

Once the false canine tooth popped out, I knew I was saved, as I had been on a previous occasion, when, totally frustrated in a last desperate attempt to get me to go to bed, he had lunged for me in anger and had been stopped dead in mid-flight by dental failure. This false tooth replaced one Dad had lost in a fight back in his neighborhood as a kid. It broke off whenever he got really angry and put extra pressure on it, usually on a weekend, and he had to go around looking like a hoodlum with a front tooth missing—a terrible humiliation to one who put such stock in his appearance—until he could get in to see his dentist on Monday.

Such was life with my father. I would die a thousand deaths, embarrassed and apologetic for him and mortified for myself, but he had his methods and got things done. Clerks obeyed him, employees feared him, clients respected him. All—with rare exceptions, such as the Porges Hardware staff—complied with his wishes. At the office, the job always got done—Dad's way.

I always felt our family was unusual, different from others, partly because of the trauma of war, but partly because our family was formed by two unique and very different individuals. Most of my life, I was an outsider trying to fit in. Only as a teen, when I found groups which worked hard on joint projects such as theater companies, did I feel I belonged. Our furious activity drained us of energy, called for our last ounce of creative inspiration and made us forget our inhibitions and ignore our differences, uniting us in a common cause. But in ordinary, everyday situations, I felt like an alien, never at ease with my peers, sharing few of their interests and scorning their tastes and passions.

But if anything Mom and Dad, each from a family that had raised itself up from poverty, always said we were better—because we tried harder, thought more about things and made better choices. Later I learned our lives were not that different from other families: in those postwar days many lived in good homes, dressed well, attended good schools and did things most families did together. Even though Mom and Dad had made us feel the distinction between "us," with our better plan of living and "them," many other families in the late 40s and early 50s were going through the same self betterment process, There turned out to be fewer of "them" and more of "us" in an emerging and vastly expanding middle class.

But we were different in another significant way: my parents were from families of different faiths—and because they both felt alienated from their religious roots—they defiantly refused to subject their children to either of their family religions and their associated cultures.

Dad had consciously reformed himself. He recalled the self-imposed segregation of the Jews from the rest of society in the neighborhood where he grew up. He felt that adopting the telltale mannerisms, speech oddities, accents and dress of his family, friends and neighbors would shut him out of economic and social life in the booming American mainstream. He identified these limitations very young and strove desperately to cleanse himself of ghetto habits. He severed Yiddish expressions from his vocabulary, adopted standard pronunciation and dressed like his peers—especially after he was on his own in college.

While he encouraged me to hang out with my Jewish friends and loved them dearly, his antennae were out for signs of ethnic speech mannerisms, habits and actions. When he encountered them he corrected me mercilessly. While he did not discourage me from the practice of religion, I found it difficult to separate the two: if I wanted to be Jewish I would have to join the Jewish Community Center for recreation with my friends, and, while he had allowed me to join the YMCA so I could learn to swim and attend camp, membership in the JCCA was strongly discouraged..

Mom had a different reason to be estranged from her faith. She felt injured and limited by the burden of guilt that the Catholic Church imposed on her as a child. As we walked down 55th Street near St. Thomas Apostle school, which she had attended, she pointed out the St. Joseph nuns. They wore stiff-starched collars, white headpieces and frontal masks, the severely starched fabric completely encircling and pinching their faces. The rest of their bodies was shrouded in yards of the blackest wool, winter and summer. Mom told me about Sister Mary Agnes, who terrified her as a second grader by telling her that her conscience sat like a little bird on her left shoulder, spying on her every word and deed.

As a result, we attended neither church nor temple. Saturdays and Sundays were family time—for trips to the Museum of Science and Industry, special breakfasts together and visits with grandparents. When I approached my teens and my Jewish friends were preparing for bar mitzvahs and Christians were nearing confirmation, my parents told me I could select a religion of my choice. When you're a child, you know nothing about how to do that, so I began attending the Church of the Disciples of Christ with our neighbor, my friend Mary Frances, whose father was a minister. I had petty objections: I wanted the lead in the Christmas pageant, although my mother archly pointed out that Jesus would have been a short-lived role. I soon got bored with this activity, and I chose to stop attending. Dad would encourage me to attend reform Jewish services on the high holidays with his mother, and I did, but it made no lasting impression. I was awed at the unveiling of the Torah from its niche on the altar and the tale it told of the long and turbulent history of the Jews. Recalling my father's discouragement of any social involvement which made me appear Jewish, I was not sufficiently motivated to adopt this faith, either.

A memorable encounter with religion in my birth family was at the age of 13, when my Irish maternal grandfather died. We attended his funeral at Holy Name Cathedral, where he was given a high mass and a fine eulogy. Since he never attended, we assumed this praise was due to his generosity in supporting the church and his sensitivity in building their Cathedral school. In conducting me through this fine limestone-clad building, Grandpa showed me, for example, how he made sure that the blackboards in the classrooms were mounted at the correct height for the students in each grade—a fine touch that preceded the many school design innovations the Saarinens and Perkins & Will were to introduce to the American schoolhouse beginning in the 1950s. The archbishop's gratitude was also due, I'm sure, to my grandfather's careful limits on his construction charges to the cathedral treasury. During the priest's remarks I was distracted and embarrassed by Mom muttering in a stage whisper, "Well, if you'd had any kind words for *us* during his lifetime, perhaps some of his seven grandchildren would have been raised as Catholics!"

Thus we were reared, not without religious and moral principles, but without a formal "religion," that could identify us with a social group and a religious sect which would make orderly classification possible among friends, teachers and institutions. Even at camp or in the military, when it was time for services and for Catholics to go here, Jews to go there and Protestants to go somewhere else, I was often left sitting alone on the bleachers with one or two other like-minded individualists. But my family had made me fiercely proud of my non-affiliation. Even in filling out forms that asked for "Religion," I defiantly entered, "None."

Despite my ineptitude for sports, Dad loved to do things with his children and made a big effort after the war to spend time with us. When I was in seventh grade and my sister was in second, I expressed a desire to have a bicycle. He determined that, first, I should learn how to ride one, and he found a concessionaire renting bicycles at the edge of Jackson Park, near 57th Street and Stony Island Avenue. He, my sister and I would go out there on Saturday or Sunday mornings; he taught us both to ride, running alongside and propping the bike by the seat until we had attained balancing speed, and then letting go to prove we could stay up on our own. This was just before he showed me how to earn my own bicycle, which I did by selling subscriptions to the Chicago Daily News.

While he was growing up, Dad had lived in Englewood district on the city's South Side, just west of the park—site of the Columbian Exposition, the 1893 World's Fair. One Sunday morning as the three of us were riding, we sped across the first of two oriental bridges leading from the Wooded Island, a crown jewel of Frederick W. Olmstead's landscape plan for that fair. I was riding in the lead, with Dad following close behind and Linda bringing up the rear. As I approached the steep grade up to the second bridge, my foot slipped backward on the pedal, activating the Bendix brake instead of propelling the bike ahead, and my bike suddenly slowed down. To avoid hitting me, Dad hit his brakes; he flew off the bike into the air. The next thing I knew he was unconscious on the ground.

Chapter 13--Homecoming--Scrambled Eggs

Linda and I stood over him, both screaming, "Daddy, Daddy! To complete my state of total panic, a bearded vagrant in shabby clothes, fresh off a bender in the taverns on nearby 63rd Street, wandered by and said, "Oh, don't worry about him, he's dead!" Just at this moment Dad came to and said, "I'm all right," through half-open eyes, which then closed again. His Marine training to tuck and roll as he landed on the pavement had probably saved his life.

My adolescence and late teens brought on some rough times in my relationship with Dad. Probably because he had felt deprived of me in my early years, he wanted to hold on longer and found it difficult to free me to grow toward adulthood. In 1966 I saw a movie that characterized my situation perfectly: "You're a Big Boy Now," Francis Ford Coppola's thesis film at UCLA.

In this zany, offbeat classic, a young man named Bernard Chanticleer, over-sheltered by his parents, is just beginning to discover girls at almost 20 years of age. His tyrannical father is the curator of rare books—including the erotica collection where he whiles away his on-duty hours—at the New York Public Library. His son also works there as a book runner, gliding through the stacks on roller skates. When his father makes Bernard move out of the family home to become more self-reliant, he insists on selecting his son's living quarters and arranges for him to rent in a rooming house where a spinster landlady named Miss Thing rules the entry from her first-floor apartment. At night, she lets her misogynistic pet rooster roam the hall. Whenever a woman other than Miss Thing enters, the rooster attacks. It is a good system, as far as Bernard's overprotective mother is concerned. Bernard, meanwhile, is obsessed with sex and infatuated with Barbara Darling, his man-hating go-go dancing idol, who torments and baits him just to show she is more woman than he can handle. Frustrated, he eventually manages to lure Amy, a nice girl he has met at the library, back to his pad, in hopes of finally losing his virginity. The rooster attacks her, shredding the girl's stockings, ripping her clothing and inflicting scratches. After the fracas Miss Thing calls on Bernard's father at the library and pronounces, "I cannot tolerate this. I run a respectable boardinghouse!" His father retorts, "And I run a respectable son!".

Just so, I thought: he's not all that different from Dad.

In the climactic scene Bernard steals the priceless Gutenberg Bible in his father's care and runs with it held high above his head through the streets of New York, providing for me, in my mid-twenties, my first taste of vicarious rebellion, a good laugh at the whole state of affairs and validation: perhaps I really was the only sane person in my family!

In truth, I was a chip off the old block; the similarity to my father was comical. I was headstrong, stubborn and willful, and yet at times felt dominated, manipulated and demeaned. Once I lost a check Dad had given me for college expenses and asked him to replace it. He did, but not without a price. He made it out to Peter Dumbo Green and told me the bank wouldn't cash it unless my endorsement was identical to the payee's name. Thoroughly humiliated, I complied. But I never lost another check.

When I was thirteen, to further my education and give me an insider's look at publishing, Dad proudly presented me with the prerelease galley proofs he received as an adman's perk of Ernest Hemingway's novella, *The Old Man and the Sea*. When I read it I felt, like the old man himself, battered by struggle, wind and storm—a survivor, not the worse, but the stronger for my exposure to the tribulations of my youth. It may have been a battle of titans, but, like Dad's war with the Marine Corps, the glory was not in victory or defeat, but in the struggle. While he lived, it was a draw. When he was gone, I grieved for many years over loss of this worthy competitor, who was also my mentor and my best friend.

Peter and Ben sparring

CHAPTER 14

MAKING UP FOR LOST TIME

I wish I could tell you about the South Pacific. The way it actually was. The endless ocean. The infinite specs of coral we called islands. Coconut palms nodding gracefully toward the ocean. Reefs upon which waves broke into spray, and inner lagoons, lovely beyond description.

I wish I could tell you about the sweating jungle, the full moon rising behind the volcanoes, and the waiting. The waiting. The timeless, repetitive waiting.

But whenever I try to talk about the South Pacific, the people intervene. I try to tell somebody what the steaming Hebrides were like, and the first thing you know, I'm telling about the old Tonkinese woman who used to sell human heads. As souvenirs. For fifty dollars!

Or somebody asks me, "What was Guadalcanal actually like?" and before I can describe that godforsaken backwash of the world, I'm rambling on about the Remittance Man who lived among the Japs who sent us radio news of their movements. That is, he sent us the news until one day.

—James A. Michener, *Tales of the South Pacific*, 1947

"Hey, Green," said Lenny, in his gruff, Seabee voice, "You're an artist, aren't you? I need you to do the boat on my stomach. Come an hour before the cast call tonight so you can draw it."

I was thus approached during the dress rehearsal of *South Pacific* by Leonard Stone—in his faded blue shirt with sleeves rolled, slouchy dungarees and weather-beaten sailor hat—who played the role of Luther Billis. So great was my delight in having this important part in creating his character, I could barely resist saluting, saying. "Aye-aye, sir!" It was the talk of our family dinner table as I bolted down my meal so I could show up earlier than usual.

Launching Billis's Belly

When I sat down in the scene shop to do this elaborate make-up job for Billis—Stone, that is—he handed me one of those indelible pencils with one sharpened end red and the other blue, and told me to create a two-masted schooner precisely in the center of his belly. Using both colors I drew a graceful sailing ship, straining in the wind, headed from left to right, with several square sails billowing out toward the bow. The two masts sloped gracefully from front to rear, accentuating the impression of speed. Checking the mirror, he scorned my first attempt: "Naw, dammit, that's not it!" he cursed like a sailor, as he scrubbed off my efforts with a wet cloth. "Here's how to do it!" He grabbed a scrap of brown wrapping paper and with emphatic strokes drew the same ship, but foursquare, its masts perfectly vertical and sails trapezoidal and flat, with lines much thicker and bolder than I had dared inscribe on his famous abdomen. Finally, he was satisfied, and I was invited to come back every night to reestablish the accepted design.

That night I got a front row seat for the action. Owing to our penny-pinching producer's tight budget, I, along with the other male apprentices, joined the singers and dancers, assuming positions around the perimeter of the round stage floor as the onstage military audience. When the lights came up, Billis appeared in his grass skirt and halter top made of half coconut shells, blonde wig and smeared lipstick. As

Chapter 14-Making Up for Lost Time

the chorus broke into "A Hundred and One Pounds of Fun," he edged his way toward center stage.

The trombone blared at the conclusion of the third line and the verse ended. The orchestra repeated the tune, and Marvin, our punch-drunk drummer, launched into his drum solo, his black hair flying: BOOM- boom-ba-doom-doom, BOOM-boom-ba-doom-doom. Billis sprang into action. His hips gyrated, the grass skirt swayed and the blond mop flopped. He was in his element, in total control. He relaxed, lifted one cup of his halter top, took out a pack of cigarettes and matches, lit one and replaced the pack. As his audience of sailors and soldiers, we clapped, hooted and cheered. Gripping his smoke tightly with his lips, he puffed, raised both arms and started to bump and grind.

The ship caught the wind. The waterline undulated; the hull bobbed on the swells of his gut; sails alternately billowed and collapsed in the gale, and foam splashed from Billis's stomach as the schooner knifed through the waves. When I saw how Lenny performed the number, I immediately knew why he didn't need to have any motion expressed in the line work of my drawing. In assuming the total effect rested on my artistry, I had forgotten to allow for his!

I set down this episode in my own early career only to explain how I learned about South Pacific, helping to design and build scenery for shows at this professional summer stock company. A faint reflection of the horrible reality of war, this production showed the funny side of the military; it suited the postwar mood of many Americans, especially Dad. An evening at the theater was one of the many luxuries Dad could enjoy again. something he could do for his family- once he returned from the Pacific theater.

After he had reestablished his broadcasting and advertising career, still craving the warmth of the tropics, Dad planned elaborate family vacations in the Florida Keys. On one such trip I found myself aboard a deep sea fishing boat at eight o'clock in the morning.

"Wa-a-ahnd, boah, wahnd!" hollered Captain Angus in my ear. At 17, slight of build, I could barely fill the fishing chair, much less crank the heavy duty Star-drag reel, mounted on a fishing rod the thickness of a table leg, which the captain had thrust in my hands. Now

I had a worse problem: a huge bottom-fish had taken the anchovy bait and settled in for a good fight. Moreover, as I wound, the dead weight at the end of the steel wire he used for fishing line resisted and more line went out than came in. Eventually I got the hang of it and the monster tired. About an hour later Angus hauled my catch over the gunwale with a gaffe, and both my prize, a 30-pound grouper, and I lay spent and exhausted on the deck.

Dad had roused me from a sound slumber at 5:30, hours before the time I liked to wake up on vacation. He prepared our breakfast and a bag lunch, and with Ralph, another guest at our hotel, drove at dawn in our rented Ford to Whale Harbor, a short run on U.S. 1 from the hotel in Islamorada on Lower Matecumbe Key.

They had arranged to split the cost of chartering a vessel for a day of deep sea fishing in the waters of the Gulf Stream. We arrived at the docks early on this April morning, as the sun broke through the remaining clouds on the eastern horizon. A stiff offshore breeze, the remnant of a squall that passed through overnight, promised a clearing and warming trend. Before us a dozen or more slips projected from a manmade crushed coral jetty, which enclosed a rectangular marina. Captains and mates were preparing the three or four boats still in the harbor to set out for the day. We soon located the *Muriel II*. Unlike the sleek sport fishing craft we had seen in harbors and in ads for Florida, she was a sturdy, stocky boat, painted white with two outriggers stowed upright at its sides.

As we approached, a solidly built man in matching gray shirt and work pants backed out of the cabin and plopped several life preserver cushions on the benches. He noticed our group.

"Howdy! Ah'm Cap'n Angus Boatwright," he boomed in a thick, Florida twang. He straightened to his full height. Under the visor of a worn Greek fisherman's cap, his high cheekbones and well-tanned leathery face revealed a nautical squint in his deep blue eyes. Muscular arms projected from his short sleeves. He offered a meaty palm to Dad, who had organized the expedition, and greeted Ralph and me.

"We gonna fahnd yew some *fish*, boah!" he said to me, and invited us to climb aboard. Dad did so and I handed him gear—jackets, cameras, beer and sack lunches and hopped on. A partially enclosed cabin served as

Chapter 14-Making Up for Lost Time

the wheelhouse, where some add-on video screens and radio components crowded the dashboard. Simple benches lined the sides and two swivel-mounted, varnished wood fighting seats dominated the stern.

Soon the captain started his powerful twin diesel engines, cast off and set out We nosed out of the narrow neck of the harbor; he opened the throttle wide, and we roared into the bay. A light chop was on the water. As the sun began to warm us from the chilling rush of sea air, the scrubby low shoreline of the Keys receded and gorgeous azure patterns on the shallow reef bottom alternated with deeper patches of royal blue. Dad, normally tense and in control at his office in Chicago, seemed totally transformed. Reclining in one of the fishing chairs, in Bermuda shorts with his feet on the rear fish locker that doubled as a seat, he chatted with Ralph, who occupied the other chair at his right. As he sunned himself under his familiar khaki fishing hat, with both a brim and a bill, he was the picture of total relaxation. Ralph, who was bigger, overweight and not accustomed to the sea, appeared less at ease.

The aquamarine of the coral flats gave way to deep green; the night's steady winds had roiled the water enough to make our 24-foot fishing craft rise and fall rhythmically as we plowed through a 6- to 8-foot swell. I was feeling a bit queasy myself. The captain observed our condition. "Focus your eyes ahead on the horizon. You probably had too much milk for breakfast. That'll do it every time."

After we had been under way for about an hour, I had just begun to get my sea legs, unconsciously compensating for the rocking of the boat by alternating flexure in my knees, and was beginning to feel like an old salt, when I noticed the rocking subside and watched as we crossed a clear line of demarcation into calmer, ultramarine-colored water. The captain pulled right on the wheel to resist a strong drift.

"Here's the Gulf Stream," Angus announced. I marveled that this famous current, so vital to moderating the climate of northern Europe, and of such interest to sailors, was so easy to recognize. Apparently it was also important to the fish, and, consequently to our guide.

The captain slowed the engines, changed course to parallel the line in the water and flipped a switch. The screen in front of him glowed with phosphorescent blips, each accompanied by an audible beep, which faded and then reappeared as each burst of energy refreshed the image.

We chugged along at this pace for a while. Suddenly, the blips and beeps increased in number and frequency, in a staccato rhythm that stimulated the captain and aroused Dad's curiosity.

"What's that?" Dad asked, as he refocused his attention and accustomed his eyes to the dim interior of the cabin.

"Here they are!" exclaimed Angus, "On the edge of the reef."

"How do you know?" asked Dad, puzzled.

"I can see 'em with the Sonar!" exclaimed Angus proudly.

Pan-fishing in the shallows

Dad and Ralph had the first turn to fish. Angus baited larger hooks than I had ever seen with 8-inch mackerel. The two men got strikes almost immediately.

"Whee!" Dad squealed as he felt the tug, watched his line play out and yanked his pole up to set the hook. This was a sporty fish, causing Dad a thrilling struggle. When he got it landed on the deck it was beautiful in form—handsomely tapered from its snubbed nose back to a concave-peaked dorsal fin to its perfectly regular tail fins, with a subtle tawny stripe down the mid line tinting its sleek silver surface.

"Ambah-jack!" roared the captain, "Mighty nice size, too. Maybe 40 pounds."

Over the next two hours the three of us hauled in twenty more fish—mackerel, jack, pompano and grouper—almost filling the huge locker at the stern. I was thrilled to catch a dolphin, a blunt-headed fish with a beautiful, continuous blue dorsal fin and a speckled yellow and green body that lost its radiant colors minutes after it was pulled from the water. This is a different genus than the playful marine mammal most people associate with the name—in Florida the latter creatures are called por-

Chapter 14-Making Up for Lost Time

poises in order to make the distinction. We had watched them entertain at a tourist attraction called Theater of the Sea, where Jeannie, the kissing porpoise, gave hourly performances.

When the frantic activity subsided, we took a break to eat our lunches. while the captain took us out to troll in deeper water. Ralph and Dad again cast out their lines. It was only a few minutes later when Dad got a massive strike. It bent his pole almost to the waterline. He had to set his feet against the gunwale to avoid being hauled out of the boat by an undersea monster.

"Z-Z-z-z-zzz," went the reel, as the force of the fish exceeded the drag setting and paid out more line. Dad yelped and wound furiously. He had very little line left when his cranking started to gain on the undersea creature. He gained for a few minutes until the fish, with redoubled energy, made another lunge, taking back all the distance he had gained. With his faced reddened, his teeth set and the veins of his forehead bulging, Dad began to wind again. After almost an hour of solid work, he drew the fish close to the boat.

The captain peered over the side. We looked as a huge shape loomed up near the suface.

"Hamma-head! At least eleven feet," the captain bellowed. Simultaneously the monster eyed the dark shape of the hull above it in the water, recoiled in terror and took out half the line again. Dad braced and held on. The captain revved the engines, trolling faster in an attempt to tire the fiend. Sweating profusely despite the fresh ocean breeze, Dad resumed the struggle. An eternity elapsed while, straining his sore arms, he reeled in the fish once more. Taking no chances this time, Angus got out his boat hook and held it ready. He leaned over, gaffed the fish by its primitive gills, grabbed the line and had Dad hold it high. Ralph grabbed the

Ben with a tarpon.

gaffe pole and held the shark partially out of the water. Its two eyes were spread some 20 inches apart, their beady protrusions at the extreme hammer ends of his skull staring angrily.

The creature bared triangular teeth in the ugly gash of his jaws. Captain Angus pulled out his automatic pistol and fired one shot at an indentation located dead center in his head. He would have had to miss badly, I later joked, to avoid getting him right between the eyes. I snapped photos in rapid succession. The monster slumped, lifeless. The captain grabbed his pliers and cut the steel line, as the deadly predator slid back into the depths and became the prey of other sea creatures.

"We won't miss him," Angus said with satisfaction. Although we had already released some fish alive that day, he noted that the great hammerhead shark—this one was a large specimen of its species, weighing over 500 pounds—are angry predators, sometimes even cannibalistic, and consume all types of game fish, octopus and crustaceans."Those bad ones ruin the fishing for everybody."

Back at the marina, Angus offered us as much of the day's catch as we could carry. Even so, he still had 300 pounds of fish to take to market. Gulls, pelicans and cormorants swooped in and scooped up the scraps, excess bait and fish parts he dumped in the water.

That night at Sid & Roxie's *Green Turtle Inn*, after an appetizer of Roxie's famous turtle flipper chowder, with just a dash of sherry for flavor, we dined on Dad's own amberjack, garnished with almonds, seasoned and broiled to perfection, with Key lime pie for dessert. We were living off the land and the sea, enjoying the fruits of our day's hard labor. It was an unforgettable feast, complete with sea adventures that we recounted well into the night.

Back at college two years later, on Saturday, April 23, 1960, I heard a news broadcast over the radio: "Captain Angus Boatwright, who docked his charter boat at Whale Harbor in the Florida Keys, departed today for the Bahamas with a mate and four fishing customers on the Muriel III. Off of Elbow Key, two Texas desperadoes out of gasoline and stranded at the lighthouse, swam out and shot the captain twice. He later died."

To hear of such a tragic ending to our gallant and unforgettable captain's life—such a big story that it made the networks—was inexpressibly sad. I later learned that the four fishermen had somehow been allowed to escape to safety before the desperadoes made off with the boat and that the murderers fled to Cuba. Angus's widow later retrieved the Muriel III. Boatwright's rifle was recovered with a jammed bullet in the chamber. Piracy was still alive in the Keys.[1]

On the many days when we were not deep sea fishing, Dad would take us to Bud 'n' Mary's dock, where we would rent an outboard skiff for a day's local fishing in the bays and shallows, on the western, Gulf of Mexico side of the Keys. Plying the inshore grass beds, mangroves and canals, using two dozen live shrimp as bait, we could pull in many pan fish of every color and description in half a day. Linda could not stand to bait her own hook with the lively, energetic crustaceans, so when she came along, Dad did it for her. Mom sat out most of these fishing jaunts; she preferred to sleep late and read her mystery novels by the pool.

Ranging from 6 to 10 inches in length and weighing ½ to 2 pounds, these fish came in all varieties. Very common were the beautiful yellow tail snapper, with its iridescent blue body, marked with yellow spots above and horizontal stripes below, a distinctive yellow stripe running along the mid-line and yellow fins, including a large, perfectly symmetrical and deeply forked caudal fin. A cousin of this fish was the mutton snapper, with yellow fins above and pink below, including the lower half of the tail, various kinds of drum fish; the Atlantic croaker; "spot," a fish without barbs below the mouth, distinguished by a dark blotch above the gills, and the "grunt," which got its name from the noises it made, to my amazement, after landing in the boat. Most of these small, inshore fish made wonderful eating. We frequently cleaned them, took them back to the Islander and had a great lunch or a big fish fry for dinner.

On all-day jaunts, we would go to another location in the afternoon, sometimes trying our hand at bonefishing, an art that Dad—as impulsive, demanding and impatient as he was in business—pursued with seemingly endless forbearance; he somehow found it in himself to sit all afternoon in absolute silence, trying to coax the wily and skittish bonefish to take his bait. Whenever he did, his efforts were repaid manyfold with a thrilling fight. In several attempts I never got a strike, nor did I even see a bonefish; when Dad later proposed all-day bonefish expeditions with a guide, I declined.

Dad and I set out one blustery March morning in a Bud 'n' Mary's outboard to try our luck. following his hunch that fish congregate around bridge piers under the highway. The sole route connecting the Keys together is the Overseas Highway, U. S. 1, a 159-mile road linking Miami with Key West. The Keys were first linked by a railroad, completed in 1912, the brainchild of Henry Flagler, a Standard Oil partner of John D. Rockefeller, who envisioned an American Riviera extending from St. Augustine to Key West. He set out in 1905 at age 75 to begin the railroad's extension from Miami into the Keys.

Portions of today's highway were constructed as early as 1917. Plans were already under way to continue the highway when the 1935 Labor Day hurricane ruined large sections of the Florida Overseas Railroad. Florida's road department bought the roadbed and built bridges for this new roadway, which was dedicated in 1938 and operated as a toll road until 1954. Flagler's vision lives on with this intriguing highway and its 42 bridges, which connect the chain of 40-plus inhabited islands in the southernmost region of the continental United States. [2]

We cast out our lines under a bridge just west of Lower Matecumbe Key and hoped for the best; Dad had heard some mighty big, old fish lurked there, feasting on the many crustaceans and small fish that twice daily were swept with the tides through the channel between the Atlantic and the Gulf. He was not disappointed. Just a few minutes later, Dad got a solid bite and felt a huge strain on the end of his line. Attempts to reel him in were limited by the strength of the line: with light tackle the drag on the reel had to be set to yield when the tension would exceed its 20-pound capacity. It was a standoff—just my old man and the sea.

The big fish wouldn't quit and neither would Dad. He let the creature drag him and our boat around the bay for four hours, while we shivered in a stiff gale. When the fish, in exasperation, I suppose, finally headed out into the Atlantic, with the tide and offshore wind behind him, Dad at last had to admit it was a draw. He cut the line, crushed that he had lost this battle with a Titan of nature.

Back at the dock, Bud expressed amazement at our story. "Why you hooked that old jewfish that hangs around under the bridge. Nobody's ever landed him. We think he weighs about 600 pounds, close to the Florida re-

Chapter 14-Making Up for Lost Time

Alice and Linda by the Islander pool, April 1961

cord!" The lifespan of this species, which is in the grouper family, is 30 to 50 years. It's just as well Dad didn't succeed. Although I don't know what the game laws were back then, today jewfish are protected from harvest in Florida waters. He might have ended up doing 30 years himself!

Dad was enchanted with the Islander, founded after the war by Leo Samuels, a Chicago lawyer who discovered the potential of the Keys for p peaceful idleness in a glorious climate. He and his wife Helen decided to develop an unpretentious resort hotel, with no entertainment, activities or unnecessary distractions from the sea, the sun, the coral sand and the rustle of subtropical breezes in the palms. Discovering the genius of the site, architect Robert Law Weed arranged two dozen, long one-story hotel blocks in a V-shaped herringbone layout, facing inward to a landscaped central corridor leading to the sea. He placed the swimming pool in the space in front of the last row of buildings. Beyond lay a coastal row of native palms, with a few shuffleboard courts, some white wood Adirondack chairs facing the water, the Atlantic beach and a fishing pier.

The buildings had single-plane sloped roofs, their high sides facing the ocean, to capture the afternoon onshore winds. Jalousie blinds on the window openings afforded continuous cross-ventilation day and night. The units were simply furnished with a studio couch along each side, a dining-game table at the central bay window and an efficiency kitchen along the rear, in front of the bathroom. I recall napping during the heat of the day in the cool interior of the room, lulled to sleep by the gentle rattle of palmetto fronds in the breeze, the sweet smell of the sea air across my face and shadows adorning the textured white walls. The resort remained in the hands of the Samuels family until 1999, when a new owner took charge and set out to improve the buildings and site without losing its 1950s look and feel, which remains at the time of this writing.

In the late afternoon, after sunning, swimming, a shower and donning a fresh pair of shorts, shirt and sandals, I entered my parents' unit through the connecting door for an Islander cocktail. This drink combined cut-up Florida fruits—oranges, grapefruit segments, pineapple, pears, peaches and bits of maraschino cherry, made abundantly and economically available in glass jars at the local grocery store. We poured the contents, with their natural juices into a tall glass and spiked the concoction to taste with rum, a genuine tropical treat.

My parents' daily drinking regimen often started with a couple of beers at lunch and continued with dinner and after-dinner drinks. While this routine might be considered dissolute today, to Mom and Dad, who had been through *both* prohibition and the war, and to me as a young collegian in a era when the rite of passage included consumption of large quantities of alcohol, it seemed perfectly appropriate adult activity.

To Dad the Islander meant having the tropical island paradise he had seen on Guam and so longed to share with Mom and his family, without fear and the smell of death hanging over the incomparable beauty of the scene—the South Pacific without the war. He was content, with his loved ones around him and time to pursue his favorite pastimes and pleasures: swimming, fishing, all he wanted to eat and drink and the company of friends and family.

Alcie and Ben had vowed to take each other for better for worse. "But when does the good stuff start?" they joked. After the war they were determined to make up to themselves and to their family for all they had sacrificed during the war. The growth economy of the post-war era—in conjunction with Dad's genius for publicizing, promoting and growing

Chapter 14-Making Up for Lost Time

businesses—cooperated and gave them enough money to treat themselves and the family to some of the things they had always wanted.

The fishing vacations in Florida were just part of the cure. When we were younger, my parents took my sister and me to the circus, to ball games and to special performances, like the Sonja Henie Ice Review. Sonja Henie, who started skating and dancing as a child, won the gold medal for figure skating at the 1928, 1932, and 1936 Winter Olympics. Born in Oslo, Norway, Henie pioneered the use of modern stage effects in figure skating. In the 1950s she took her spectacular ice productions on the road, featuring innovative choreography, lavish costumes, imaginative lighting concepts and rich musical themes. She received high critical acclaim for these shows and developed a broad and appreciative audience for ice skating. Mom, who often could watch a production or a movie and go home and recreate the dress she saw on the screen, loved the costumes. In one number, the troupe of some 30 skaters appeared as a legion of swans, gliding majestically across the ice, which had been transformed by lighting effects into a shimmering blue lagoon. She burst onto this scene in a blaze of eight carbon-arc spotlights as a sparkling white swan, doing the arabesques, and acrobatics that initiated ice skating's popularity as a spectator sport, a trend Dorothy Hammill and today's Olympic champions made magical for yet another generation.

Baseball games were an event Dad had missed during the war. Because his agency had the Wrigley account, he occasionally had access to box seats along first base line at Wrigley Field. Dad was so grateful to be back with his family and so thrilled to have the money to attend the game in style—something he had never experienced as a child—he spoiled us with anything we wanted at the games. Catching on quickly that he was a soft touch in this department, my sister and I would make sure that no vendor's cry—"Getcher pea-nuts hea-AH!"—went unheeded, and we asked Dad to buy us peanuts, soda, hot dogs and then ice cream bars. He also bought us programs and pencils and taught us how to keep a box score. Mom dealt with the stomach aches later.

One day at the ball park—Phil Wrigley was the last holdout in resisting night games—when the Chicago Cubs were hosting the New York Giants, Dad took me over to the low wall separating our seats from the first base line. He called to the Giants first baseman as he began to leave the field for the seventh inning stretch. Bud Blattner, who had just tucked his glove in his back pocket and was expecting to see Dad, came over and chatted with his former Marine buddy. This was not only my first time to meet Bud, it was also the first time I had met a real baseball player. Just observing his casual loping pace, grasping his huge hand in a relaxed handshake and seeing the texture of his pin-striped Cubs uniform close up, as well as real dirt on the base paths and foul balls we could almost reach, made baseball real for me. I became a fan at that moment and have loved the game Dad introduced me to ever since.

Before there were Disney World and Six Flags, I would beg Dad to take me to the amusement park. On a summer Saturday, my friends, Mike, Christopher and I crossed with Dad beneath a wide arched portal, its buttressing towers topped by pointed Turkish domes, and sauntered along the midway. We sampled the cotton candy and chose our rides and fun houses. Dad bought a string of tickets as long as his arm, something he could never afford as a kid, and we were in paradise. This was our long-awaited trip to Riverview, one of the last of the old-fashioned amusement parks, on the west side of Chicago.

We started out tamely enough: Mill on the Floss was a lovely float in self-guided boats past gardens, under waterfalls and through tunnels. Some of the craft were just big enough for two—it was a real tunnel of love for those old enough to care about such things. Next we got a little more daring and resolved to Shoot the Chutes. We climbed into boats with about 20 other people seated in rows and rode a lift to the top of a huge incline, some 75 feet in the air. We peered down two parallel ramps of flowing water. At the signal, an attendant released the boat and we gathered speed until my heart was in my mouth, too scared to scream, and then splashed gently into the pool at the base of the slope. We spied the Pair-O'-Chutes, the first civilian parachute jump tower in the country. Neither of my friends, Mike and Christopher, had the daredevil gene, nor did I. For Dad, it was all too real—he had been too close to plane crashes and unsuccessful parachute escapes on Guam to need this kind of excitement or force it on children, whom he wanted to shelter from such horrors. This thinking also ruled out the Blue Streak, reputed to be the world's highest and fastest roller coaster. We did ride the Flying Turns, a tamer ride, relocated from the 1933-34 World's Fair, which was heart-stopping enough for us to get our fill of excitement.

Chapter 14-Making Up for Lost Time

Dad's favorite attractions were the shooting galleries. The land for Riverview Park itself was originally assembled by a group of German-Americans who needed space for a shooting club. A Marine Sharpshooter himself, Dad liked to try his skill whenever we went to a county fair or a park like Riverview. If the game was honest, he would often win a teddy bear or other stuffed animals for my sister or me.

Since Mike was familiar with Riverview, he served as our knowing guide: he guided us to the Aladdin's Castle fun-house—a sprawling Ottoman palace with crenelated walls, towers and minarets, from the center of which loomed up a huge image of of Aladdin, beckoning all to come inside and experience his funny mirrors, air blasts, spooks and an exit slide back to ground level.

After a full day of rides, hot dogs and cotton candy, we still had many unused tickets. I watched as Dad split a long ribbon of them into parts and handed them to three young black boys standing outside the park. "Here guys," he said. "Go in and have some fun!" Overjoyed, they raced to the entry portal, eager to get in on the excitement. I suddenly realized Dad would have been one of them when he was young and poor; he got pleasure from sharing his good fortune with those not as privileged.

Only as a teenager when I worked at Music Theater did I get a sense of what Dad's life in the Marine Corps was like. Seated among the troops on the stage I could pretend I was there and realize the desperate boredom of waiting for assignment to battle, or the end of the war, and the hilarity the men devised to divert their thoughts from the seriousness of their plight

The night arrived when Mom and Dad were scheduled to see our production. After my special assignment with Billis, they were eager to find out what all the fuss was about. They had already seen *South Pacific* when the touring company played the Shubert in Chicago and had bought the 1949 original cast 78-rpm record album of the show. It was one of their favorites. At age 8 Linda picked up on it immediately, parading around the house singing, to the tune of the Seabees' Bloody Mary song, "I can't find my doggone underpants/ Now ain't that too damn bad!"

They loved the show. They were pleased at seeing their son on the stage and his handiwork on Billis's belly. Mom adored Richard Rogers's enchanting melodies and the apt Oscar Hammerstein lyrics. Dad had bonded instantly with Billis: if there ever was an enlisted man like Luther Billis—a "big dealer," a free spirit, a friend to all comers and a creative genius when it came to getting things done on an island military base—it was Dad.

Although I must admit I never saw him do a belly dance, he was a very uninhibited, if unschooled, dancer. A few years later, at Princess Rudivorivan's birthday party—a press stunt staged at a Chicago hotel to announce the actress's triumphant arrival from Thailand—Dad meticulously executed a Siamese circle dance with all the young Thais, his arms jutting at odd angles, his merry eyes wide as saucers, and got his picture in the paper.

Thai dancing

Dad knew what it was about. He had met men who risked their lives on Pacific islands, like DeBecque, the "Remittance Man" who put himself in harm's way watching for enemy ships to come down "the slot" in the Solomons. He had put on shows for the troops. He knew the men. He had lived with the terror, the waiting, the boredom and the absurd hilarity of wartime Pacific island life. He had witnessed its whole human drama played out amid the incomparable beauty of a tropical paradise.

This was a place where Dad had lived, matured and survived. South Pacific was in Dad's soul. This show, inspired by James Michener's *Tales of the South Pacific*, spoke directly to him, as the book spoke volumes for him, from its very opening lines: "I wish I could tell you about the South Pacific. The way it actually was . . ."

CHAPTER 15

WHAT MAKES BENNY RUN?

There aren't any great men. There are just great challenges that ordinary men like you and me are forced by circumstances to meet.
—attributed to Adm. William F. Halsey, Jr.

"What on earth are you bringing in here?" wailed Mom in panic as she reached the foot of the stairs to the sunken family room of our trilevel suburban house, incredulous at what she saw. "The guests are arriving in an hour. My whole party is ruined!"

She could only stare dumbfounded, as Earl "Madman" Muntz brought yet another load of audio-visual equipment—microphones, coils of heavy cable, amplifiers, lights and tripods—through the garage entry into the family room. On his final trip, he hauled in a movie camera the size of a suitcase, with a pair of huge reels on top, which looked like Mickey Mouse ears. He set it on a large wooden tripod, a wheeled affair from which three half-inch diameter cables snaked along the full length of the room, tangling with the legs of the once neatly aligned chairs. Earl surveyed his setup with satisfaction and placed a boom microphone at the opposite corner of the 30-foot room, set floodlights on collapsible stands around the perimeter and began his plugging operations.

"Alice," he said, "this only happens once in a lifetime. We've got to save it for posterity!"

My mother stared in disbelief at the U-shaped array of folding tables she, my sister Linda and I had spent the afternoon arranging, covering with her best tablecloths and neatly setting for dinner. complete with Linda's custom-designed centerpieces and party favors. They were now misaligned and nestled in a forest of stands and electronic gear, giving her festive party the appearance of a used equipment auction.

"Earl, you're crazy!" she exploded.

"Yup, I guess that's how I got my nickname," was his terse reply, as he studied his amplifier hookup. In shirtsleeves and tie, he had planted his large, well-padded frame squarely in a tiny folding chair. His eyes, deep-set beneath bushy eyebrows, fixed intently on his equipment. He hunched over his work, oblivious of all outside distractions.

Earl Muntz had come into our lives when he became Patricia Stevens' second husband. This one-time California used-car impresario turned home television marketing mogul, in his second time around as well, had fallen head over heels for the beautiful, poised and successful purveyor of feminine charm. With Dad's sure-handed promotional skill, Patricia Stevens had become household name—a model turned educator, promoting the image of success to the American working girl years before Mary Tyler Moore's fame. Her marriage to Earl meant a chance to "have it all," with a suburban ranch house, tended garden, swimming pool and fancy cars.

Patricia had started in New York as a Powers model, founded a chain of finishing schools "for models and career girls" with her first husband, Tom Fizdale—still her business partner—and made a significant contribution to the changing role of women in America. Patricia Stevens Finishing Schools' advertising was handled by my father's ad agency. As business associates and friends, Mom had invited them both to Dad's surprise birthday party. Tonight Earl had burst into our lives with a vengeance.

"Mom, maybe it would be nice to have movies of this," I said, "I'm going to be too busy tonight to take pictures myself." An ardent amateur photographer who had captured some memorable family pictures,

Chapter 15-What Makes Benny Run

I also stepped in from time to time as the family peacemaker.

Since she had cast me in a role for the evening's presentation, Mom relented. She made peace with Earl and did what she could in the remaining minutes to align the rows of tables, reset the chairs and straighten the place settings at the center of what had now become the set in her new movie studio.

She was arranging a centerpiece when the door chimed and the first guest arrived. Patricia, eschewing Earl's van—probably because there was no room in it—had come in style in her own Brougham. Well into her 40s, she still possessed the poised, glamorous image she presented to the public, with short, elegantly sculpted hair, subtle makeup and a smart cocktail dress in striking black and white. Hardening to the harsh realities of business had never dimmed her winning smile, which shone with a basic sweetness that endeared her to her business associates students, and friends alike.

This festive occasion celebrated not only Dad's 48th birthday, but also his and Mom's 20th wedding anniversary, coming in a few days on the first day of spring. Mom had invited her brother Frank and his wife, any of Dad's wartime buddies who could make the trip, associates from the radio and advertising business, and a few favorite neighbors.

The guests had all assembled by the time Dad arrived home from a business trip on a Saturday evening. Despite his ignorance of our plans, with his usual serendipity, Dad arrived at the perfect time. We heard the swing of the screen, his keys in the front door and the thud of his suitcase on the floor. Mom casually led him downstairs. We all swarmed around him and yelled "Surprise!" The party was on.

Dad was flabbergasted but, showman that he was, he grinned broadly and immediately stepped into his role as the birthday boy. We had drinks and a festive dinner, served in the family room. Although Mom always planned and prepared the food herself, for this busy occasion she had called in Earl and Eva, a devoted black couple, to do the bartending, serving and cleanup. After drinks and a fine buffet dinner, it was show time.

My mother launched into a presentation she had been creating for months. She stood at the corner of the table layout holding her her script, looking demure and wise in her horn-rimmed reading glasses.

Mom had also pressed television announcer Ed Roberts, into service as narrator. Earl Muntz, our movie director, called for "Lights, camera, action," and the show began.

We presented Dad with whiskey crate I had decorated as a treasure chest: "Pandora's Box," Mom called it, and Dad pulled out a blue leatherette album with "This Is Your Life" inscribed on it in silver script. Dad leafed nostalgically through its pages of photos, pausing to chuckle at an early shot of himself: "With hair!" he exclaimed.

"Fortunately," Mom began, "Ralph Edwards could *not* be with us tonight." Mom's well-crafted lines drew gales of laughter from the guests, aware that they were privileged witnesses to a unique spectacle. "So we settled on Ed Roberts, Ben's long-time colleague and friend, as our narrator." Ed walked up and placed a brotherly hand on Mom's shoulder, script in hand, looking very professional in his gray suit and black horn rims. The a boom microphone, lights and cameras were as natural to him as Studio B at WBBM-TV Chicago. Far from making him nervous, they only reinforced his professional demeanor. He began to deliver the script in the relaxed, confident baritone which had made his name and American Family Soap household words to all Chicagoans for the previous twenty years.

Next, I was pressed into service, certainly not for my acting talent, but at least as "the only available 16-year old who could read Ben's handwriting," to present Dad's high school autobiography. He described his humble beginnings in his own words.

"I began life on March 11, 1908, the third of four children, an only son," I read. "My parents were of Hungarian birth and had been reared under rigid orthodox Jewish principles. Both came to America at an early age, my father at fifteen, my mother at eight; and resided in the great melting pot, New York City, my birthplace."

Dad was the son of Amelia Freireich, whose family had been professionals and merchants in Budapest, and Isidor Green (or Grüen, we were told, before it was Americanized), who was also Hungarian. He was said to have lived in Buda, site of the old town and the ancient castle; she lived across the Danube in Pest, the commercial and modern governmental heart of the city. I used to joke that they must have met on the Chain Bridge over the river. They spoke German in their birth families, and may have migrated from the Austrian part of Austria-Hungary to a more tolerant Budapest in the Jewish diaspora during the waning years of the 19th century.

A generation later, Hitler's genocide destroyed many records, along with large numbers of Budapest's Jewish population, whose survival might have made it possible on my recent visit to Budapest to learn more. The Ellis Island database shows that an Izidor Grün, of Hungarian, German ethnicity, emigrated from Fiume, an Austro-Hungarian Adriatic port, on the Ultonia May 29, 1907. Another Isidor Green, who was married and of English, Hebrew ethnicity, arrived on the Oceania September 18, 1907 at age 40. Neither seems to be the right individual: Dad's father would have immigrated much earlier, probably in the mid-1890's, in order to have arrived at 15 and to have had three children by the time my father was born in New York in 1908.

"My father was neither wealthy nor extremely poor," I read, "but possessed a moderate income, sufficient to support a family of six." His tone was remarkably even-handed, as he tried to present a picture of a comfortable working family.

"My birthplace had no influence upon me," I continued, "as Chicago became my home when I was at the age of one year, because business relations had forced a change of residence. My only regret is that my father's work did not take us to the western coast. However, Chicago is an improvement over New York, although its much-spoken-of crime waves, congested traffic and automobile speeders leave room to doubt its qualifications as an ideal home-town."

Chuckles arose from the group.

Dad's family lived in the bustling and recently annexed Englewood district on the city's South Side, just west of Jackson Park—site of the Columbian Exposition, the 1893 World's Fair. He attended public school in the district and Englewood High School. During the War, in the summer of 1918, he took a trip with his mother and youngest sister "to the far-famed Isle of Manhattan." He met his New York relatives, especially his mother's sister Regina, who lived up to her name ruling her subjects, consisting of three daughters, two of whom were married. "Previous to this, our family had rented a cottage in the country each summer, but after 1918, due to the fact that my father was taken ill and suffered financially, we were unable to continue our customary plan. From then on the family fortunes varied in accordance with my father's health.

He never regained his natural vigor and a serious relapse from which he has just recovered may cause him to seek occupation in a warmer and drier clime than that which Chicago's lake front affords."

Dad's working life began early, I recited from his autobiography: "I received my first employment at the age of seven as errand boy for a neighboring shoemaker at a penny a trip. This position terminated in a dispute over my wages at the end of one week."

The guests laughed, recognizing how early Dad's scrappy streak had appeared. "Following that I conceived the idea of selling cold drinks to thirsty tennis players and, until a policeman informed me that a license was necessary, I enjoyed a successful business. My next business venture was selling Christmas cards. This I carried on for three years, my last two at grammar school and my first at high school."

He passed along this experience to me: during August of my eighth grade summer, Dad showed me how to order a stock of Christmas cards, helped me build a display case with a lid that lifted up and revealed individual compartments for each style of card and taught me a verbatim sales pitch to overcome my natural shyness in making cold calls on strangers. The venture was successful: I sold out my stock of cards well before Christmas.

"I also became a newsboy for a short time," I read, "thus gaining a qualification which should permit me to be one of those great men who started life selling newspapers."

The guests roared with laughter.

"The summer of 1924 was spent working at a racetrack," I read. "I was employed five hours a day, thus leaving me sufficient time for recreation and correspondence with friends away for the vacation. My employment brought me into contact with the strangest types of people I have ever met."

In a favorite reminiscence of his youth, Dad described how, one blistering hot midsummer day at Washington Park racetrack on Chicago's south side, he discovered the concession stands at the track had sold out of soda pop before the end of the third race. He sprang into action, out the gate and across the street. He immediately began climbing the rear porch stairs of the surrounding tenements.

"S-e-e-c-ck baby," he cried at each back door in a faked Italian accent, cradling an imaginary infant in his arms. At last he found a sympathetic mother who offered him the bucket and tin cup he sought for the "baby's" care. He filled the bucket with a garden hose, went back to the track and began hawking water by the cup. Remembering the lesson from the tennis court caper, this time he conducted his business well out of sight of the authorities.

That night, he emptied his bulging pockets on the kitchen table. "Ma, I'm rich!" he exclaimed, as his hoard of pennies, nickels, dimes and even some quarters cascaded into a large pile. I forgot to ask him if he ever returned the cup and bucket to the sympathetic woman, but at least he could now afford his own serving utensils.

In senior year of high school, he worked on Saturdays in a men's clothing store, where he gained "experience which may prove valuable in aiding me to earn my way through college" and which imparted to him a love for dressing well that stayed with him throughout his life.

"One other change I have not noted began in my third year; when I became interested in girls and dancing. My interest increased, and at the present time I enjoy the friendship of several girls, whom I consider as having some ideal qualities."

Here I laughed along with the others. Ben Green had gotten an early start as a "ladies' man," who charmed every beautiful woman he met, kissing her boldly on the lips, a habit he never abandoned. But we all knew he honored Mom above all women, and she tolerated it. But I wouldn't always welcome Dad's role as a charmer. Once when I was in college. he invited an attractive young actress to our house, upstaged me for her attention and won. I wondered why I, who was single and of an age closer to hers should have to compete with my own father.

"My junior year in high school, I joined the staff of the school paper, "a move which may greatly affect my life, as I am considering journalistic work as my career." By senior year he had become editor of the paper, "began to read more widely and better books and began to think more of *things in general* and of the future." He even got his first recognition in journalism, when, at a state press convention. "Our paper was awarded a sweepstakes prize: This victory afforded me what I believe to be the greatest thrill of my life. The present year has been my most successful and I hope future ones may surpass it," I recited.

"I have again reached the present time and am again crystal-gazing, trying to visualize the future, making plans, developing ambitions, daydreaming and castle building, enjoying an optimism that is the uncensorable pleasure of every young person."

The guests applauded, congratulated me on my portrayal.

"That fall Ben entered the University of Illinois," Ed resumed reading. "He worked part-time, managed to be a big shot on the Illini, the campus newspaper, and was asked to *stay away* the day the governor reviewed ROTC troops (he couldn't roll his puttees—those white, dressy socks the military wore on parade). The next year he attended the University of Chicago, worked as a campus reporter for the old Chicago Daily Journal, spent his spare time on the Maroon, another campus newspaper, smoked a pipe and generally deported himself in the accepted collegiate fashion, *circa* 1928."

Dad by that time had begun to exhibit his never-ending restlessness, which Mom laughingly called his *migratory instinct*. Early in his sophomore year, now at the University of Chicago, he became increasingly impatient with the slow pace and unclear objectives of academia. He told of a lecture delivered the first day of a course, in which the professor, in mock intellectual modesty, smugly proclaimed: "You aren't going to learn anything new here, you won't hear the answers to life's mysteries and you won't be able to go out and apply this knowledge tomorrow."

Dad promptly got up and strode toward the door. When the professor challenged him, "Where do you think you're going, young man?" Dad wheeled around and said, "By your own admission there is no earthly reason for me to take your course, so I'm leaving." Soon thereafter, amid the throes of his father's terminal illness, he dropped out of college to take his chances in the real world. His migratory instinct had caught up with him; he was daydreaming of a trip to France. The literary scene and the delights of Paris, already home to Ernest Hemingway, Samuel Beckett and George Orwell, beckoned to him as well.

In keeping with the delightful camaraderie of that celebration, Mom was careful to keep her script light and upbeat. But Dad's family life had a dark side—one no one ever talked about, certainly not to us children, one that I discovered only recently. In addition to the allure of Paris, the push causing him to leave Chicago at that time had more disturbing

Chapter 15-What Makes Benny Run

origins. The expense of living away at college was certainly one reason he retreated back home from the University of Illinois, but I more recently learned that Dad's urgent need to be back with his mother in Chicago was the other: a resurgence of his father's abusive behavior toward his mother and his sisters. In chatting recently with Dad's cousin, Babs Levey, the only surviving eyewitness to the family during that period, I learned that Isidor Green's lack of success in business was just part of a more complex set of issues: he was also an alcoholic and a wife-beater. Although he adored my cousin as the first grandchild, he had mistreated his daughters to the point that Ruth, the eldest, left home at an early age to get married; Sylvia never liked or trusted men well enough to marry, and Rosalie, the youngest, flourished only after her father's early demise. Ben's return home soon led to a nasty fight with his father over treatment of his mother, which resulted in his expulsion from the house. This domestic turmoil redoubled his impatience with the college scene. Babs said it was a blessing for Millie when her husband died shortly thereafter; she flourished and began to enjoy life. For my Dad, she said, it was the greatest thing that ever happened to him: it set him free.

"In Paris," Mom continued, "he fell in love with the city's charm. His favorite haunts included the American library where he whiled away many hours, the Delicatessen St. Marcel where he ate bread and cheese and drank wine, the Cafe de Lyon on the Boulevard Raspail, where they had good beer. He pursued Betty Burgess, an American from Chicago. He took her walking in the Bois de Boulogne for cocoa and honey cakes at the Turkish mosque. That was really Paris in the

Ben, young publicist

ked his way back from Europe as a mess boy, and if n carve, you know where he developed that talent. nd broke but fired with ambition. It seems he wanted to marry Betty Burgess. "That's what he thought!" my mother said.

"He returned to Chicago intoxicated with,the spirit of the times: "Everyone was rich, or about to be," Ed resumed. "He was getting into high gear and into politics." Actually Dad started his political career as a ward heeler, that lowest of the low political jobs, where duties could range from helping to get out the vote, assisting at the polls and publicizing candidates to getting coffee for ward bosses. He had fond, if scandalous, memories of those dirty days. He confided to me one day in my teens, as I was learning about the political process, how it worked in Chicago. "We'd have a Democratic and a Republican judge examining each ballot as it was tallied. Our judge (the Democrat) would have a 'short pencil.' " He showed me how it is possible to embed the broken end of a pencil lead under the fingernail of your index finger. "We'd just make sure that an occasional Republican ballot received a big mark on it so it was considered a spoiled ballot and not counted." The more things change, the more... It seems that this was merely an early, low-tech version of "hanging chad."

From politics and publicity he seized an opportunity to work in his chosen field—journalism. "He became known as the little dynamo and the Napoleon of the Northwest News!" reported my mother. "Politicians cried for his services... they even joined the polar bear club and dove into Lake Michigan to please him... and to get their pictures in the paper."

"When he left the Northwest News, he joined the personal press staff of Mayor William Hale Thompson," Ed read on. "With this job went a roadster that said 'Office of the Mayor,' a press pass, and a taste for high living which never left him." From there he formed his own publicity business, in partnership with Tom Fizdale, with whom he would be associated in various roles for many years. His accounts included promo- ... Molly, the National Barn Dance and such lo- ...kler, Ann Seymour, Joan Blaine and Betty ...ee days were fast drawing to a close," Ed related. "On the tennis courts, in the summer of 1935, he was introduced by Katherine Chandler, to a blonde by the name of Alice Herlihy. But he was chasing another blonde at the time and he never seemed to be able to remember the aforementioned blonde's name or even that he'd been introduced to her."

On their first real date, they went to the Artist's Ball. To make sure he established

Alice and Ben—first date.

himself in her mind as the life of the party, he pulled a tablecloth from under a table full of Drake glasses to demonstrate his manual dexterity. Failing this, when he learned the manager wanted a word with him, he made off with one of the hotel elevators, in which he played hide-and-seek for the next hour with anyone who would chase him. Meanwhile, Alice sat, all dressed up like a Degas ballet dancer, waiting for her first dance. After two hours of this, when she had decided to go home (she just lived across the street) her hero returned. He had been asked to leave and then was reinstated to the good graces of the management by Marjorie Livingston, an opera singer of some influence, who thought Ben was cute. Here is a picture of Ben apologizing to Alice for the first time.

Alice Joan Judith Herlihy was the youngest child of Francis Jeremiah (F. J.) Herlihy and Mary Howard, both Irish immigrants; they met in a Chicago boarding house where Mary made the beds and served meals. Her older brother, Frank, Jr., like my father, was also the second youngest of four, and two older sisters, Mae and Helen. She was born in Lewistown, Montana, in 1913, where her father, a young engineer, was in charge of construction of all bridges on the Puget Sound line west of Butte—and the Great Falls-Lewistown line—of the Milwaukee Railway Company. After completing this assignment, he acted as an independent consultant and built a financial stake through an assignment in Montreal. He took charge of construction for a six-mile long aqueduct, part of an electric power development, much of it through solid rock, a $3.5 million project in 1914 (the equivalent of about $100 million today).

Although Mary at a slight 5'3" was dwarfed by her 6-foot-2 heavy framed husband, he was no match for her when she disagreed with him. Her quiet, measured tones, "Now, Frank..." she would say firmly, were the perfect foil for his hot, Black-Irish temper. But each had Irish charm. Mary's was lavished on her grandchildren. Despite his profane, intimidating bluster, F. J. also had a huge soft spot for his family, friends and employees, who at various times included all five of his brothers; he ruled benevolently. All who knew him loved him, including his loyal employees, who became like family over his 40 years in business. His ability to charm the birds off the trees—not to mention politicians, clients and friends—was the key to his business achievement.

Although shorter than her towering Papa, Ben at 5'-6"—was someone Alice could look up to, with her father's drive, determination and winning personality. The two men even shared the same flaws, including an inability to hold on to money, which was offset and partly caused by their extreme generosity to others, and by a certain immodest tendency toward self-promotion and conspicuous display, countered as well in each man by extraordinary personal charm.

In Mom, Dad saw a beautiful, witty and brainy girl—unlike the many ordinary girls that showered him with attention—his equal in every way, and clearly his superior in taste and refinement. What Dad saw in her family was success—something he craved. He would sit with F. J. by the hour and listen to him explain how he planned a project, the way to organize materials at the job site and the key things to remember in submitting a bid. When I reached my teens Dad would advise me, "To win a girl you've got to broaden her world." It is evident that while he had certainly opened her eyes to Chicago, Alice also broadened *his* vision. He told of a shopping trip to Marshall Field's, where he accompanied Mom and her sister Helen as they looked for silk stockings. When they found the ones they wanted, between them they bought a dozen pair. To him this represented wealth beyond his wildest imagination.

"It seems Alice had her mind made up to get married," Ed read. "Usually, in cases of this kind, there are two sides to the question. This time there were three. Alice's father, who said, 'You can't marry that guy. He can't even buy pork chops.' Ben's mother, who said. 'Pork chops? Couldn't you look around a little longer and find a nice Jewish girl?' And, last but not least Ben, who said, 'I don't want to get married yet!' "

"So on Thursday, the 19th of March," Mom read from her script, "over a stein of Bock beer in the Auditorium Hotel bar, I asked Ben to be my husband. He said, 'no.' So I agreed to wait until the 21st, of March, that is, the first day of spring. Meanwhile, I was taking no chances, so we were married by Judge Casey in his chambers the following day. Then on Saturday, in the Thorndike-Hilton Chapel at the University of Chicago, we really sewed it up."

Now the carefree bachelor had two mouths to feed. "True, the bride went to work as a press agent for a while," Ed read, "but most of her paycheck seemed to go for silly hats, of which she has always been ex-

Chapter 15-What Makes Benny Run

tremely fond, and income tax was a real problem. They paid $13.00 that first year." As they started their married life in a rented flat on Chicago's near north side, Mom and Dad would count the pocket change on the dresser each morning and split it equally as their cash for the day. Breakfast was shared at Walgreen's. The best that could be said about the restaurant was that the coffee was hot and the orange juice was wet. But they were together and in love, and nothing else mattered. One year ran into the next and their married bliss increased, while Dad's talent and Mom's charm propelled his career into high gear.

Next my father went to work for the Plan for Hospital Care as Director of Public Relations. Bob Cunningham, long-time editor of Modern Hospital magazine and a lifelong friend, in a letter read at the party, recorded his contribution to a very new concept: health care insurance. "In 1936 a friend of yours, Perry Adelemen, organized the Plan for Hospital Care—forerunner of today's Blue Cross with its millions of members—and you became its first director of public relations. You believed in the idea that the Plan would help people pay for the costs of their illness, and, besides, the proposition offered promise of continued gainful employment, a consideration that's not to be sneered at in 1936—remember?

"Due in roughly equal parts to the soundness of the idea, and the skill with which you publicized it, the hospital plan flourished beyond your wildest dreams. In fact, it burgeoned so rapidly that the number of people who signed up and paid their fees outran the ability of their officers, other than yourself, to keep count of who had paid and who hadn't, and who owed what for whose hospital bill. When finally the trustees of the plan became a little nervous and called in an sub- cription cards in their little shoebox files and the cash in the desk drawers, you were one of only a few held blameless for the shambles. And so, in 1939 you left this half-world of doctors, hospital administrators and social welfare executives for the clean, pure atmosphere of the advertising business."

"But all else paled before the great

Son and father

event of that year," Mom continued. "On May, 1939. Ben became a father. One got the impression that only one child was born that year, and his name was Peter Green. Those of you who remember Ben in those days will recall he was willing to talk extensively on any subject as long as it was his son Pete."

Now there was another mouth to feed and Dad moved—with that restless, unfailing migratory instinct of his—to H. W. Kastor and Sons, Advertising, where he worked at both promotion and production. Ginny Smith (later, von Tresckow), who was office manager at the time, recalled in her letter to the party that he launched a publicity campaign for *Painted Dreams*—"something utterly foreign to us" up to that time—and worked several of her "best girls" to the point of nervous breakdowns. Still dissatisfied, he requested that he hire his own secretary. Ginny said that "wouldn't be difficult, since we paid such high salaries—$15 a week!" at which Ben roared, invited her home for dinner to meet Alice and the family and made a life-long friend.

Painted Dreams, a weekly radio drama for which Dad was producer and director, was written at that time by Kay Chase, whose verse on the subject of those melodramatic years included a paean to Ben Green. Kay, one of the party guests, smartly dressed in a very feminine gray silk dress, her chestnut hair flowing and her dark eyes twinkling behind oversized reading glasses, assumed her position at center stage—her script at the ready— and delivered her memoir.

Kay Chase

How Green Was My Ally

For eight long years this weary Chase
Pursued a dream, at pitiless pace...

Chapter 15 - What Makes Benny Run

A Painted Dream—if you'll pardon the phrase—
Which still induces a slight malaise,

But which meant to imply, to me and to you,
That we all paint dreams and they do come true.

Eight long years of sweet old sayings,
Eight long years of pious prayings . . .

Eight long years of joy and sorrow,
Eight long years of "Listen tomorrow" . . .

Till she was nearly non compos mentis,
Putting words in the mouths of Hill and Prentiss,

And herself and Murphy, and a long procession
Of other actors in search of expression.

Flynn had flitted, Flynn had fled -
But Mother Moynihan was not yet dead.

Reincarnate in Connie Crowder,
Her brogue got broader, her prayers got louder

And for the future there still was hope –
For along came American Family Soap!

Though Kastor might cause a horrible bollox,
Kastor and Green were not Castor and Pollux.

Green was predictable when Kastor was perverse
He went from good to better, they from bad to worse.

And so did the show. Instead of hearts and flowers,
Now it was melodrama . . . dangerous hours . . .

Sabotage and suicide . . . arson, murder, rape . . .
Or, from them, preposterous implausible escape.

But none for the writer! In all this inanity
Green was the only link with sanity.

Green who would sympathize, Green who would cheer,
Green who would anyway lend an ear.

Green who would have an idea or a hunch,
Green who would anyway buy your lunch.

Green who went on through two tough years
Mopping up blood, perspiration, and tears.

Which ought to suggest that the weary Chase
And the right bright Green won the old rat-race . . .

For right is might, and virtue wins,
And even Agencies shall suffer for their sins . . .

Ben stages a shot with Connie Crowder, April, 1942

Chapter 15-What Makes Benny Run

> *But the sweet old sayings must be a con—*
> *For the show went off... But the friendship went on.*
>
> *So a toast—and I think you'll see what I mean—*
> *When I give you my favorite color: GREEN!*

"But the balmy days were drawing to a close," Ed continued. "Ben's GREETINGS from Uncle Sam and his daughter, Linda, with a feminine sense of the dramatic, arrived the same day. Our hero fast-talked himself into the Marine Corps infantry at the age of 36."

About the time Dad was called for his physical exam, in early spring 1944, Mom's sister, Helen, a practicing psychoanalyst who lived with her family in Boston, wrote a newsy and supportive letter discussing preparations for Dad's induction: "Much as it may ease the situation for both of you, this doesn't do away with the reality that you are right up against the fact of separation. So you go up for your physical Wednesday, Ben. We shall be waiting to hear how many days of grace they'll give you after that. For your sake, I hope more and more that the commission will go through. But I'm so convinced that you'll do a good and cheerful job of accepting your part in this war, whatever it is, and I need not be concerned on that score. I'm sure of another thing too—that you won't have any psycho-neurotic breakdown, such as thousands of others are having. We see them constantly in the clinics here, discharged after short periods of service. You are one of the few really mentally healthy people I know, Ben. Did I ever tell you that before? If not, it's high time...."

That was something: Helen, who had studied with Freud, pronouncing Dad sane, when lots of people were saying he was crazy to be enlisting in the Marines!

"So Ben Green, husband, father and fine fellow," Ed read, "became 958730 and was sent promptly to the boondocks at San Diego."

Dad set off with optimism and enthusiasm. Other than what it said on his train ticket to San Diego and the promise of a commission, he had no idea of where he was headed or what awaited him. Mom faced his departure with dread, knowing that whatever happened, it would take him further and further away from us before he returned—if he returned at all. Little did she realize what one man could accomplish within the vast scenario of a world war; nor did she have any concept of the impact it might have on her family.

Ed resumed his narration: "But this story can only be told first-hand. I give you the man who was the best friend Ben ever had. The man who taught him how to get a fully packed sea-bag off the ground... and here he is: Jim Morrow."

Jimmy Morrow was a huge, powerful Irishman, with a round face, crew cut, thick arms and a barrel chest, well-adapted to his life's work in a machine shop. He had a heart of gold, with a gentle air, which immediately assured he could never hurt a flea. He rose from his totally inadequate metal folding chair to his full 5-foot, ten-inch height and addressed the guests from the corner of the table. "The Marine Corps may not remember Ben Green, but Ben Green will never forget the Marine Corps," he said, He presented Dad with a few wartime mementos, some yen and a couple of Japanese ration books and recalled: "Last of all, a couple of reminders of a swell time we had in Hollywood and L.A. about twelve years ago, and in case you have forgotten, a clipping to prove we did shoot 100 percent on the rifle range."

Jimmy Morrow

"I can tell you I'm proud and happy to have shared a small part of your life: may it be long and happy"

Ben rose and approached Jimmy, who gave him a huge bear hug. There was no doubt among the assembled company that these two were the dearest of friends.

"From boot camp," Ed continued, "he was transferred to Mare Island, California, to a Guard Company, where he was assigned to the bond bank detail guarding money from the base in the company of a beautiful WAC. They never lost any money during his tenure of duty, but they almost lost a Jeep the morning he discharged his .45 through the battery by mistake. He used his gift of gab to great advantage that time; claimed they'd never been given training with a .45 at boot camp—his testimony resulted in

Chapter 15-What Makes Benny Run

having a course in this weapon organized at Mare Island. Instead of being court-martialed as he expected, he got his first and only stripe by making a good impression on the colonel before whom he was called on the carpet. In his spare time he worked as a bartender at the officer's club."

"I always thought he got that stripe for loading the colonel's martinis." rejoined Alice, to the delight of her audience.

"This job enabled him to stay in the largest, permanent, floating crap game in the Marine Corps. Mike Wallace has a few well-chosen words to contribute here," continued Alice, and she read excerpts from Mike's letter:

"Remember—Ben Green—when a grubby young announcer from Dee-troit came into your office back in 1941, looking for a handout, and you promised him all the Drene Shampoo he could drink if he'd work on Knickerbocker Playhouse? And how everything went all right until Bob Jennings demanded the cash return on the bottle?

"Remember how that sterling young man (not you Ben—me!)—now overseas, defending his country's flag—wrote, in grave concern, because he heard that you were back in the states, a Marine war casualty! Only to find that you developed SCIATICA shaking drinks and scooping things out of the cash register behind the bar of the Officers' Club!"

"In January, he was sent to Camp Pendleton and then overseas to Guam," Ed resumed. "On the troop ship, you guessed it . . . he was on mess duty all 43 days and in the poker game all 43 nights. He lost $200 in record time and had to borrow 50 cents to get back into the nickel and dime game, but this story has a happy ending. When he finally reached his destination, he sent home his winnings for the trip, a money order for $500. I wish we could produce Blackie from Brooklyn tonight. He was a card shark who liked Ben and refused to let Ben play when he, Blackie, was cheating. He played with his aces back-to-back and yet he walked 10 miles one Sunday on Guam to pay Ben back $20 he owed him from aboard ship.

"On Guam he was assigned to the Ninth Marines. But not for long. He wrote home saying he'd heard his first intelligent lecture in the Marine Corps, a remark his Captain did not take kindly. Immediately, if not sooner, he was transferred to a supply depot, heaving 100-pound cases around with something less than abandon. Soon after his return to his unit, he was transferred once more.—through his own lobbying 'to do something useful this war' and that ever-present *migratory instinct* — this time to radio station WXLI, the Armed Forces Radio Station on Guam. For him, it was almost as good as going home. But nothing is perfect. The captain in charge of the station was broom-happy. No program went out over the air until the station was CLEAN…do you understand, men? CLEAN. Happily the captain was shipped to Japan, but more about that later."

The party guests were just finishing their dessert—Alice's special angel food birthday cake with a topping of crushed fresh strawberries, one of Ben's favorites. Ed Roberts, in his booming baritone, further mellowed by a good meal and couple of Scotch and sodas, resumed the narrative.

"1945 October 28 . . . oh!" Ed exclaimed. "That beautiful ruptured duck. Back home and broke again. Pete was 6, Linda, 2, and she didn't know her father from the man on the cover of Time."

"But it was love at first sight!" chirped Linda.

"It was wonderful!" exclaimed Alice.

"Once more a civilian," Ed continued, "has anyone suggested that Ben was ever anything but? . . . he returned to Kastor. By Christmas that year, old friends were returning from the war in droves. The house on Blackstone became a local branch of the USO."

"That big, old empty house where I had rattled around with the kids for nearly two years was suddenly jumping," Alice resumed. "As fast as the Marines were discharged at Great Lakes, they charged upon the Greens. I developed a case of post-war nerves mixing drinks for them. And the Sea Stories . . . how often I had to put my hands over Pete's ears when the reminiscing began.

"Orin Tovrov remembers that post-war period vividly, so I'll let him tell it." Alice read from Orin's letter. "Life is a rushing river . . . Whatever happened to Don Herbert, for whom we were all trying to get a job? . . . You live in Glencoe now, but in Glencoe you have no room or root cellar or tool shed as cold as that guestroom on Blackstone; excellent preparation for my later life on Cape Cod." Orin, the guests all knew, was the creator and perennial writer of the daytime serial, Ma Perkins, a great chapter in radio history.

"And speaking of Don Herbert," Ed continued, "He not only got a job, he became Mr. Wizard, the idol of millions of budding scientists, including Pete and Linda. He has a word to add here." Alice read Don's letter, which noted that he remembered their meeting just after the war, expressed gratitude for the kindness Ben had shown when he helped Don get a job in broadcasting after a long period of unemployment and invited him to visit his family whenever he came east.

"And Mike Wallace had a postscript to add here," said Alice as she began to read. "... and then, Ben, when the Great War was over ... remember how you scoffed at his sea stories? Cheated at tennis with him? And replaced him with Vince Gottschalk on the Evans Fur commercials? Yes, Ben Green, God help us, This Is Your Life!!!"

Mike moved on, to be certain. He began the Chez Show, and then the Mike and Buff Show, his first foray into the interviewing game, with his second wife, Buff Cobb, daughter of Irvin S. Cobb. Soon afterwards he was drafted by NBC to come to New York for The Mike Wallace Interview, and then came 60 Minutes.

"When he left Kastor," Ed continued, "Ben worked briefly with Chuck Acree, doing a show called *Man on the Farm*. From there he jumped to Arthur Meyerhoff and Company, where he may still be seen if you look quickly and have nothing the matter with your blinking reactions. But no story of our Ben's life would be complete without mention of his secretaries ... a list of those who have come and gone through the years would read like a telephone directory. Starting with Evelyn Lindeman and ending with his present gal Friday, Shirley Grossman, there were many good ones and bad ones in between but he always preferred those who fought back."

Ben, the ad man

"But it's still the same old story," Ed read on, "Whenever Ben has discovered the perfect secretary, Like Maggie, some other guy has discovered her simultaneously, and married her.

Despite being driven to distraction, his assistants and associates respected, even admired, my father. Soon after that party Shirley Grossman secretly entered Dad in the "Best Boss" contest.

Because of her articulate and convincing letter, in which she said,

Ann Sothern, Ben, and Shirley Grossman

"He takes a personal interest in me, but not personally," he won first prize, which included a photo shoot and publicity with Ann Sothern, star of the popular television sitcom, Private Secretary.

I picked up the script again and continued, "There's been a lot of talk about advertising. But what about Dad's *interesting* business: the Patricia Steven's schools? Those beautiful girls..."

"Ben soon discovered that although his work at the agency was demanding," Ed continued, "he did have his evenings and an occasional Saturday free... so... he started looking for a business on the side, which he found with Patricia Stevens in her franchise setup. He acquired the Indianapolis franchise five years ago... and recently added Cleveland.

"I saw him looking at a map the other night... I'm worried..." interjected my mother.

"Don't worry, Mom," I chimed in, "You know Dad. Remember what Chuck Mills wrote for this occasion?" She read: "This is your party—so I feel quite at home. You will recall that I always feel at home at other people's houses. You are the guy I have always sat down on most. That's why I was so baffled by your reaction to our being so 'at home' at the Norbach's on Waikiki Beach. I felt that whole episode in Hawaii was somehow very representative... I had wheels and 'rank,' but I was on the beach and you were flying!"

"At this point," Mom continued, "I want to say something that's been in my heart since we first had this idea."

"You were the one who said we had to keep it gay, Mommy," Linda reminded. "The light touch, remember? You told Pete and me that one of Daddy's most wonderful qualities was that he remembered only the happy things in life."

Chapter 15-What Makes Benny Run

"But this is a happy thought . . . a new thought for me. When a woman marries a man, she marries his friends too, whether she likes it or not. There have been many through the years that I could take or leave alone, and I guess I got my first comeuppance about friends when Pete was eight. Dad had invited someone for the night and I said we didn't have enough room."

"And I said, 'If there's room in the heart, there's room in the home.'"

"I still don't know where you heard that."

"Mom," where else?" I said, "I read it in a comic strip, the Toodles!"

"Many of the people who replied to my request for memories," Mom added, "were flat on their backs, far from home or busier than 40 dogs but I do want you know that the replies were 105 per cent and all in before the script was finished."

"Now we'll have to turn Ed from narrator to character for a moment," Alice interjected. "He's another wonderful friend from that period in our lives. Here he is: one of Chicago's finest announcers and the only man who has done soap commercials for 20 years without foaming at the mouth. Remember. Ed. No commercials."

"There's a side of Ben you may not know," Ed began. "Ever since Ben has lived in Glencoe, he has prided himself on returning to nature. The only problem is the odd time of day he chooses to do it. It's what he does between the hours of 5 and 9 in the morning. In his typical go-getter fashion, it's a point of honor that he lead the *first* foursome to tee off at the Glencoe Public Golf Course, which by the way, is just two blocks from his house. After carefully plotting with the course starter all week long, he secures the first slot, at 6 a.m. on Saturday! He then invites three of his more—or less—willing friends to come over to the house before the crack of dawn and proceeds to prepare a complete breakfast for them. And this is no coffee and roll affair: it's the works! It includes orange juice, bacon or sausage, scrambled eggs, toast and huge quantities of rich, black Thomas J. Webb coffee, occasionally varying the menu with some Broadcast brand corned beef hash. Oops! I forgot, Alice, no commercials, but I couldn't stop plugging Ben's accounts. He then considers his subjects sufficiently fortified to tackle the fairways in the fog. With that *migratory instinct*, which apparently has never left him, he leads us into the gloom for yet another adventure.

"But it all began in broadcasting. While I hate to boost his ego any more than we already have tonight, I have to admit that his creative vision, willingness to try new things and dogged persistence ever since those early days have challenged us to exceed our capabilities and accomplish seemingly impossible tasks. While he can be incredibly demanding at the office and in the studio, he remains, above all, a dear friend."

As the Walter Cronkite, Mom's media idol, might say, "And that's the way it was—nostalgia, corn and all—on that Saturday evening, March 10, 1956." A boy who had a difficult childhood but wouldn't look back had grown up. He was too afraid of financial embarrassment to stop running, boundlessly confident of his abilities to solve any problem and never forgot those who helped him along the way, nor the nation that made it possible. We owe it to Ben, Alice, his family, all those wonderful friends—and a lot of other great Americans with his same spirit—to remember.

While Dad was an ordinary man—head of a family, soldier and businessman—never rising to high public office, great literary or artistic distinction or heroism in battle or life situations, he was faced with some extraordinary challenges and met them with determination, skill and grace. He never shied from difficulty. He risked his life, liberty, property and reputation for important causes he believed in: such causes as defeating aggressor nations, advancing unrepresented minorities and providing equal pay for women. And yet he did it in his own way—idealistic, creative, with the system when possible and against the system when he found it smothering the individual. He is part of a great American tradition that sometimes is forgotten by our elected representatives: help all members of society to rise together and all will benefit.

Ben with Eleanor Roosevelt

Dad had had once met Eleanor Roosevelt. The former First Lady was known for loyalty to her children, especially her son

Chapter 15-What Makes Benny Run

Elliott. Named for her father, and like him in many ways, Elliott was her favorite child and the one for whom she felt the most responsibility. Never shy about exploiting the Roosevelt name, Elliott wrote numerous mystery novels, with Eleanor Roosevelt featured as a famous sleuth. She was always eager to help him and promote his books, even accompanying him on book tours. On one such occasion in Chicago, Dad tied her visit in with one of his client promotions and met this remarkable woman, whom he so much admired and who had so much influence on domestic policy during her husband's presidency.

I recalled some of the other life lessons Dad had taught me, for example how to "dress for success." When I was ready to go off to Yale for my freshman year, Dad took the day off from work and made a formal date with me to go downtown. His purpose, or so I thought, was to buy me some school clothes. Since he had not finished college himself, he was bursting with pride that I had been admitted to one of the top schools in the country. Reflecting on his own experience, he feared I would be among my "betters," but he knew that I could overcome any Midwestern social crudity that might be apparent to Easterners by dressing like them. We were not only shopping, we were acquiring my "college man's wardrobe" and the mental attitudes that went along with it.

He had learned the men's clothing business shortly after he dropped out of college in his sophomore year, when his father died. He went on to work in a department store that offered quality men's wear. He had an eye for color harmony—subtle was best: "See the little thread of yellow that is worked through that Harris Tweed weave? This is a beautiful jacket," he said, and he bought it for me.

We combed the downtown department stores: Marshall Field's, Brooks Brothers, and several smaller men's stores. But their selections in my size (36 short) were limited, and we could not find anything satisfactory. At one point when I got bored with shopping and was rude to a salesman, he brought me up sharply. He reminded me from his own experience how hard the man works and explained that he only would get paid if we bought something. He himself was scrupulously polite to each individual who waited on us, making sure to thank him even if we could find nothing to buy. But when we arrived at Maurice L. Rothschild, we struck gold. Our salesman was a master and the selection was immense. Like kids in a candy store, we could hardly decide which of the many handsome garments available I should try on. We settled on a basic navy wool suit with a faint pinstripe, a Harris Tweed gray wool jacket with a vertical stripe and a dark brown suit that complemented my hair color. Dad said it fit me like a dream—I agreed. The next step was to find the right accessories. Dad showed me how to select a shirt that contrasts nicely with and picks up tones found in the suit fabric. He carried the sport jacket over to the tie counter and showed me how to decide what went well together. As a result of our educational shopping trip, I went off to college with a fine new wardrobe and the confidence that I could hold my own in any group because of the way I dressed.

When I enlisted in the Army I confronted a different clothing problem. During my first week in basic training at Fort Dix, New Jersey, I was issued enough gear to fill two duffel bags and naturally given only one to contain them. I was measured, fitted and suited on the spot; I staggered out of the clothing center with all my new possessions on my back—two sets of fatigues, an Army green dress uniform, khaki shirts and pants comprising my Class A uniform, three styles of hat—fatigue cap, garrison cap and billed saucer dress hat—shorts, T-shirts, socks, combat boots, dress shoes, belts (leather and canvas), a brass belt buckle and numerous brass buttons and insignia, which I had no idea how to install—the makings of a complete soldier. The challenge, I later learned, was maintenance. The guys in my platoon—from Terry Fox, the tall bossy one, to Irwin Gurland, a portly, smart guy Fox picked on, whom I had befriended on our first day there—were impressed with the way we looked when we tried on our new duds. Little did we know that every waking moment for the next eight weeks would be devoted to trips to base Laundromats, visits to the tailor shop and cleaning off layers of mud and spit-shining our boots and shoes. We even filled hours that were supposed to be devoted to sleep doing the rest of our chores, including mopping the barracks floors from the dirt we had tracked in and endlessly disassembling, cleaning and reassembling our M-1 rifles.

Then there was the matter of storage. We were each given only one foot locker, half of a metal cabinet and one duffel bag to contain our possessions. On inspection day, we had to demonstrate to the in-

Chapter 15-What Makes Benny Run

specting officer's satisfaction that each shirt, dress uniform and pair of pants was stored in its correct location on hangers arranged in the correct order; that our foot lockers, when opened, contained nothing but neatly folded clothes, and that each additional issued item such as canteen, mess kit, entrenching tool (a collapsible shovel), poncho and helmet was displayed in the proper configuration, open to show all loose parts, on the tautly stretched blanket on the neatly made upper or lower bunk.

Peter as a Corpsman

During the day, and some nights, there was plenty of training going on. We marched, we drilled, we went to class and we spent hours on the rifle range. We hit the dusty trail, marched through rain and slogged through mud for eight solid weeks. There were times when we thought we'd never keep up with the maintenance chores. While these activities were instructive and sometimes even interesting, they somehow don't stick in my mind as vividly as the daily chores involved in keeping 60 pounds of clothing and equipment clean, in top repair and ready for battle. Perhaps it's because these were the activities we could do together on our own time. As we polished our boots for hours on end, there was time to get to know Bill East, the Princeton grad with glasses, a nervous type, who said, "I never eat when I travel; it's too upsetting." There were trips to the Laundromat with Wally Webb, a fellow architect. He would take along the latest copy of Architectural Record magazine; we would debate while our clothes tumbled in the dryer over the optimum design for an urban airport, whether it was better to have passengers walk on long concourses to reach the gates or to use Eero Saarinen's new idea of transporting people from the terminal to the gates on special buses. As we polished our belt buckles and brass insignia, we learned about each other's families and shared our dreams.

Although we thought it would never arrive, at the end of eight weeks graduation day rolled around. In a final burst of maintenance mad-ness, we prepared for hours, shining, polishing, pressing, brushing, and preening to look our best in our dress greens, khaki shirts, black neckties and black dress oxfords. Along with 40 other platoons we massed at the parade ground and sat on the bleachers to receive our final instructions. At the signal we all took the field and formed into our squads, platoons and companies. Whistles blew; commands were sharply issued, and they were relayed from the Colonel to the captains to the platoon sergeants, who gave the signal to the men. The Commanding General, his wife and dignitaries, and soldiers' families who lived close enough to the post to travel there, viewed the scene from the reviewing stand. A final whistle blew, the band struck up a march and we moved out, proceeding in the sparkling sunshine of a crisp fall day along the field to the beat of the big bass drum, in lockstep with our heads held high. We were tough, we were disciplined, and we knew we were now soldiers. How did we know? It was the same principle Dad had taught me back in the Maurice L. Rothschild department store: in our sartorial splendor, we were dressed for success!

One anecdote about Dad and his clothes reveals a lot about his character. One of his clients, a seafood company, had put him on the Board of Directors as a measure of respect for his advertising, public relations and marketing expertise. In Tampa he instituted an annual luncheon, each year presenting one of the great economic or international thinkers of the day. He had built this event, the Trident Luncheon, into a prestigious, not-to-be-missed affair for the leaders of the Tampa Bay business community. Among the distinguished speakers Dad invited and hosted at the event were Arthur Schlesinger, Arthur Goldberg and Walter Heller. In 1972, he even arranged for Past President Lyndon B. Johnson to address the gathering, however the luncheon was canceled because of President Johnson's death. After the sudden death of his beloved client in 1973, the event was renamed the Leo D. Levinson Memorial Luncheon. Motivated by the memory of his good client and dear friend, Dad redoubled his efforts to find outstanding speakers, and his list included Paul McCracken and Dr. Milton Friedman. After Abba Eban had retired as Foreign Minister for Israel, he resolved to see if this most eloquent of statesmen would be available to address the luncheon.

To initiate his contact he called Tel Aviv and talked to Mr. Eban's office. As was his custom, he made friends with his principal assistant,

Chapter 15-What Makes Benny Run

who said she would talk with the Foreign Minister and, if he would be so kind as to call at the same time the next day, she would have an answer.

When he called back, she said that because of his travel plans Foreign Minister would have to make that appointment himself; but he would be pleased to talk to Dad at 11 a.m. (Tel Aviv time) the following Tuesday. Allowing 8 hours' time differential, Dad went to bed early the night before and set his alarm for 2 a.m. He awoke, showered, shaved, put on his best suit and tie and made coffee. When I asked him later why he couldn't just do it in his pajamas, he was shocked. "Is that any way to greet the Foreign Minister?" he replied. He was supremely confident that immaculate dress was inextricably entwined with top performance. It worked. At precisely 3 a.m. he placed the call. He had a most cordial chat with Abba Eban, rearranged the luncheon date to coordinate with the Foreign Minister's American travel schedule and made the agreement right then over the telephone. All reports were that this was the most memorable luncheon that the company ever gave. I still have an image of Dad standing alone in the living room of his Chicago apartment in the middle of the night, dressed in his finest, chatting confidently with this distinguished world leader.

What had motivated a married man with two children to volunteer for the U.S. Marines in the first place? What enabled him to rebound from each disappointment and to emerge from the world's largest war—alive, accomplished and available to take charge of his family again back home? He believed in the cause.

Ben was not alone: an entire generation of Americans felt as strongly as he did about the way of life they were given and how strongly they would fight to defend it. As with so many of that magnificent era, it started with an American's love of life, idealistic goals, love of country and the opportunities it afforded, but in Ben's case there was more to it. His boundless self confidence and resourcefulness had served him well. He was smart, talented and a good organizer; he made friends easily and was steadfast in his loyalty to them. He often said, "My friends can do no wrong." He used his contacts, and he was not afraid to ask for what he wanted, because he believed in himself and felt that he *deserved* what he wanted.

Today we realize how different our lives would have been if Dad had failed to make it back home. Of course, dumb luck had a lot to do with his safe return. Many brave Americans did not make it back, and their loved ones, sons, daughters and grandchildren alive today were deprived of the opportunity to learn firsthand of their experience. On the other hand, the baseball and tennis players and Ben in his radio station role, after all, had better conditions . . . safer, softer jobs than the poor guys that hit the beaches.

I asked Bud Blattner how he reconciled his fortunate position in his own assignment with the guys in combat. Bud said, "We were where they put us. I didn't want the war; not one of these kids wanted the war. There were hundreds of thousands of sailors on Hawaii (Oahu). The Marines were the aggressive fighting force on the islands. We in the Navy had the Seabees, but the rest of us were on ships. We idolized the Seabees, because they made life bearable for us: they made the homes, the canteens, the roads.

"I never felt self-conscious: we did patrols in the jungle—we had to go through the same physical regimen. I never said: 'Don't you dare send me into combat!' *They* selected *me* to go to Bainbridge for the physical training program . . . You do what you're told. We toured the forward area in a DC-3—Pelelieu, Kwajalein—trying to hit a little spot of sand in an ocean that extended as far as the eye could see. You had no control over what to do: the only control was what you did once you were assigned. . .

. "If you chickened out, you had a miserable life. You had to hunker down. If told to go over the top, you did it. You didn't have to apologize. You made a joke about your blunders. A guy would try to shoot a Jap out of a tree, stumble over a log and almost shoot himself: he would laugh at himself. We didn't brag, but instead told the funny stories. Only the pseudo-heroes were hated—the ones whose stories got better each time they retold them. Those who had been through it could tell they were never there. You're under rigid restriction—shape up or they'll really ship you out. Anybody who enlisted and spent a reasonable amount of time in the service was a hero. We're very lucky we're still alive. My God, I could never have believed I would live!

"All these guys were heroes for what they had done," Bud concluded. "They had all given up a lot in life to be there. They didn't plan to be there. But they made the best of it. They lived the times and even forgot counting the days. One day was like the next.

"When I was at Pearl Harbor, Riggs and I were stationed at the Royal Hawaiian Hotel, which was the submariner station. Those guys would come back pale and thin after five months out. We had recreation programs, horseshoes, tennis—whatever they wanted. All they wanted to do was sit under a tree and have a beer. There was mutual admiration for everyone who was doing his job. We thought how fortunate we were that we weren't in that submarine. It would have bothered me to have evaded the draft. I didn't resent Mickey Wittick because they didn't send him and he stayed to play baseball. Bob Feller was really in combat, as Chief Petty Officer on a cruiser. He had a ship blown out from under him. (He resumed his duties as pitcher for the Cleveland Indians in 1945, and by 1956 had completed 18 seasons with a win-loss record of 266–162.) I had a career that could really be damaged by a period of inactivity for 3½ years," Bud continued. I tried to avoid career paralysis by staying in shape. We didn't know what was going to happen. This war was progressing island by island. It might take another two years to invade Japan." [20]

Those who survived came home to support, nurture and love their families. They came home to an even more prosperous America than they had left—one they helped to preserve—and to prosperity they would help to increase. Many did not return—non-combat heroes such as Glenn Miller, whose music memorialized an era, and the fighting men like Ben's buddy, Charlie Donati, who could lift a steel rail all by himself and who wouldn't let Ben go into a bar without him as his bodyguard—and millions of sons, daughters, dads, moms, uncles and cousins—all of those, we remember and pay our tribute of eternal gratitude and respect.

They were all heroes—those in combat and those in support. They put their lives on the line to do what had to be done. Modern critics have said that today's leaders have used this "good war," if such a thing can be imagined, to justify bad wars ever since. Only time and history will tell. But our American fighting men and women are the same: they are still serving with honor today in over 100 countries around the world. Keeping alive our memory of them—their good times and bad, their joys and sorrows, their follies and their wisdom—is the only way we can possibly repay them for their dedication and sacrifice.

ENDNOTES

Dates not otherwise identified refer to original letters by Benjamin J. Green.

CHAPTER 1. THE CALIFORNIAN
1 Green, Benjamin J. My War with the United States Marines, presented to the Chicago Literary Club, Feb. 8, 1965. Chapter 1, "The Sea Bag."
2 Saturday, May 13, 1944.
3 Tuesday, May 9, 1944.
4 The Comic Strip Project, at http://hometown.aol.com/comicsproj/creditsSZ.html, records that Stan Baer and his wife, Betsy wrote THE TOODLES from 1941 though 1965, while the artist from 1941 through 1958 was Rod Ruth.
5 Green, Benjamin J. My War with the United States Marines, presented to the Chicago Literary Club, Feb. 8, 1965. Chapter 2, "Rifle Butts."
6 Tuesday, June 6, 1944.

CHAPTER 2. SAN FRANCISCO CHRONICLES
1 Wednesday, July 5, 1944, aboard the train to San Francisco.
2 Wilson, Mike, 2002. A History for Marine Barracks, Mare Island, at http://images.military.com/HomePage/UnitPageHistory/1,13506,711977,766866,00.html.
3 Denger, Mark J, CWO1, California Naval History, The Early Submarines of Mare Island, The California State Military Museum, at http://militarymuseum.org/SubMareIsland.html.
4 July 14, 1944.
5 Housing conditions. Saturday, July 14, 1944.
6 Alfie Frankenstein. Sunday, July 23, 1944.
7 Marines with Joe Aspley. Saturday, August 6, 1944.
8 Visit with with Clemmie and shopping. Sunday, August 13, 1944
9 Green, Benjamin J., My War with the United States Marines, Chapter 6 "Charlie Donati," presented to Chicago Literary Club, Feb. 8, 1965

CHAPTER 3 HOME ECONOMICS
1 Alice Green, *Between Us Girls,* No. 2, June, 1944.
2 O'Dell, Cary. *Women Pioneers in Television.* Jefferson, North Carolina: McFarland, 1996, on the website of the Museum of Broadcast Communications, www.mbcnet.com.
3 Campbell, D'Ann, *Women at War with America: Private Lives in a Patriotic Era.* Harvard University Press (Cambridge, Mass., and London),

1984. Pp. 165-6.
4 Alice Herlihy Green, *A Tale of Two Cities,* 1965.

CHAPTER 4. THE POLITICIAN
1 July 18, 1944.
2 Hecht, Ben, *A Child of the Century,* Playbill/ Ballantine (New York), 1954,1970., Pp. 533-4.
3 Hecht, *op. cit.,* Pp. 551-2.
4 Wednesday, July 19, 1944.
5 Green, Benjamin J., *My War with the United States Marines,* Chapter 4, "Special; Training—The .45", presented to the Chicago Literary Club, Feb. 8, 1965.
6 Friday, December 22, 1944.
7 Wednesday December 20, 1944.
8 Original letter from Myron L. Wallace, Ensign, U. S. Naval Reserve, December 4, 1944.

CHAPTER 5. TRANSPORTED TO GUAM
1 Monday, and Tuesday, Dec. 26, 1944, 8 a.m.
2 Thursday, December 28, 1944, Noon, The Day.
3 Helen Herlihy Tartakoff to Alice Herlihy Green, Friday, February 23, 1945.
4 Smith, Holland M., and Finch, Peter, *Coral and Brass,* Charles Scribners Sons (New York), 1949, p. 52.
5 *Ibid.,* p. 34.
6 Sunday, January 14, 1945.
7 February 8, 1945 (Postmark).
8 Friday, February 23, 1945.
9 Benjamin J. Green, *My War with the U. S. Marines,* Chapter 5, "The Letter." Presented to the Chicago Literary Club, Feb. 8, 1965.
10 Thursday, March 22, 1945.
11 Tuesday, March 27, 1945.
12 Monday, April 16, 1945.
13 Sunday, April 22, 1945.
14 Wednesday, April 18, 1945.

CHAPTER 5 TRANSPORTED TO GUAM (cont'd)

15 Thursday, May 3, 1945.
16 Friday, May 11, 1945.
17 Wednesday, May 9, 1945
18 Smith, *op. cit.*, p. 201.
19 Herbert, Kevin, *Maximum Effort: The B-29s against Japan*, Sunflower University Press (Manhattan, KS), 1983. Foreword, P. ii.
20 Herbert, Kevin, *op. cit.*, P. ii.

CHAPTER 6. CAMBRIDGE BEACH

1 Hayes, Helen, with Lewis Funke, *A Gift of Joy*, M. Evans and Company, Inc. (New York), 1965. P. 187.
2 *The New York Times*, July 28, 1945.
3 Wednesday, May 17, 1944.

CHAPTER 7. ARMED FORCES RADIO STATION WXLI

1 Wednesday, May 23, 1945. Noon.
2 Wednesday, May 23, 1945. Noon.
3 Tuesday, June 26, 1945, 7:30 PM.
4 Thursday, June 28, 1945, 7 PM.
5 Wednesday, June 27, 1945.
6 Saturday, July 7, 1945.

CHAPTER 8. HERE'S GUAM

1 Background Memorandum #44, For release 2300, 19 July, 1945 (0900 19 July, 1945, EWT), U. S Pacific Fleet and Pacific Ocean Areas, Advance Headquarters, Guam.
2 Sunday, July 22, 9:30 AM.
3 Rogers, Robert F, *Destiny's Landfall: A History of Guam*, University of Hawaii Press (Honolulu), 1995, p. 95.
4 *Ibid.*, p. 190.
5 *Ibid.*, p. 210.
6 Monday, July 23, 1945, 3:30 PM.
7 Monday, July 23, 1945, 3:30 PM.

CHAPTER 9. THE HIGHEST RANKING PRIVATE ON GUAM

1 Christman, Trent, *Brass Button Broadcasters*, Turner Publishing Co. (Paducah, KY), 1992, pp. 14-19.
2 From *The Kwaj Lodge*, an article posted at http://radiodx.com/spdxr/WXLG.htm. This article was originally published in the Kwajalein Hourglass, August 29, 2000. Copyright to Kwajalein Hourglass. Permission to use is under request with publisher. For the moment, it forms part of the Radio Heritage Collection (c). All rights reserved to Ragusa Media Group, PO Box 14339, Wellington, New Zealand. This material is licenced on a non-exclusive basis to South Pacific DX Resource hosted on radiodx.com for a period of five years from July 1 2001. Author: Eugene Sims, Kwaj Historian.

CHAPTER 10. THE SCOOP
1 Sunday morning, 4 a.m., August 12, 1945
2 Tuesday, August 14, 1945 … A little after midnight.
3 University of Missouri-Kansas City, *The War in the Pacific: The War's Voices*, at http://www.umkc.edu/lib/spec-col/ww2/PacificTheater/voices.htm.
4 Interview with Bud Blattner, held Sep. 14, 2000 at Lake Ozark. Missouri. 18 *Ibid*.
5 Green, Benjamin J., "Beer for the Troops," from *My War with the U. S. Marines*, presented to the Chicago Literary Club, Feb. 8, 1965.

CHAPTER 11. WAITING FOR B. J. DAY
1 Tuesday, August 14, 1945, A little after midnight.
2 Tuesday, September 4, 1945, 9:45 p.m.
3 Friday, August 17, 1945.
4 Sunday, August 26, 1945.
5 Monday, August 27, 1945.
6 Friday, August 31, 1945.
7 VJ Day … 6 p.m., Sunday, September 2, 1945.
8 Tuesday, September 4, 1945, 9:45 p.m.

9 Wednesday, September 5, 1945.
10 Interview with Bud Blattner, Held Sep. 14, 2000 by phone in Lake Ozark, Missouri.
11 Friday, October 5, 1945, 10 AM.

CHAPTER 12. LIBERTY SHIPS: THE PRIVATEER

1 Saturday, September 15, 1945
2 Monday, September 17, 1945.
3 Tuesday, September 18, 1945.
4 Wednesday, September 19, 1945.
5 Monday, October 1, 1945, Noon.
6 Monday, October 1, 1945.
7 Wednesday, October 1, 1945.
8 Friday, October 5, 1945, 10 AM

CHAPTER 13. HOMECOMING-SCRAMBLED EGGS
1 http://www.keyshistory.org/lowermatecumbekey.html.
2 Rocky Mountain News (Denver, CO); 5/21/2000.

CHAPTER 14. MAKING UP FOR LOST TIME
1 *The Chicago American*, Wed., July 24, 1957.

CHAPTER 15. WHAT MAKES BENNY RUN?

Acknowledgements

Thanks to all the fine people who believed in this project and encouraged me: the late Mary Oates Johnson, for giving me the courage to attempt it in the first place; Leslie Epstein, author, writing professor, patient reader and thoughtful critic of my earliest chapters, and my other Yale classmates, who asked what I would do with the last third of my life; Catherine Rankovic, author and workshop professor, who nurtured my nonfiction storytelling skills; Larry Fiquette, leader, and the other members of our Saturday memoirs group, and Bettye Dew, for reading and critiquing my manuscript, providing numerous constructive suggestions for improvement.

I would be remiss if I didn't also acknowledge the participation of those featured in this story. Benjamin J. Green wrote 400 letters home and six post-war essays. Alice Herlihy Green preserved those letters and wrote a biographical script for his "This Is Your Life" party. Babette (Babs) Levey, Dad's niece, was there when he was young and remembered. My sister, Linda Green-Metzler, preserved her memories, the family photo archives and several key documents. The late Bud Blattner was as much a friend and collaborator for me as he was for Dad; his journalistic skills, honed over years of radio broadcasting, brought some of the flavor of life in 1945 on Guam to these pages. Mike Wallace remembered us after all these years and encouraged my work on this book as far back as 2001. To all of you and to others still living mentioned in this nonfiction work: I hope that in attempting to be factual I have not seemed unkind. To me these memories of you are precious, and I thank you for being part of our lives.

In this new, completely revised edition, with a new publisher, the chapters have been rewritten, combined, re-edited and reformatted for a better presentation and an easier reading experience.

—Peter H. Green
St. Louis, Missouri,
March, 2014

ABOUT THE AUTHOR

Peter H. Green

A writer, architect and city planner, Peter found his father's 400 World War II letters, his humorous war stories, his mother's writings and his family's funny doings too good a tale to keep to himself, so he launched a second career as a writer. His first book recounted the often hilarious antics and serious achievements of his dad's Word War II adventure, *Dad's War with the United States Marines*, Seaboard Press, 2005. re-issued in March 2014 by Greenskills Press. His first novel, *Crimes of Design*, a Patrick MacKenna mystery, an intrigue of murder and sabotage set in St. Louis during the highest flood of record, which first appeared in 2012 from L&L Dreamspell, will be republished, along with the second in this series, *Fatal Designs*, by Greenskills Press in 2014. He lives in St. Louis with his wife Connie, and has two married daughters and three grandchildren. The story of his the last pet his family owned, "The Night We Ruined the Dog," can be found onhis website.

His website is: www.peterhgreen.com
Facebook page: www.facebook.com/AuthorPeter Green
Twitter handle: https://twitter.com/writerpeter
LinkedIn ID: Peter H. Green

Before you go, If you enjoyed this book , please leave a review comment at this book's Amazon Page : https://www.amazon.com/Bens-War-U-S-Marines-ebook/dp/B00ISYPDCU/

ALSO BY PETER H. GREEN

Nonfiction

Ben's War with the U. S. Marines

Patrick MacKenna Mysteries

Crimes of Design

Fatal Designs

www.ingramcontent.com/pod-product-compliance
Lightning Source LLC
Chambersburg PA
CBHW030312080526
44584CB00012B/536